FROM THE HARP
TO THE EAGLE

by

Peter Durkee

ASHRIDGE PRESS

Published and distributed by
Ashridge Press
A subsidiary of Country Books

ISBN 1 901214 07 9

© 2003 Peter Durkee

The rights of Peter Durkee as author of this work has
been asserted by him in accordance with the
Copyright, Designs & Patents Act 1993

All rights reserved. No part of this publication may be
reproduced, stored in a retrieval system or
transmitted in any form or by any means,
electronic, mechanical, photocopying
recording or otherwise, without the
prior permission of the author and
publisher.

Design, typesetting and production:
Country Books, Little Longstone,
Bakewell, Derbyshire DE45 1NN

Tel/Fax: 01629 640670
e-mail: dickrichardson@country-books.co.uk

Printed and bound by: Antony Rowe Ltd, Chippenham, Wiltshire

CONTENTS

Chapter	1	Platten Hall	1
Chapter	2	The Wedding	11
Chapter	3	Dublin	21
Chapter	4	Drogheda	32
Chapter	5	Rape and Murder	40
Chapter	6	The Black Bird	49
Chapter	7	Indian Bridge	61
Chapter	8	The Jacaranda Tree	72
Chapter	9	Preparing for Invasion	84
Chapter	10	The Invasion	92
Chapter	11	Cane-Cutting	110
Chapter	12	Jamaica	126
Chapter	13	Farley Hill	143
Chapter	14	Land of The Eagle	158
Chapter	15	Martha	176
Chapter	16	Months of Scorn	190
Chapter	17	The Court Case	204
Chapter	18	The Appeal	221
		Epilogue	234
		Family Tree	236

ILLUSTRATIONS

Map of Drogheda	33
Map of Barbados	62
The 'hall' of settler's house	166

Acknowledgement

I should like to express my thanks to
Bernice Gunderson of the Society of Genealogy of Durkee, California.

References

Society of Genealogy of Durkee Inc.,
   4100 East Theresa Street, Long Beach, CA 90814-1758
Cromwell, Our Chief of Men Antonia Fraser
Oliver Cromwell John Buchan
English Costume of 17th Century Iris Brooke
Discovery of North America Michele Ryan
Little England Gary A Puckram
New England Village GM Chandler
Sins of Our Fathers James Pope-Hennessey
Scotland Farewell Donald Mackay
History of the United States George Bancroft
History of Ipswich, Essex & Hamilton Joseph B Pelt
American Museum, Claverton, Bath.
Maritime Museum, Falmouth
The Boston Records and Files

Chapter 1
PLATTEN HALL 1649

'The King is dead! The King is dead! They've killed our King!' William Durgy repeated to himself as he rode his black mare up the valley of the Boyne from Drogheda to his home at Platten Hall.

William knew the news he was taking home would alter his life and the lives of all his family. The peace he had known in Ireland was to be shattered by war!

The ground was hard with a white hoar-frost and his mare's hooves rang loud through the silent night. It was late in the evening and a clear moon shone in the cloudless sky. William was sixteen and a good horseman, as was befitting the son of Sir William Durgy. Horses had been a natural part of his life since his father had sat him on the back of one when he was three years old.

At that time his mother, Lady Elizabeth, had been full of foreboding. Their first born son, another William, had died in a hunting accident in 1632 so she had not liked the idea of their latest offspring being taught to ride so early.

'It'll be the best way for him to learn,' his father had said.

William loved horses and in particular his own Black Bess. He had been spending his time with Pete Flaherty, the ostler at an inn in Drogheda, when they heard the news just brought by courier from England. William had started home at a full gallop but then realised the ground was too hard for the horse. The news could wait for the extra time a more reasonable pace would take.

After all, he thought, nothing can happen tomorrow! If anything was to happen it would take months. As Catholics and Royalists his family were sure to be enemies of the Protestants and Parliamentarians who had executed King Charles 1.

After riding for an hour he neared Platten Hall, quickened his pace, and galloped into the stable yard. Patrick, the stable boy, ran out to grab the bridle.

'The King is dead! The King is dead! They have killed our King!' William shouted excitedly.

'This is bad news, master William. I'll take Bess and give her a rub down while you tell your father.'

William strode hurriedly through the kitchen, throwing his hat and riding crop on an oak chest as he crossed the entrance hall and entered the music room. Here a large log fire radiated warmth and comfort, in welcome relief from the cold outside and he blinked as his eyes met the soft light of the candles. His mother was sitting by the fire doing some needlework; his father sat opposite reading a book. Sister Sarah was playing the harp.

'The King is dead! They have killed our King!' William repeated excitedly.

'Where did you hear this, son?' His father shut his book and looked up. He was a short man, with a round kindly face, usually smiling and friendly. Tonight he looked up showing some concern.

'In Drogheda tonight, sir. A messenger arrived from London and the news is all over town.'

'This is bad news indeed but after hearing about the trial in London I have been expecting it.'

'How dreadful,' Lady Elizabeth cried, 'How dare they do this?'

'What do you think will happen, sir? Does this mean war?'

'Cromwell must now come to Ireland. He will want to avenge the massacre of '41 but it will take some time for him to muster an army, raise the funds and organise a fleet to invade us. I will go and see Ormonde tomorrow.'

Sarah had stopped playing on hearing William's news. Her eyes widening anxiously. 'What does this mean, Father? I hope it'll not alter my wedding date'.

'Have no fear, daughter, we will have you wed in June whatever happens.'

Nineteen year old Sarah had long dark hair and brown eyes, she was engaged to be married to Michael O'Leary and live on his farm outside the North of Drogheda.

'I fear this means there will be more fighting,' Lady Elizabeth shook her head, putting her needlework on her lap.

'Never mind, mother, we'll beat them, kill Cromwell and put Prince Charles on the throne.' William assured her.

'You make it sound simple, my son, but I'm afraid there is more to it than that.' Sir William said. 'Cromwell's armies have never been defeated and if he comes here, as he must, he'll bring a large force with him. He has many sympathisers here, too. Before he comes, maybe we can invite Prince Charles and declare him King in Ireland. It'll mean an early start if I'm to see Ormonde, so I'll retire now.' He rose and pulled the bell cord by the fireplace. The man servant appeared at once, almost as if he had been waiting outside, listening and expecting to be called.

'Tell Maureen to place the warming pan in our bed, we are retiring now.'

'Yes, sir.'

Lady Elizabeth put her needlework carefully in the work box by her side. 'William, I do not like the thought of you riding alone at this time of night from Drogheda. I wish you had stayed with Charles.'

'But, mother, I had to bring the news at once.'

'It would have kept till the morning! You are so impetuous,' she shook her head and rose to leave the room. She was tall and upright, her back hair neatly arranged, the curls on the front tied with black ribbon. Her full length black, satin dress brushed the floor as she walked with her usual air of elegance. 'Good night to you both, don't stay up too long.'

'Do you really think there'll be more fighting, William?' Sarah asked after her parents had left the room.

'Yes, as father says, Cromwell is bound to come to Ireland as we are the last supporters of the King left.'

'But will it be before June?'

'I don't think so. It'll take him a long time to rise an army and ship it over here. I would think it'll be after June but before the winter.'

'And then what? Do you think they will reach here?'

'I don't know. If we could take Dublin before he arrives, then he would not have another good port near here to use.'

'I'm afraid, William, I wish he would not come at all! And what will happen to Charles and Robert?'

Charles, their oldest brother, was a grain merchant; Robert, two years older than William, worked with a wool merchant. Both were married and lived in Drogheda.

'They will fight like the rest of us. Don't worry, sister, we'll defeat him and put Prince Charles on the throne.'

'I don't want war. I suppose Michael will have to fight too.'

'Yes, we will all be in the army to fight those Roundheads.'

'But why not accept the new Parliament? Are we not going to fight a lost cause?'

'We Royalists will never give way. We must defeat Cromwell and put Prince Charles on the throne. Don't worry Sarah, it will be all right, you'll see.' William was full of enthusiasm and eagerly looked forward to the fight, although he had never fired his musket at an enemy before, only at deer for the pot, and at wolves.

Sarah was made of less stern stuff. 'I'm afraid, William,' she said again and began to cry. William went over and put his arm round her shoulder. 'Hush, have no fear, Sarah. We'll be all right. We'll kill Cromwell and restore the monarchy. Don't cry, go to bed now and pray for God's protection.'

She looked up at him and smiled faintly. 'You are so brave, William, but I wonder if you are too young to realise what could happen?'

The next morning Sir William rode to see Ormonde who lived at Trim, about twenty miles further up the River Boyne. Whilst riding he was able to think about his own position in the pending war. His forebears had lived in Ireland for over three hundred years since Sir John D'Arcy had been made Lord Chief Justice of Ireland by Edward II, in 1323. He held this office until he died in 1359. He had married Jane, the widow of Thomas Fitzgerald, Earl of Kildare, and daughter of Richard de Burgo, the "Red Earl" of Ulster and Lord of Connaught. All the D'Arcys who adopted the name of Durgy were descended from that marriage.

Sir William was a Catholic and a faithful supporter of the executed

King Charles. He was determined not to give way to any invasion by Cromwell. He thought of the man he was going to visit, James Butler Ormonde, 12th Earl of Ormonde, who was of English descent, a Royalist like Sir William, and considered Ireland his homeland. He was intelligent, commanding and, above all, trustworthy; a born leader and dashing cavalier. His natural qualities had made him one of the King's most promising assets in Ireland. A Protestant, brought up in England, he nevertheless belonged to Ireland, where his family, of Norman descent, had lived since the twelfth century.

On arrival at Trim, Sir William was shown into Lord Ormonde's oak panelled study. Over the fireplace hung a large painting of King Charles, in a dark blue suit and wearing the insignia of the Garter, sitting in a chair with his Queen standing beside him and his two younger children seated on the floor. As Sir William entered, Ormonde rose from his desk, walked up to him and looked at him straight in the eye. He was tall, fair and blue eyed, clean-shaven but for a slight moustach. 'How good of you to come, William,' he said offering his hand.

'Have you heard the news, James?' Sir William asked.

'Yes, indeed. I must say it has horrified me.'

'Do you agree this means Cromwell will now have to come to Ireland?'

'Yes, but I think that is unlikely at present. It will take time to raise the money and the ships for such an operation. However, there are already strong forces in Ireland in favour of the Commonwealth and I think we'll have to defeat them first and secure the ports. Will you have a madeira? After your long ride you must feel like a little refreshment.'

Sir William nodded briefly.

While pouring the drinks Ormonde continued thinking aloud. 'We have too many people in favour of the Commonwealth to give us any peace of mind. Even Aston's grandmother, that Lady Wilmot, I cannot be too sure of her sympathies. She is an important figure in Drogheda and expresses her opinions very forcefully among the ladies of the town. She could influence the feeling in Drogheda. I think we must secure our position especially in the ports of Drogheda, Dublin and Wexford. We have already invited Prince Rupert to come to Ireland and support us. He has a squadron of ships in the Scilly Isles.'

'Do you think he will accept?'

'It is too early to say yet. But if he did, he could engage Cromwell's fleet before it reached Ireland. In the meantime, we must proclaim Charles II king. This will encourage the Royalist sympathisers to support us including, I hope, Lord Inchiquin with his army.'

They continued to discuss the situation for some time before being joined by Sir Arthur Aston and the Colonels Byrne, Wall and Warren. Sir Arthur Aston was an old Catholic veteran who stumped in on his wooden leg. He had lost his leg fighting the Turks in Poland before the Civil War, had fought at Edgehill, defended Reading against Essex, and had been governor of Oxford. He was a short man and full of confidence.

'This is going to be a pretty kettle of fish, James. We are going to have a fight on our hands.'

'I agree with you, we have just been discussing our tactics. We must hold the ports at Drogheda, Dublin and Wexford. Possibly Prince Rupert will bring his fleet over from the Scilly Isles. George Monk has assured me of his support and I hope Lord Inchiquin will too.'

Their discussion was to continue for several hours.

That morning, Michael O'Leary rode along the River Boyne to Platten Hall to see Sarah. The large, imposing building never failed to impress him. In the centre, the front door had a pillared portico approached by a wide set of steps. On either side were three large leaded windows and on the first and second floors a row of seven windows the same size. At each end on the top of the wall was a large stone acorn.

Patrick came from the stable and after he took charge of the horse, Michael went up the steps and pulled the knob of the door bell. A servant opened the door.

'Good morning, sir,' she said.

'I have come to see Miss Sarah.'

'She's in the parlour with my lady, sir.'

'Thank you, I know the way.' He handed his hat and riding crop to the servant. In the centre of the hall a wide staircase, with mahogany banisters, led to the landing above. To his right two doors led to the sitting room and music room and to his left two doors led to the parlour and the dining room. He entered the parlour.

'Good morning, Lady Elizabeth. Good morning Sarah.' He bowed slightly to them both.

'How nice of you to come all this way on such a cold morning,' Lady Elizabeth closed the book she was reading.

'It was a pleasure, my Lady, I assure you. I had to come to see how you had taken the news from London.'

'Such dreadful news, I don't know how they could dare execute the King. The whole country, indeed the whole of Europe, must be horrified.'

'Indeed, my Lady, it is dreadful news. I fear it means Cromwell must invade Ireland now we are the sole supporters of the King left.'

'Not before our wedding, Michael, I hope?' Sarah asked.

'I doubt it. These things take time.'

'I expect you two would like to talk together? Sarah, why don't you put on your shawl and take a walk down to the river? Although it is cold, it is a beautiful sunny morning. The fresh air will do you good.'

'Yes, mother,' Sarah replied, smiling at Michael, 'I will only be a minute.' Sarah left and shortly returned wearing a blue hooded cloak. She looked very pretty, Michael thought.

'I'm ready, Michael,' she said.

He took her arm and together they left the room, walked through the entrance hall and into the main hall at the end, through the hall and out onto the terrace at the back of the house. The white frost on the lawn dazzled in the bright sunshine, stretched right down to the bank of the river Boyne. There was a thin gossamer mist hanging over the smooth water.

Michael put his arm round Sarah and turned her to face him. 'You're so pretty, my darling, I do love you so,'

'I love you too, darling,' she replied, smiling up at him. They stood there embracing and kissed a long passionate kiss.

She glanced over Michael's shoulder. 'Mother is watching us'.

'I'm sure she does not disapprove.' Hand in hand, they descended the steps from the terrace and slowly walked down to the river's edge. Sarah watched two swans gliding silently by and a robin pecking at small insects on the water's edge. She thought it was such a peaceful

scene and hard to imagine that it would ever be disrupted by war.
'I'm worried about the news, Michael. Cromwell will not come before our wedding, will he?' Sarah's tone was agitated.
'No, my love, don't be so anxious'
'It is what will happen after that frightens me.'
'Be not afraid, my darling. We will fight them and defeat them.' He held her in her arms and she looked up at him.
'That's what William says. I hope you are both right. I would that there'd be no fighting. Must you fight too?'
'I must do my duty, my darling.'
'I want to live in peace in our home.'
'So do I. God willing, we shall.' She clung closer to him and felt safe in his embrace, even if it was to be a short time.

That same morning William was once again at the inn in Drogheda. Here the activity and the horses were not the only attractions for him. Maeve, one of the maids at the inn, was seventeen, a buxom, hearty girl who enjoyed spending her time with William in the hayloft over the stables, whenever the opportunity arose.
'Hullo, William. What does thee think of the news?'
'Come with me into the hayloft, my beauty, and we can talk.' They climbed the ladder to the hay loft and settled down comfortably. William embraced Maeve and kissed her. She liked being kissed and responded eagerly, clasping her arms round him.
'Oh, I do like that William! But tell me, what does this news from London mean and why is everyone so excited?'
'Now that the King is dead, Ireland will proclaim Prince Charles as King. Cromwell and the Parliament have declared they will not have a king, so as Ireland is part of the kingdom they will have to come here to fight us before we will accept them.'
'Do ye think they'll come here?'
'Yes, of course.'
'Will ye fight, William ?'
'Certainly I will.'
'Oh, I don't see why ye should. Why not leave it to the soldiers?'

'But we'll all be soldiers. We will be fighting for our King and country. My father is a direct descendant of Sir John D'Arcy of England, who came here three hundred years ago.'

'So ye be an Englishman, William!' she exclaimed.

'No, I'm Irish. Our family have had Platten Hall as our family home for over three hundred years.'

'Why can't the English leave us to ourselves to support the King, and they support who they like?' she asked.

'Then we would invite Prince Charles to come here and raise an army to invade England!'

'We could never do that! I don't think the war will happen here. They'll fight near Dublin and the bigger towns.' She nestled her head against his shoulder and was happy to think war would never reach them. William gently undid her bodice and fondled her breast. Maeve sighed with contentment.

Their serenity was broken by the sound of two travellers entering the stable below with their horses.

'I wonder where the groom is?' One of them asked.

'If the whole town is as unprepared as this stable we'll have no trouble taking it over.' The second man remarked.

'I've no doubt there are plenty of Irish here who'll greet us with open arms. Hey there! Anyone here to take our horses?' He shouted.

William gently pushed Maeve aside and hurried down the ladder to the stable below.

'Here, sir. I'll take them.'

'A feed of oats and a good brush down mind ye, lad.'

'Yes, sir! Where are you from, sir?'

'Dublin. We're here to see if this town is ready for the Commonwealth troops when they come. We don't want the Royalists to hold it, do we lad? Ye don't have anything to do with those Royalists, do ye?' William did not reply and the visitors strode off to the inn.

Maeve hurriedly rearranged her dress and came down the ladder. 'I'd better be back. They'll be calling for me next.'

'You heard what they said?' William asked, 'they're after Drogheda already!'

'I'll be going. See ye later, Englishman!' she teasingly prodded him in the ribs as she ran out of the stable.

'I'm not English. I'm Irish and proud of it,' he shouted after her.

Chapter 2

THE WEDDING

It was one bright, sunny day in May when William was with Pete Flaherty in the stable.

'You should go to the Duleek Gate, boy,' Pete said, 'I hear that Lord Inchiquin's men are coming. Lord Ormonde has at last persuaded him to bring his army to defend Drogheda. It'll be a great sight to see.'

'Aren't you coming?' William asked.

'I've more important things to do here, boy, you go.'

William ran down St. Peter's Street, Ship Street, across the bridge to Duleek Street and joined a group of people mounting the narrow, stone steps leading to the top of Duleek Gate. He pushed his way through the crowd lining the wall. They were all talking excitedly, delighted at the prospect of the army coming to defend their city.

'We'll show that farmer Cromwell what the Irish are made of.'

He looked across the open country and in the distance he could see the army marching towards the town. Leading the column was Lord Inchiquin himself sitting bolt upright on his horse, the white plume on his cavalier's hat waving in the slight breeze, his sword dangling at his side. Following him were the pipes and drums beating a marching tune. Then some two hundred cavalry, their bright uniforms glinting in the sunlight and, stretching far down the road, the foot soldiers carrying their muskets and pikes. It was a magnificent sight and the onlookers cheered and waved their hats and kerchiefs.

The gate was opened and the column marched beneath the onlookers into the town. William ran down the steps and followed the troops across the bridge, back down St.Peter's Street to the square around St.Peter's

Church. Here the column halted and William returned to the hostelry. Maeve was in the stable.

'Where you been, William? I were looking for thee.'

'I've been to see the army arriving. It was a wonderful sight. Now Drogheda will be safe – the army is here to protect us.'

'I can't stay – the officers will be coming to the inn and I'll be busy.'

'And I shall have more horses to groom. There are over three hundred cavalry and two thousand soldiers here now. Billets will have to be found for all of them in the town. We are going to be very busy'.

On his way home that evening, after stabling and grooming ten of the officer's horses, William was stopped at Duleek Gate by the soldiers who were now guarding it. 'Where ye going, boy?'

'To my home at Platten Hall. My father is Captain of one of the companies. My name is Durgy.'

'Pass, Durgy.'

When he reached Platten Hall he found his mother and Sarah in the drawing room. 'Lord Inchiquin's men have arrived at Drogheda and the town is full of soldiers,' he told them.

'It is good to think we shall be well defended,' his mother replied, 'but I wish it were not necessary.'

'Everyone we asked to the wedding has accepted,' Sarah told William excitedly. She was not interested in the army. 'The musicians have been engaged and Robert will be an usher and Charles best man. I hope you will be an usher, William.'

'Yes, Sarah, I'll be an usher. What will I have to do?'

'Show the guests to their sets in the church. Surely you know that? Michael's guests to the right and my guests to the left.'

'Which church?'

'Which Church! William, have you no idea what the arrangements are? St. Mary's church, of course. And after the wedding they are all coming back here for the reception.'

'I hope it doesn't rain.'

'It's going to be a lovely fine day.' She assured him.

Saturday, the 9th of June, was indeed a fine day. In fact it was very hot and William was glad to be inside the church where it was cooler. The wedding was to be at 10 o'clock in the morning and the guests began to arrive half an hour before. William and Robert did their duty as ushers.

Lady Wilmot entered the church. She was over eighty and leaned heavily on her walking stick. Tall and slightly bent, wearing a black hat with a wide rim and mauve feather floating from the top, she was an imposing sight. A gold pomander hung from the belt of her high-waisted black dress. She wore mauve silk gloves and waved a mauve silk handkerchief in front of her nose as if she felt the heat and, being a Protestant, disapproved of the stale smell of incense in the church.

'The heat is too much for me, young man,' she told William.

'I'll show you to your seat, Lady Wilmot,' and he led her to a seat on the left.

'I'll sit where I like," she said, 'and somewhere where I can hear and see what is going on.' She went to sit in the front pew on the right.

'But, Lady Wilmot, the groom and best man will sit here. Please take the pew behind.'

'Oh, very well, then. But I don't see why I can't sit where I like!'

Michael O'Leary and Charles arrived and sat in front of her. Michael wore a brown, waist length jacket, buttoned at the back with full length sleeves and white lace embroidered shoulder cape. His brown breeches were tucked below the knee into stockings tied with ribbon. He had blue bows of ribbon on his love locks. Charles was dressed in his cavalry uniform with his sword at his side. He was a tall, upright young man of twenty-two and looked very elegant in his uniform.

Soon the church was nearly full and the clock struck the hour. The organist was softly playing suitable music. Everyone waited for the bride to arrive.

After waiting quarter of an hour Father O'Neill came scurrying up the aisle and approached William and Robert.

'What is the cause of the delay, my sons, do you know?' He asked breathlessly.

'No, Father. I left home two hours ago and everything was all right then.' William replied. He went outside to see if they were coming. 'They're not in sight yet, Father.'

After half an hour all the guests were muttering to each other and getting restive. The organist was reaching the end of his repertoire.

Michael was wondering what could be causing the delay. Surely Sarah was going to come? What could have happened? Has she been taken ill or had an accident?

Lady Wilmot put out an imperious hand as Father O'Neill passed.

'How much longer must we wait here?' Michael leaned over to hear the reply.

'The bride will soon be here, my Lady, I'm sure.' He and Michael hoped he was right.

At 10.35 the organ began playing the music selected to greet the bride and Lady Durgy came down the aisle looking very agitated. Michael looked round to see her. She wore a dark blue silk dress with a low waisted bodice, long sleeves with lace cuffs, and long richly ornamented stomacher which reached the floor. Her hair was drawn back with a small curled fringe in front and curls over her ears tied with dark blue ribbon. She had dropped pearl earrings and a strand of pearl necklace with a pearl ornament between her breasts. She sat behind Lady Wilmot.

'I should sit behind the groom,' she whispered to William who had followed her.

'Lady Wilmot insisted on sitting there,' William whispered. 'Why are you so late?'

'We lost a wheel on the way here.'

Michael beckoned to William. 'What has happened?' he asked and William told him.

Sarah followed holding her father's arm, resplendent in a beautiful dark green satin dress with a long pointed bodice, short sleeves above puffed shift sleeves with lace trimmed cuffs. Her skirt was opened in the front to reveal a patterned underskirt. Her hair was drawn back with a small knot and her low neck was outlined with a deep lace edged collar. She smiled happily as she went up the aisle. Michael turned to see her come down the aisle and smiled at her.

Sir William, Sarah, Michael, and Charles stood in a row before the altar rail.

'I hear you lost a wheel,' Michael whispered to Sarah, 'Were you hurt?'

'No, my love, I was not hurt.'
An attendant sprinkled the rail with holy rose-water.
Father O'Neill began the service with a clear loud voice.
When he came to the question, 'Michael, wilt thou have this woman to thy wedded wife......?' Michael looked at Sarah, and smiling replied, 'I will,' loudly and clearly.
Lady Wilmot had her hand up to her ear to catch the reply.
'Sarah, wilt thou have this man to thy wedded husband...'
'I will,' she replied shyly looking into Michael's eyes.
'Who giveth this woman to be married to this man?'
Sir William held Sarah's hand forward and the two plighted their troth to each other, holding hands.

Charles then produced the ring and laid it on the opened prayer book held by Father O'Neill.

'Say after me; with this ring I thee wed, with my body I thee worship, and with all my worldly goods I thee endow; In the Name of the Father, and of the Son, and of the Holy Ghost. Amen.'

The church filled with the aroma of incense. Lady Wilmot waved her handkerchief more fiercely.

The Mass followed in Latin with prayers, hymns and a long sermon by Father O'Neill who could not resist mentioning the perils of the forthcoming military activities and praying for the safety of this young couple.

As the happy couple came out of the church into the bright sunlight, they stood by the door for a few seconds listening to the sound of the bells of St. Mary echoing across the town. A large crowd had gathered to watch as the bride and groom entered their carriage and the guests sought their own carriages and horses. William saw Maeve among the onlookers and waved to her as he mounted his horse. She waved back.

The procession proceeded through Duleek Gate, unchallenged by the guards, and along the road to Platten Hall. Sir William and Lady Durgy arrived ahead of their guests to find William already there. Then the bride and groom arrived and stood by the front door greeting and shaking hands with the guests as they entered.

Lady Wilmot was almost the last to arrive.

'That journey shook me up,' the old lady complained, still frantically waving her handkerchief before her nose. 'The heat y'know and I'm sure my coachman deliberately found every pot-hole on the way.'

'Come through to the terrace, Lady Wilmot, and I'll find a seat for you in the shade.' Lady Durgy took her arm and led the old lady, shuffling along with her stick, through the entrance hall, through the main dining hall to the terrace.

'Here you are, Lady Wilmot, a comfortable chair in the shade. I'll send for some refreshment for you,' she suggested.

'Thank you. I could try a brandy.'

That was not what Lady Durgy had in mind! But she asked a servant to bring one.

'I don't see what all this fuss over Cromwell is about,' the old lady shouted, 'that king was a traitor and deserved to lose his head.'

'Hush, my dear, you'll be overheard.'

'Hush woman? Who are you to hush an old woman. Am I not entitled to voice my own opinion? Hush, indeed! I will not hush!'

'I must see to my other guests. Here is your brandy, I hope it will make you feel better.'

'Is that it?' Lady Wilmot asked the servant girl. 'Not a very big one, is it? You'd better fetch me another!'

At the far end of the terrace a small band of musicians, a harpist, three fiddlers and two flautists, now began playing. Some couples came on to the lawn to dance and across the lawn a group of Royalist officers were standing around the drinks table. There was Lord Inchiquin, Sir Arthur Aston, James Ormonde and those officers of the Royalist forces recently active in the successful operations in the area, dressed in their colourful uniforms of the time, their swords hanging by their sides.

'We are doing well, sir.' Colonel Wall said to Ormonde, 'let's drink to our further successes.'

'Indeed, by all means. But we have a long way to go yet. The most important place to hold is Dublin. I plan to move our forces down there and occupy the town as soon as possible. If Cromwell is planning to come to Ireland, as he must, he will need Dublin to land his forces. I hear Colonel Jones only has a small force there.'

'A toast then, to success in Dublin!'

They all raised their glasses: 'Success in Dublin.'

'A toast to the King. King Charles the Second, may he soon reign over us. The King, gentlemen!'

'The King,' they all chorused.

Lady Wilmot heard them and raised her glass. 'To Cromwell,' she shouted, 'may God protect him.' The music drowned her voice and she drank her toast alone.

'Ladies and gentlemen,' the butler announced, 'Dinner is served.'

Inside the main hall two rows of tables were laid down the length of the hall. The bride and groom, O'Leary's parents, Sir William and Lady Durgy sat at a shorter row across the end, by the window. Lady Wilmot managed to find a seat near the top table and Sir Arthur Aston sat on the row opposite her with his back to her.

'Would Father O'Neill please say grace?' Sir William asked. Father O'Neill rose and clasped his hands in front of him.

'Dear Lord, we thank you for what we are about to receive. We thank you for our company here, especially the young bride and groom and we pray for peace in the land. Amen.'

He sat down and the guests all chorused, 'Amen.'

They were served with silver bowls of vegetable soup and the general conversation became subdued whilst the company consumed the soup.

Grilled trout was next on the menu. Sir Arthur Aston was busy describing the battle of Edgehill to the two officers sitting next to him, using his knife, spoon and the salt cellar to show the position of the combatants.

A saddle of lamb followed with bread and green vegetables. The silver goblets were filled with French red wine and the whole company enjoyed their meal, to the accompaniment of the musicians on the terrace outside the open doors.

After dinner the guests went back to the terrace and several danced on the lawn. Sarah and Michael went round the guests to thank them for coming and for the presents they had been given.

'So you will be a farmer's wife, Sarah,' Sir Arthur Aston said.

'Yes, sir. I have had some training on my father's estate.'

'I'm sure you've had good training at that, too. And you, Michael, will be joining Sir William's company and leaving your wife to run the farm?'

Michael had no wish to be reminded of his expected duty.

'I hope I shall be able to spend some time with my wife before that eventuality arises, sir.'

'We shall be going to Dublin next month, I expect. But that will be a minor engagement. I wish you both a long and happy life.'

'Thank you, sir.'

'By the way,' Sir Arthur added, 'I don't like the look of that weather,' pointing to black clouds building up on the horizon.

The other guests had also seen the approaching summer storm and began saying farewell as they did not wish to be caught on their way home.

'Please order my carriage, Lady Durgy,' Lady Wilmot asked. 'It was bad enough driving here in the heat, I don't want to be stuck in the mud.'

'Certainly, Lady Wilmot, but I'm sorry you have to leave so soon.'

Lady Wilmot turned to Sarah standing nearby. 'Young lady,' she said, 'late at your wedding and a storm on your wedding day! That bodes evil times ahead.'

Sarah turned away and ran to Michael, crying.

'Sarah, my love, what is the matter?'

'Oh, Michael,' she sobbed, 'that Lady Wilmot has just said a terrible thing to me. She says a storm on our wedding day is bad luck!'

'Hush now, don't heed such talk. Just an old woman's superstition!' But Sarah had difficulty in suppressing her tears. She was convinced Lady Wilmot was right and that the impending war would bring her great sorrow.

The clouds came over quickly and there was a flash of lightning followed by a loud crash of thunder. As the rain poured down the remaining guests and musicians hurried inside the hall.

The carriages and horses were brought round to the front of the house and the guests hurriedly departed. Lady Wilmot looked particularly annoyed as if the Durgys themselves were responsible for the storm.

'Why not stay the night here, Sarah?' her mother suggested.

'What do you think, Michael?' Sarah asked.

'I think that would be very wise, if you don't mind. We don't want to be stuck in the mud on the way to Drogheda.'

Robert and Charles and their wives decided to stay as well so after all the other guests had left they moved into the parlour.

Charles sat on the settle next to William. 'How fares my young brother?' He asked.

'Very well, thank you, Charles.'

'I suppose all this talk of war means nothing to you?'

'Brother, I hope to be fighting with you. I can handle a musket and am looking forward to the fray.'

'Take care, my young one, fighting is a dangerous game. You can get hurt, you know.'

'I'll take care. I shall be with father.'

Sarah was still upset by Lady Wilmot's remark and Michael and her mother had difficulty in calming her down and trying to make her forget it.

'Let us have some music,' Lady Durgy suggested. Sarah was persuaded to play the harp and her mother accompanied on the spinnet.

When it was time for bed, Sarah went to her room with her maid to help her undress. The other ladies said their 'good nights' and left the gentlemen to have a last drink of claret.

'So Lord Ormonde proposes to take Dublin, sir?' Charles asked his father.

'Yes, but it will take several weeks to raise a force big enough. We already have three regiments under Colonels Byrne, Wall and Warren in Drogheda. We cannot afford to move them or Cromwell might use Drogheda to land in Ireland. Once we can occupy Dublin Cromwell will not have a decent port to land in, except Wexford in the South and that would be too far away for him.'

Michael was depressed by all this talk of war. He wanted to live a quiet life with his new bride on his farm, but he knew if there was war he would have to fight alongside the rest of the family. He excused himself to go to bed.

'Good night, Michael, my son,' said Sir William. 'Sleep well in spite of the storm.

Michael knocked on Sarah's bedroom door and entered as another flash of lightning showed outside the window.

'Oh, Michael,' Sarah cried from her bed, her voice almost drowned by a loud clap of thunder, 'I hate this storm, it frightens me and it's lasting so long. Do you think our guests will be all right?'

'I hope Lady Wilmot is stuck in a large puddle!'

'Michael, that is not a kind thing to say!'

'Well, she was not kind to you. Even if she believes such an old wive's tale she shouldn't have said it to you!'

'Hurry up and come to bed. I never thought I would spend my marriage night in my own bed!'

'Tis better than joining Lady Wilmot in that puddle!' he laughed. While he was undressing Sarah asked, 'Will you really have to go with the army to Dublin?'

'I'm afraid so, my love.'

'When will that be, next month?'

'So they say, but you know how long it takes to organise these things.'

'Let's forget the war, Michael, hurry up and get into bed.'

'With great pleasure Mrs O'Leary!'

He joined Sarah in bed and soon they were cuddling and exchanging words of love, the storm still raging outside, Lady Wilmot and the rest of the world was forgotten.

Chapter 3

DUBLIN

A huge cloud of dust rose as the long column of soldiers marched from Drogheda to Dublin on a hot sunny day, the 30th of July. William and his father were part of the contingent of some 8000 foot soldiers and 300 cavalry which set off to march the twenty odd miles to Dublin.

William could hardly contain his excitement which communicated itself to his mount, so that he had to pull sharply on the reins to restrain it from breaking into a canter. To be riding alongside his father into his first battle – could anything be more wonderful? A smile of pure pleasure curled his lips, then faded as he recalled his mother's fears, her pleading for him not to go, to stay at home. Fortunately Sir William had not agreed.

'He will be with me, have no fear. I will take care of him and it will be a good experience for him. We are taking a large force there and we expect Jones to give way without a fight. It will be all right, God willing.'

'But he does not have to go, does he? He's too young!'

'He's over sixteen now. He's a young man. There are plenty of his age going.'

So, unwillingly, she had to give way and here was William riding with all these soldiers to battle. It was thrilling. They would take Dublin and deny Cromwell a port to use. Perhaps he would even give up the idea of coming to Ireland at all!

'Ormonde has decided to split his army into two parts,' his father explained as they rode. 'He will place half on the North side of the river Liffey and half on the South side. The first task of the force on the South side will be to take the castle which we think is lightly defended. We will be with the force going to the North side of the river.'

The contingent going to the South of the river were ahead and they planned to cross at Rathmines. Michael O'Leary was in this group, so William did not see him.

'Will we be fighting as soon as we get to Dublin, sir?' William asked.

'No, William. First we will ask them to surrender. Colonel Jones is in command of the forces inside Dublin and we believe he has only about two thousand men. When he sees our huge force outside the walls he will have little choice. If he accepts we take the town without a fight. If he refuses and we attack we offer no quarter.'

'You think he will surrender then, sir?'

'If he doesn't he will surely be defeated with a great loss of life.'

William and his father camped outside the North walls of Dublin in the evening. They were in reserve and part of the force furthest from the wall. They put up their tent and expected to stay for some time, waiting for Jones to surrender. They could see across the river where the other half of Ormonde's army was setting up camp near the castle.

The next day the demand to surrender was taken to Colonel Jones under a white flag. The reply was sent under a red flag – Colonel Jones refused, much to everyone's surprise.

Michael O'leary, on the other side of the river, had no wish to do any fighting. He wanted to stay with Sarah at home and enjoy a quiet life on his farm. But he could not be seen to refuse to support his in-laws so, reluctantly, he had joined the force leaving a tearful Sarah behind.

As soon as they arrived outside the castle they began building earthworks at Bogotrath to deny the Commonwealth horses access to the grazing areas.

They attacked the castle with scaling ladders on the morning of August 1st. Michael was among the soldiers ordered to climb one of the ladders and storm the battlements. There was one soldier ahead of him as he climbed the wooden ladder with difficulty, his musket slung over his shoulder. When they had almost reached the top, the defenders pushed the ladder away from the wall and sent it sideways, striking the ladder alongside sending them both down together. Michael felt himself falling, helplessly grasping the ladder for support. While he was falling, his life flashed before him; his childhood, his marriage and he imagined clasping Sarah close to him. He fell on the ground, hitting his head on a stone.

Many of the scaling ladders met with the same fate and those who succeeded in reaching the battlements were quickly despatched by the defenders. The attack was repulsed and Ormonde decided to withdraw for the time being.

This action could be seen by the force on the other side of the river.

'I don't understand it,' Sir William said, 'I would have thought they could have taken that castle easily. Even if they were beaten back the first time, they could have tried again, but as far as I can see from here they are doing nothing.'

Later that afternoon he received a message from Ormonde saying he had decided to wait for artillery to bombard the castle and not try to scale the battlements again until it arrived.

That night William was sitting with his father outside their small tent looking at the moonless, cloudless sky brilliant with stars.

'Why don't we attack the town at once, sir?' William asked, eager for action.

'We have asked them to surrender and they have refused. Ormonde considers we are not strong enough to attack without the artillery to bombard the city walls.'

'I hoped they would give way,sir.'

'So did I. But after what we saw today at the castle and Jones refusal, I wonder how many soldiers he has in Dublin? We didn't think they had any alternative but to give in. As you see, we have nearly eight thousand men here and we believe they have only about two thousand in Dublin. Now I have my doubts, perhaps he refused because he has had reinforcements from England. We don't know.'

An hour before dawn William was shaken awake by his father.

'Wake up, wake up, William!' vaguely he heard his father calling, 'There is something happening across the river.'

He rubbed his eyes with the back of his hand and wearily sat up. Over the river he could see tents on fire and hear the sound of musket fire. It was difficult to see exactly what was happening, but clearly the force on the right bank was being attacked by a large army of Commonwealth troops. A soldier approached Sir William.

'The sentries have spotted a small patrol on the left flank, sir. It has been decided to stand the company to, but not to worry Ormonde yet. He is being heavily attacked . We think they are only trying to see how many we are here.'

Before they could take up their positions the defences on the left flank were faced by a major, surprise attack. William and his father, who were about two hundred yards away, saw the enemy in large numbers running right through their camp. During the next hour William saw and heard his first taste of battle. The sound of the muskets, the shouting of the attackers and the cries of the injured was deafening. The air was filled with the smell of gunpowder and smoke from burning tents. He was unable to do anything himself as he could not see what to fire at in the dark. Across the river the battle sounded even louder and it looked as though the whole camp was on fire.

'We are being overrun,' his father said, 'we must withdraw. We will take up a new position and see if we can counter attack at dawn.'

They withdrew with a large number of their detachment. By dawn, the whole of Ormonde's camp on the right bank was defeated. Two thousand of Ormonde's soldiers were taken prisoner and over three hundred were killed. The whole army had been in such confusion during the night they fled in headlong panic, leaving their ammunition and baggage. Ormonde tried in vain to rally his men. They crossed the river and joined the force on the North bank which had already withdrawn.

That morning, Ormonde had no alternative but to march back to Drogheda with the remainder of the army. To make matters worse, the weather broke and it was raining. William was disillusioned. Here he was, marching all the way back to Drogheda in the mud, tired, wet and defeated, not having fired a shot. He had been so confident they could walk into Dublin without a fight, instead they had been surprised by the defenders. Cromwell would be able to use the port of Dublin after all.

Lady Wilmot, who lived in Drogheda, invited a group of her friends to a meeting at her house. There were about eight of them and they all admired the old lady for her forthright opinions and vivacity.

'Thank you, ladies, for accepting my invitation,' she addressed them as soon as they sat down. 'After the battle at Rathmines, everyone in Drogheda is very disheartened. If the Royalists can be defeated when they out-numbered the enemy four to one, what will happen when Cromwell's experienced troops arrive here? So I am going to ask you to support me to persuade my son and the commander of the forces, Sir Edmund Varney, to surrender when Cromwell arrives.'

'But Lady Wilmot, my dear,' they chorused, 'how do you think we could possibly do that? They are so determined to defeat Cromwell.'

'Ladies, as you know, if we surrender there will be no fighting. If we do not, there will be a terrible loss of life. You may not agree with me when I say that in my opinion the King was rightly accused of treason and deserved to be beheaded. But we must accept that the Commonwealth, led by Cromwell, is now the head of the legitimate government of England. The English have accepted him and there is peace in the land there now. Why should we not accept the Commonwealth and live in peace here?'

'I do not agree with you about the King, Lady Wilmot,' Lady Varney said, 'but I do see your point in saving lives.'

'Remember, ladies,' Lady Wilmot proceeded, 'they thought they could take Dublin, but instead Ormonde, with his force of over eight thousand was defeated by Jones with a mere two thousand. They have a better army than we have and when Cromwell comes he will bring a bigger army, better armed. We have no hope of winning and we should surrender.'

They continued the discussion for some time and a few of the ladies agreed with her, but most of them did not express any opinion. They all departed with their own thoughts.

William was recovering from his first experience of battle; but life had to go on and he was grooming a horse in the hostelry stable on a sunny morning in August when Father O'Neill came in.

'My son,' he said,'I am going to Dublin to find out what the situation is there. Sir Arthur Aston wants to know how many troops there are. Would you like to come with me?'

'Oh yes, Father,' William replied eagerly,'I'd enjoy that.'

'I shall not be wearing my priest's clothing, of course, and I could say you are my son.'

'Very well, Father. When do we leave?'

'Early tomorrow morning, from here. I will see you then, my son. May God go with us.'

When William went home that evening he told his mother he was going to Dublin with Father O'Neill.

'Oh, I wish you wouldn't William. Will it be safe? We have Sarah back here at home very distressed because she has not heard what happened to Michael. And she is expecting a baby. Poor child she spends her time crying her eyes out. One loss is enough, we don't want you risking your life.'

'I would not think there will be any risk,' Sir William said, 'In fact I think it would be a very interesting trip. You go, my boy, you'll be all right with Father O'Neill.'

So early the next day Father O'Neill arrived at the stable wearing a high-crowned hat, with no feather or hat band, a loose coat with no frills, a plain collar band and short leather boots in the current Commonwealth fashion. He and William rode to Dublin and they talked on the way.

'I heard that all Catholic priests in Dublin were either killed or fled the city, Father. Are you not taking a risk going there?'

'Yes, that is so. That is why I am dressed like this and you are coming with me, as my son. As you know, I cannot marry, so if I were a Catholic priest I would not have a son.'

'I see, Father. How are we going to find out what we want to know?'

'We will ride down to the dock area and put up at an inn. People talk in those places. You are to say as little as possible. You always call me "father" anyway, and I call you son, so that will come naturally.'

'I know the parliament men are against the Roman Catholics and are killing all catholic priests, and that must be one reason why you are supporting the Royalists,' William said,'but apart from that, why do you think we should fight and not just surrender and so save lives? You must be against killing, aren't you, Father?'

'We must stand up and fight for what we believe is right. I know Jesus said "turn the other cheek", but when it comes to the point that the enemy is going to kill you if you do not kill him first, then you have every right to defend yourself. Cromwell was responsible for killing the king; they need not have done so, they could have banished him from the country. I do not want to live in a country ruled by such men.'

'My father tells me Lady Wilmot is talking of surrendering, is she not right when she says she wants to save lives?' William asked.

'No, my son, we must defeat this man. We must put Prince Charles on the throne.'

'Michael O'Leary is missing after the battle at Rathmines.' William continued. 'Sarah is distraught, she does not know if he is a prisoner or if he is dead. How many more have we got to lose?'

'Yes, I heard about Michael and I have done my best to console your sister, but these are hard times, and we must be prepared to face our losses. God has his own reasons for giving us our sorrows, perhaps it will be that we shall grow up the better for our suffering. Out of the hottest fire comes the purest gold; have faith, my son, things always turn out for the better if you have faith.'

'I had faith we would take Dublin without a fight, but look what good that did!'

'There is a difference between having faith and blind hope. We lost that battle because we did not know how strong they were in Dublin. That is why we are going now to find out just what troops they do have there.'

Approaching the outskirts of the city, near where William had camped with his father, they stopped to look at a large army camp. A sentry came up to them.

'What are you doing here?' he demanded.

'We are on our way to the town to do some business. I see you have many soldiers here, you will soon defeat those Royalists with that lot,' Father O'Neill replied.

'Aye, that we will. And in a few days another fleet is arriving with Cromwell himself, so I'm told.'

'Glad to hear it. God be with you.' Out of earshot, he turned to William, 'You see, my son, already we have learned important news and we are not yet in the town.'

'I find it hard, Father, to be so enthusiastic about defeating the Royalists,' William declared.

'You must learn to play your part. Today, we are supporting the Commonwealth.'

They rode on through the narrow streets of Dublin, crowded with soldiers, down to the dock area and found an inn. They handed their horses over to the groom and went inside. The small room was dark, filled with tobacco smoke and crowded with soldiers drinking.

'Good day to you,' Father O'Neill said to the inn-keeper, 'can you give us a meal and a bed for the night?'

'Good day to you, sir. A meal, yes sir, a bed is more difficult. I am fully booked with army officers, they are all here to meet the fleet expected tomorrow, but I'll see what I can do for you. Will you have a tankard while I get the meal ready?'

'Thank you. One for me and one for my son here.'

They sat at a large table in the middle of the room where a number of officers were already sitting drinking and talking together. No-one took any notice of the newcomers.

'Yes,' one of them was saying, 'we took those Irish rebels by surprise at Rathmines. They didn't know we had a good five thousand already and more will arrive tomorrow with Cromwell. He will land at Ringsend; but I hear the field pieces are delayed and the weather is rough at sea. The men will not be fit to move on for a few days. Then we will march North and finish them off.'

'Excuse me, sir,' Father O'Neill said to the speaker, 'but we are from the country and have not heard what happened at Rathmines. Is it true that only one thousand of you routed eight thousand of the rebel leader Ormonde?'

William had difficulty in keeping a straight face as he heard Father O'Neill acting the innocent country bumpkin.

'God's teeth, man, I can assure you it is quite true. Mind you, we did have five thousand and not one thousand. More had just arrived from England, thank the good Lord, and I doubt Ormonde had eight thousand men. Mind you, he made a big mistake splitting his force.'

'Did he, sir? And how come he did that?'

'Well, you see, he put one half on the North side of the river and the other on the South side. Neither of those would have been strong enough to deal with our lot, but if they had all been together we would have had a more difficult time.'

'I suppose you know all about military strategy. I'm afraid it is beyond me. I wonder why Ormonde was so foolish to make what you say was a mistake?'

The innkeeper brought them two tankards of beer and bowls of food.

'Fraid I've no room for you tonight, sir. But you are welcome to sleep here on the settles, if you've a mind.'

'Thank you, my good man. We'll do that.'

'You'll not get a good night's sleep in here tonight,' the officer said, 'if I were you I'd find lodgings in the town. You might even find a good woman too!' he added giving Father O'Neill a gentle push on his arm. 'Know what I mean? As for Ormonde, why did he make that mistake? Because he's a fool, that's why. He's incapable of leading an army. Far too full of his own importance. We'll go North and slaughter the lot of them. We'll treat them as they treated us in '41.'

'I hope you do.' Father O'Neill replied and William nearly blew the broth out of his spoon with amazement.

After they had eaten they left the inn and walked outside.

'My son, you heard them say Cromwell arrives tomorrow at Ringsend. That is walking distance from here. We will go there early and find what we can see and hear.'

'Yes, Father, as the officer said we are not going to have much sleep tonight, I fear, so we shall be glad to go out early. I had much difficulty keeping myself from laughing as I heard what you said to the officer.'

'You must learn to play your part with conviction. We would have learnt nothing if we said we supported the Royalists. We would probably have been thrown out of the inn!'

At dawn the next morning they walked to Ringsend. There was a morning mist, but it looked as though they were going to have another hot summer's day. The town was crowded even at that early hour. The local farmers and their wives were selling their wares taking advantage of the extra trade. They were beseeched to buy eggs, chickens, ducks, butter and cheese. At the dockside they found a large crowd standing around waiting for the ships to arrive.

'I hear five thousand troops are coming,' they heard one man say. 'They'll soon defeat those Royalists, then we shall have peace.'

At last, the ships came into sight and William saw the first one, the *John*, draw up along the quayside. When the mooring ropes had been secured, a gangway was let down and Cromwell himself stood at the top. His arrival was greeted by the great guns on the city walls firing a salute. William saw he was not a tall man but held himself up very straight. He had a round face, a fat bulbous nose and looked very pale. He was dressed in a plain brown leather jacket and trousers with high boots. He took off his hat with a flourish, paused for the guns to silence, then addressed the waiting crowd:

'As God has brought me hither in safety, so I doubt not but, by His divine providence, to restore you all to your just liberty and property; and that those of you whose heart's affections are real for the carrying on of the great work against the barbarous and blood thirsty Irish...'

'How dare he say that,' William muttered angrily.

'Silence, son,' Father O'Neill implored.

'... and the rest of their adherents and confederates,' Cromwell continued,'for the propagation of the Gospel of Christ, the establishing of truth and peace and restoring the bleeding nation to its former happiness and tranquillity, will find favour and protection from the Parliament of England and receive such endowments and gratuities as should be answerable to their merits.'

This oration was received with much cheering and waving of hats, with Father O'Neill waving his as eagerly as the rest.

'Cheer, boy, cheer,' he entreated William.

William did his best to appear enthusiastic.

Cromwell strode down the gangway, climbed into the waiting carriage and was driven off, without a backwards glance at the crowd, escorted by a cavalry of horses.

The crowd melted away while William and Father O'Neill made their way back to the inn. They stayed there for two more days, going to Ringsend and watching what was happening. On the second day they saw a large fleet appearing.

'That must be over sixty ships out there!' Father O'Neill exclaimed,'I think it is time we went back to Drogheda to tell Aston the news. The army is likely to be bigger than we expected.'

Father O'Neill paid the innkeeper for their food and lodging, such as it was, and they rode back along the track to Drogheda. On the way they passed a gibbet with a man hanging from the arm and a crowd standing by looking on. William was horrified and frightened to see such a sight. He had heard of such punishment being meted out, but never seen it before,

'What's this vagrant done?' Father O'Neill asked one of the crowd, apparently showing he was unmoved by the sight.

'He's one of Cromwell's soldiers, sir. Caught stealing a chicken and strung up by his own officers.'

'Serve him right.' Father O'Neill said.

'We will support a leader like Cromwell who is so severe with his own men; and they also pay us for all the food we give them.'

'Surely Cromwell must be a good man.' Father O'Neill agreed.

'I agree with you, sir. The Commonwealth army will soon be marching through and, God willing, will quickly defeat the rebels and we shall have peace.'

'I hope you are right. Now we must be on our way, good day to you.'

'And good day to you, sir.'

William and Father O'Neill rode on.

'What a terrible sight,' William said.

'Yes, my son, terrible. I nearly crossed myself when I saw it, but stopped just in time. I don't like it,' Father O'Neill added, 'all the people seem to support Cromwell. We have not heard one word in favour of the Royalists on our whole journey.'

'If Cromwell treats his own men like that, I wouldn't like to be one of his prisoners,' William said, 'I shall dream of that man hanging there!'

Chapter 4
DROGHEDA

On the 3rd of September William was in the hay-loft with Maeve.

'Oh, William, I'm frightened. They tell me the Roundheads are already at the gate. What will happen now?'

'Haven't you been up on the wall to see them?'

'Oh, no. I haven't time to go.'

'My father tells me they have 10,000 foot soldiers and 5000 cavalry, but they will not attack at once. They are waiting for their siege guns, then they will first ask us to surrender and when we refuse they will lay siege and try to starve us out.'

'But suppose they do attack at once?'

'The town is well defended. On the East we have the Dale and the walls on the South and West are strong, they will never get in. Even if they do take the South side of the city we still have the river to prevent them taking the rest of the city. We shall defeat them. I expect Ormonde will wait for them to tire of sitting outside the walls and attack from the rear.'

Both lovers secretly thought that perhaps this was the last chance they would have to be together for some time. Mutually they allowed their kissing and cuddling to proceed further than they had before. William had his first experience of making love and found that life had more to live for than he knew before! Now he was more than ever determined to do his part in defeating the enemy at the gate.

'Oh, Will'm!' Maeve stretched out on the hay. 'Ye do love me, Will'm, don't thee?'

'Of course, Maeve my darling. I shall fight to protect you and when

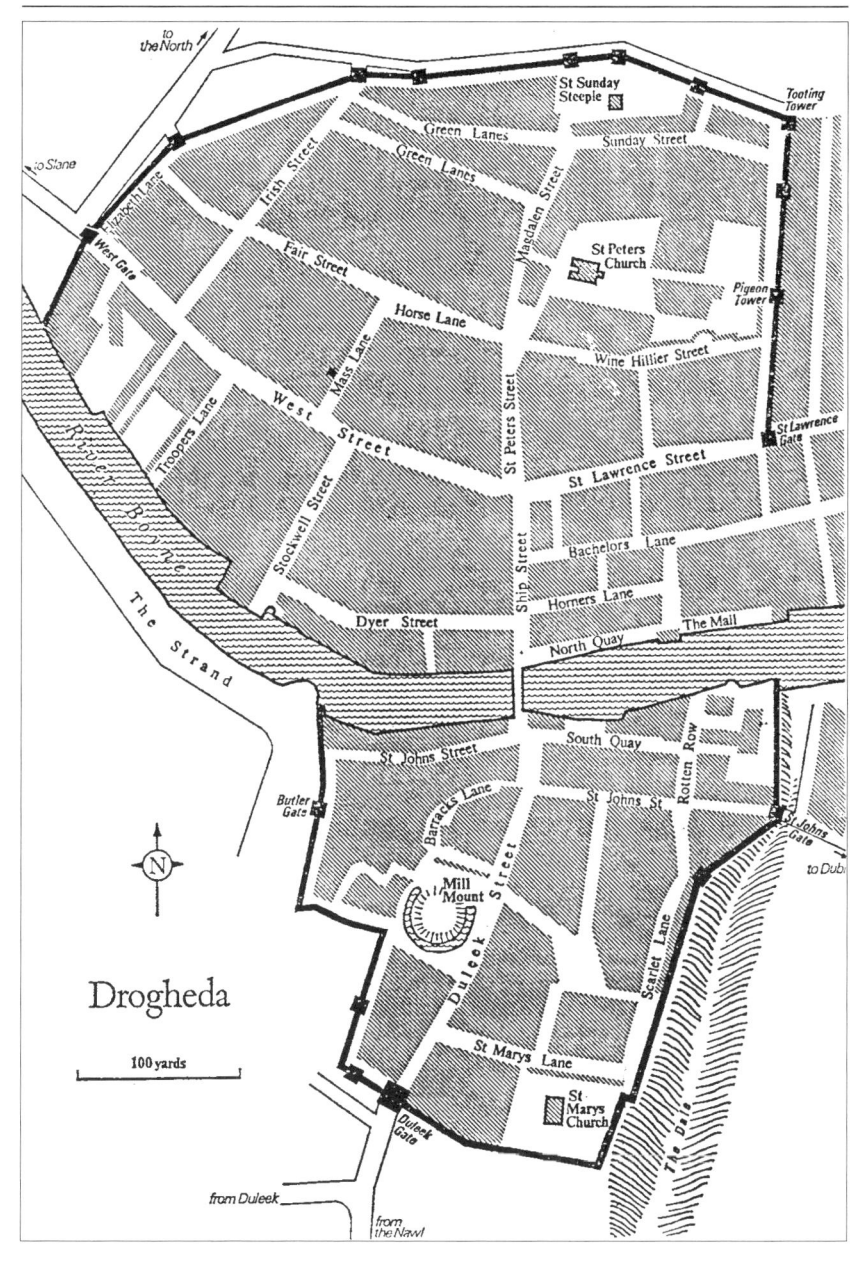

Drogheda

this war is over we will be married,' he promised, in spite of the fact his parents knew nothing of his liaison and he had given no thought of obtaining their approval.

Not everyone in the city had the same resolve. Sir Arthur Aston had heard that his grandmother, Lady Wilmot, was actively seeking to encourage the ladies of the town to petition for a surrender, and decided to visit her to attempt to dissuade her.

Ushered into her drawing room he found her sitting in an oak arm chair with a glass of perry on the table beside her.

'Good afternoon, Arthur,' she said smiling. 'Have you come for refreshment or just a friendly visit?'

He stumped across the room on his wooden leg and stood before her.

'For neither,' he snapped.

'Well, at least sit down.'

'No, I will not. I shall not stay long. Is it true I hear you are seeking to surrender to Cromwell?' he demanded.

'Most certainly it is,' she clenched her hands on her lap and stared at him with determination. 'I never could understand why you support that King. He was a murderer, guilty of treason, fairly tried and quite rightly executed. Cromwell is the elected leader of the Parliament of England and has every right to seek our support.'

'I have always been faithful to my King,' Aston declared, 'and he was not fairly tried. I will not give way to this upstart farmer. We shall defeat him and put Prince Charles on the throne, as is right. I will not have you encouraging the people to surrender.'

'But you know the rules of war as well as I do. If we surrender before the fighting starts the combatants will be merely disarmed. If they refuse and the walls are breached we can expect no quarter, many civilians will be killed with the soldiers as it is impossible to recognise only combatants.'

'Yes, yes, of course I know,' Aston impatiently stumped around, 'but the walls of Drogheda cannot be breached and we are going to defeat Cromwell,' he paused. 'We must, then Prince Charles will be made king.'

'I'm only interested in saving lives. With the forces Cromwell has brought, you have not a hope of defeating him. Arthur, be realistic and face the truth.'

'We will never surrender. I cannot allow you to stay and continue to talk of it. You shall be moved out of the town immediately. My soldiers will be here tomorrow to escort you.' Without a further word he left the room, his wooden leg echoing on the polished floor.

The West gate was still open and he rode out to see Ormonde.

'I have discovered that Lady Wilmot is planning to plead for surrender. I am having her escorted out of the town tomorrow.'

'In that case I shall arrange for her to be accommodated at Mellefont. In view of her age and quality we should show some respect.'

'I would rather make powder of her, grandmother or not!' Ormonde smiled at Aston's outburst.

'Has Cromwell asked for a surrender?' he asked.

'Not yet. He had as well save his breath, he will need it. We are well defended and anyone who takes Drogheda can take hell itself. We shall hold the town to the last man.'

'I hope you are right, Arthur. Hopefully, the two perils of any siege, Colonel Hunger and Major Sickness, will weaken the Parliament forces so that we can defeat them in the field later. However, keep me informed of events.'

'I will, be sure of that.' Sir Arthur took his leave and returned to Drogheda.

On the 10th September, William was on the wall above Duleek Gate with his father, Sir Arthur Aston, Sir Edmund Varney and other officers, observing Cromwell's camp bathed in bright sunlight outside, when they saw a soldier approaching carrying a white flag. The gate was opened to allow him in and he was escorted to Sir Arthur. He handed him a message which Sir Arthur read aloud to his fellow officers.

'Having brought the army belonging to the Parliament of England to this place, to reduce it to obedience, to the end effusion of blood may be prevented, I call upon you to surrender. If this is refused you will have no cause to blame me.'

'What do you think, gentlemen? This is the big moment. Fight or surrender?'

'Fight, sir, fight!' They all chorused.

'Then fight it shall be. May God be with us.'

Aston refused to surrender and the white flag was replaced by a red flag. William saw the soldier carrying the red flag. He knew what that meant and he looked with some misgiving at the guns installed on a hill south of the town. He knew, with a sinking feeling in his stomach, fighting was now about to begin. He felt this was going to be worse than his experience at Rathmines. He was afraid, but did his best not to show it.

The guns opened fire immediately and pounded the south wall and the church of St.Mary. William's ears rang with the noise of the cannonade; his nose was filled with the smell of the explosives and the dust of the broken wall. Again, there was nothing he could fire at, his musket was useless against those guns out of range. The church tower collapsed. Charles, William's eldest brother, was on the church tower. He and all the other defenders with him were killed.

This was William's first known loss. He was badly shaken when he heard it. He had known soldiers would be killed, but he had not expected to lose any of his family, not anyone so close to him. Charles, his own brother who had told him to take care. He could not help tears coming to his eyes, but he had to watch the enemy and be prepared to fire his musket. He wiped the tears away with the back of his hand and stared straight ahead.

Those guns, they were far more powerful than he thought possible! The whole church tower had been brought down and already, on the first day, the wall had been breached near the church. That wall was not as strong as he had thought.

He saw the Parliament foot surge towards the breach and they were immediately met with fierce hand to hand fighting by the defenders. From his position on the wall above Duleek Gate, William was able to fire his musket at the swarming enemy but was not aware that he hit any of them; at least he was doing his best. Those few who succeeded in gaining an entrance were cut down by the Royalist cavalry. The breach was not big enough for the Parliament cavalry to gain entrance, so Cromwell withdrew his men. He had lost Colonel James Castle, in command of a regiment of foot, shot in the head, and a number of other officers. He admitted the defenders had fought with reckless courage and in view of the natural advantages of the defences, decided to withdraw for the day.

Aston, like William, was amazed that the cannons could do so much damage in so short a time. He realised that the next day the enemy would try again. There was now no time for Ormonde to organise any help. An attack in the open against the enemy rear was their only hope. Failing that, he had to reinforce his defences inside the city. So he ordered a triple line of earth works to be built, running from the church west across to Mill Mount. William was among the work party which spent all night digging and building these trenches.

The next day the cannonade opened up again, pounding the outer walls all day. At five o'clock Cromwell gave the word to storm the breaches made. William was behind the third inner earth rampart with Robert and his father nearby. The defenders succeeded in repelling the enemy.

They withdrew, regrouped and immediately attacked again. Once more they were repelled and withdrew.

'We are winning!' William shouted to Robert with delight, 'We've won the day!'

'Not yet, William, they'll be back again.' Robert warned him.

Finally, Cromwell himself led an assault and succeeded in taking up a position on the ruins of the church. He now had a firing line straight along the earth-works and, with the arrival of reinforcements led by Colonel Ewer, they were able to clear them of the defenders.

William's father shouted to Robert and William, 'Get out of it, boys! Get across the bridge quickly, before it is raised.'

William ran down Duleek Street with Robert to the bridge. There were hundreds of panic-driven soldiers eager to cross the narrow bridge. The enemy was close behind and if the bridge was lifted before they could cross they faced certain desperate hand to hand fighting which they knew they could not win. Finally he and Robert managed to cross and ran down Ship Street and St Lawrence Street to St Lawrence Gate where they mounted the wall above. There was panic everywhere. Shopkeepers were boarding up their windows and everyone was asking what had happened. White sheets indicating surrender were hanging from several windows upstairs.

They took up a new position on the top of the city wall by Pigeon's Tower.

The Roundheads reached the bridge before it could be raised and were soon all over the town.

Durgy, Aston and many other officers and men had retreated to Mill Mount. Some Parliament officers shouted to them to surrender.

Aston said, 'Gentlemen, I think we must admit defeat. We must surrender.' Forlornly and hopefully, they waved a white flag.

'No surrender. No quarter. Kill them all,' Cromwell ordered. He was by now in a white heat of passion. The fighting had been harder than he expected and his losses were heavy. Much to the defenders surprise, as they had thrown down their weapons, the Parliament forces attacked and quickly overcame any resistance. All the defenders were killed, including Sir William Durgy, Colonel Wall and Aston himself. The soldiers tore off Aston's wooden leg, believing it was filled with gold; when they found none they hit him over the head with it!

From his position on Pigeon's Tower William could see some defenders taking up a position on top of St. Peter's church steeple. The Roundheads entered the church, piled up the pews inside and set them alight. When Cromwell arrived on the scene the church was burning fiercely.

'God damn me, God confound me; I burn ! I burn!' Cried one of the men on the church steeple.

'The man blasphemes!' Cromwell called out. Another man fell from the steeple but miraculously was able to limp away. 'Spare that man,' Cromwell ordered, 'God has saved him.'

William could see heavy fighting near the church. At the height of the fighting he saw Maeve and some of the other servants run across the road from the inn, which was on fire.

'Maeve!' He called out to her. She stopped and looked up at the wall. 'William!' She called back. As she momentarily stood there, a chance shot hit her in the back and he saw her fall on the road. William was overcome with anguish and cried aloud, 'Oh God! Oh God! Why?' What could he do to save her? He could not desert his post. He hoped to see her rise, but instead she just lay there and he was helpless.

At the same time he saw Cromwell himself on his horse at the end of the road, surrounded by his officers. Crying with sorrow and shaking with anger he reloaded, took aim and fired. He missed. By the time he could re-charge his musket, Cromwell had gone. He had had his chance to fulfil all his bravado and he had missed. He knew he would regret that for many years to come. He sank on his knees behind the wall and cried bitterly.

'Come on,' Robert beseeched him, 'we can still fire at them below.'
'It's hopeless,' William cried, 'we are all going to be killed.'
'At least we must not give up without a fight.'

They stayed on the wall all night with about 120 other officers and men, including Father O'Neill, not dressed as a priest, now holding a musket, firing the odd shot at any enemy they could see. The killing went on all through the night and later he heard about a thousand were killed, all the Catholic priests being especially picked out to be knocked on the head.

The next day they continued to fire at any Roundhead they could see, until a force of soldiers stormed the wall. After a brief skirmish on the steps, which cost the lives of many Roundheads, all the Royalist officers were shot and about a hundred and ten others, including William, Robert and Father O'Neill were captured. They were lined up against the wall facing the town, their hands tied behind their backs and orders were given to knock every tenth man on the head.

William looked across the buildings of Drogheda and wondered if this was to be his last sight of the town he loved. He had lost Maeve and his brother Charles. He assumed his father was dead too. Was he now to meet his death? He heard them counting. 'Seven... eight...nine...ten'. The second tenth man was Robert. William shuddered as he heard the blow on his head. Was he to be next? Was the whole Durgy family to be wiped out?

'One...two...three...four...five,' they were slowly getting nearer to William. The suspense was nerve wracking. Any minute now would he too be cracked on the head from behind? He stared at the town below and said a quick prayer.'Please, God. Not me!'

Chapter 5
RAPE AND MURDER

On the 15th September a rider galloped into the yard at Platten Hall. He was tired and covered with dust, his horse was sweating. Patrick was not there to take the horse so he stabled it himself. He knocked on the kitchen door. Without opening it a maid called out, 'Who is it?'

'A messenger from Drogheda, I must see Lady Durgy.'

She opened the door slightly and peered at the visitor. 'Who are you?' she asked nervously.

'You don't know me, but I have news from Drogheda and must see Lady Durgy.'

She let him in, 'We have to be careful until we know what has happened at Drogheda.'

'That is what I have come to tell you. I'm afraid it is very bad news. Drogheda has fallen and Sir William is dead.'

'Oh no! Dear Lord!' She sat at the table and burst out crying. 'Oh no, no, no! The master dead! Dear Lord!'

'I must see Lady Durgy,' he insisted, 'Where is she?'

'In the drawing room,' she said between tears, wiping her eyes with the corner of her apron.

'You must show me the way, girl, I don't know the house.'

'Give me a minute, sir,' she pleaded. She wiped her eyes finally and stood up. 'Follow me sir, I'll take you there.'

He followed her to the drawing room and she knocked on the door.

'Come in,' Lady Elizabeth said. 'Why, Maureen, whatever's the matter, you've been crying!'

'Sorry, my Lady, but it's dreadful,' she started crying again 'There's a messenger from Drogheda to see you, my Lady.'

'Then show him in.'

The man came in, holding his hat in his hand. 'Madam, Lady Durgy,' he uttered in confusion, 'I'm afraid I have very bad news.'

She rose and came towards him. 'Tell me, sir, what has happened?'

'Drogheda has fallen, my Lady. Sir William is dead!'

Her face went white and she drew herself up, clenching her hands in front of her. She was a brave woman, but this was testing her to the limit. 'Oh no! This is what I feared. Forgive me while I sit down.'

He stood before her, feeling embarrassed. 'Of course. Is there anything I can do for you? I'm sorry to have to bring such news, my Lady, but someone had to tell you.'

'Thank you, it was good of you to come. I knew in my heart all along that Cromwell's army would be too strong.' She looked up at him. 'I wonder what will happen now? Have you any news of my sons? They were all at Drogheda.'

'I am afraid we think they are all dead, my lady.'

'Oh, dear God! Not all of them?' she cried.

'Yes, my Lady. The massacre was terrible. The walls collapsed on the second day after a heavy bombardment and the Roundheads murdered all the priests and hundreds of soldiers and residents. Over two thousand were killed. Once they were inside the town we never had a chance. Somehow, the draw bridge over the river was never raised. Many buildings and the churches were destroyed. It was shocking.' He shook his head with the memory of it.

Lady Durgy stood up and offered her hand. 'It must have been terrible! Thank you for coming, now please leave me. Maureen will give you refreshment in the kitchen.'

'Yes, my Lady, thank you.' He bowed and backed out of the room, quietly shutting the door behind him.

Elizabeth fell on her knees and prayed. She did not cry, but she prayed for strength to face whatever must come next. She took her rosary from her pocket and fingered the beads for a long time in the silence of the room.

Eventually she rose, straightened her dress and decided to tell Sarah. She dreaded having to tell Sarah who was already so distressed at the loss of her own husband, but this was something she must steel herself to do. She left the room and climbed the stairs wearily; she knocked on Sarah's bedroom door. Sarah had spent a lot of her time alone in her room since Michael had failed to return from Dublin. Her pregnancy was making her feel very sick and she was certain Michael was dead; but she prayed he might still be alive, perhaps a prisoner in Dublin. She had been sitting by the window and had seen the messenger ride up the drive. Perhaps he had brought some good news?

'Come in,' Sarah said hopefully.

Elizabeth entered and found Sarah still sitting by the window.'Sarah, I've just had very bad news.'

'I saw the rider come up the drive, I hoped he would bring some good news. Michael is dead, isn't he?'

'We still do not know, but Drogheda has fallen and father is dead.'

'Oh, dear God, no!' Sarah cried, rising and coming towards her mother. She put her arms round her and burst into tears. 'This war, oh how many more do we have to lose?' she cried, 'Mother, how dreadful – what will happen now?'

Elizabeth tried to comfort her and they clung together.

'Be brave, my daughter. I don't know what will happen now, but we must carry on and look after our home and the estate. I want you to help me bear this terrible loss.'

'I will, mother, but I feel so ill. The baby makes me sick and I do so grieve for Michael. Now father is dead. Oh dear God! Is there any news of Charles, Robert or William?'

'Yes, Sarah. I am told they too are possibly all dead,' she replied struggling not to cry herself.

Sarah burst into more tears. 'Oh no! Not all of them!'

'All of them! Yes, all of them, Sarah. They tell me the massacre was dreadful, the walls collapsed and the Roundheads just poured in and killed everybody.'

'Mother, how can we carry on? What is there to live for?'

'We must pray that God will save us. We must be brave and carry on with His help.'

They held close together, comforting each other and looked out of the window. They saw the rider, the messenger of evil tidings, ride down the drive.

'Now come, Sarah,' Elizabeth unclasped her arms and stood upright determinedly, 'we have work to do. I want you to get dressed and come with me to see the bailiff. He must be told and instructions must be given about the estate.'

'Oh, mother, I couldn't go now. Is it safe to leave the house? Suppose Cromwell's troops arrive here?'

'They'll be too busy in Drogheda to come here yet. We must go today, or tomorrow may be too late. It'll do you good to get out and I don't want to go alone. I'll wait for you downstairs.'

'I don't know how you can do it, mother!'

'We must keep ourselves occupied, it will do no good just sitting and grieving. Father would want us to carry on with our lives.'

Elizabeth went down to the kitchen and found the maids all crying and weeping. 'Come, come, girls, there's work to do. There's the dinner to cook and I want the dog-cart got ready.'

'But my Lady,' Maureen said, 'We are so distressed at the sad news. We are so sorry for you.'

'Yes, yes, thank you, all of you. It is terrible but we must carry on. Sir William would not want us to grieve for ever. We must trust in God to give us strength and the will to go on.'

'Yes, my Lady. Is there any news of master William and the others?'

'I'm afraid they are all dead,' Elizabeth struggled not to show her grief, 'William, Robert and Charles. It is dreadful!'

'Oh no, my Lady!' they all cried, 'We are so sorry.'

'Now Sarah and I are going to see the bailiff.' Elizabeth recovered herself and tried to smile.

'Yes, my lady,' Maureen said, 'I'll help you saddle the horse.'

When the horse and cart were ready Sarah came into the yard and climbed onto the seat next to her mother. They drove away to see the bailiff who lived in the nearby village of Donore.

They arrived to find the villagers gathered together in the middle of the track going through the cluster of thatched cottages excitedly discussing the news. A few of the children were unconcernedly playing with a ball. The bailiff came up to Lady Elizabeth and Sarah. 'Good day to you, my Lady. Have you heard the news?'

'Yes, Thomas, dreadful, isn't it?'

'Is there any news of Sir William, my Lady?'

'Yes, I am sorry to say he was killed and our three sons too.'

'Oh, my Lady, how tragic! I am distressed to hear it. What will you do now?'

'We must carry on. I have come to tell you I will be managing the estate and I want you to help me as you served Sir William these many years past.'

'Yes, my Lady. Very well. May I come to see you tomorrow. Today the whole village is terrified the Roundheads will come at any time and they don't know what to do.'

'Just do nothing, Thomas. Tell the villagers to accept them, don't fight them or you will all be killed. There's no point in fighting them now. Accept what has happened and try to live and carry on working peacefully.'

'As you say, my Lady.'

Elizabeth and Sarah drove back to Platten Hall.

The midday meal was now ready and Sarah sat and stared at her plate. 'Come, Sarah,' her mother persuaded her, ' you must try and eat something.'

She picked at her food and ate a little. Her mother tried to eat without showing any concern, but in her heart she found it a struggle. She had difficulty swallowing the food, but did her best to encourage Sarah.

After eating half of the food, Sarah went up to her room and Elizabeth went into the drawing room. She took out her needlework and tried to occupy her mind, but very soon her eyes were filled with tears and she could not see to work. She dropped her work, held her hands to her face and burst out crying. Her body shook with sobbing and she could not stop.

'All of them,' she cried, 'Dear God! All of them!'

Sarah entered the room. 'Mother!' she exclaimed, 'Mother!' and came over to her, sat beside her on the sofa and put her arms round her. 'I know, I know how it feels. I have cried and cried for many days. Now we grieve together.'

'I'll be all right in a minute,' her mother said, 'I tried not to cry but it suddenly came over me. I am not as strong willed as I thought. I must pull myself together. It does no good just to cry.'

'Mother, you must cry. You cannot keep it in your heart. You should cry. But why, why do we have to have these wars? Dublin and now Drogheda. When will it all end? I so wanted to live in peace with Michael on our farm. Now we have nothing, nothing to live for.'

'You must not think like that, my child. You have Michael's baby. We must plan for the future. Cromwell will not do anything to us here.'

'I hope you are right, Mother.'

'Surely they will not attack defenceless women, like us? What for?'

'I don't know, Mother. But I'm afraid. Oh, Mother, I'm so afraid. Lady Wilmot's words after my wedding – they haunt me!'

'Rubbish, my child. Have faith, we must put ourselves in God's hands.'

'You are so brave. I wish I was.'

After another sleepless night, the next day a second messenger arrived, this time from Lord Ormonde.

'Lady Elizabeth,' he said, 'I have an invitation from Sir James for you and your daughter to come and stay with him.'

'Please thank him,' Elizabeth replied, 'but we must stay here and look after Platten Hall and the estate.'

'But Lady Elizabeth, he asked me to tell you he expects Cromwell's army to come this way any day now and they will not spare Platten Hall. Your life is in danger, my Lady, I beseech you to accept his invitation.'

'I cannot see why they should take any account us. Surely they are not going to murder defenceless women? But if it is God's will that we die, I'd rather die here. We stay here and God willing we shall be spared.'

'If that is your final answer, my Lady, I must accept it, but I know Sir James will be very sorry. He cannot spare any soldiers to defend you.'

'I would rather there were no soldiers here. They are not going to murder us if we are alone, but if soldiers were here that would be different.'

'I would not like to say, my Lady. They spared no-one in Drogheda.'

'That was in the battle. We stay here,' she repeated, 'this is our home and we must stay.'

'As you say, my Lady. May God be with you and protect you.'

He rode back to Trim full of misgiving. While he admired Lady Elizabeth's courage and determination he thought she did not fully realise the danger she was in.

But Elizabeth came from a long line of one of the noblest families of Ireland and had been brought up to believe the rest of the World would look up to her and no-one would want to do her any harm. Nevertheless, she instructed the servants to shutter all the ground floor windows and not to answer any one at the door. The only windows without shutters were the big ones in the main hall at the back. She had all the doors leading from the main hall locked and told the maids to keep the kitchen fire as low as possible to show little smoke from the chimney. As all the male servants had joined the army, there were only the three maids, Lady Elizabeth and Sarah in the house waiting for whatever was to come. She hoped that when and if the Roundheads came they would think the house was empty.

They did not have to wait long. One morning, four days later, a troop of ten Roundheads rode up the drive. They hammered on the front door.

'Open up in the name of the Commonwealth!' they shouted.

There was no reply.

Elizabeth was in Sarah's bedroom and Sarah was still in bed. She went to the window, cautiously looked through the leaded window and indistinctly saw soldiers standing around the front door. There appeared to be no officer with them. They looked an untidy lot, their uniforms torn and dusty.

The soldiers went round to the stables and found two horses. They knew then that the place was not empty. They went to the back onto the terrace and found the unshuttered main hall windows. They smashed the windows with their muskets and entered the hall.

'All these doors are locked, corporal,' one of the soldiers said.

'Smash them down,' he ordered.

Elizabeth heard them banging on the hall doors and she ran down to the gun room. There was no shot nor powder, Sir William had taken all the guns and powder with him. As she heard the doors of the hall being broken down she found a pistol. Could she threaten them with an unloaded pistol? She decided that would not do and searched around for some other weapon. A dagger which she could hide up her sleeve?

Although she was frightened she was determined not to give in without a struggle.

By now some of the soldiers were in the kitchen and she heard the maids screaming. Other soldiers were upstairs and they had opened Sarah's bedroom door. Elizabeth paused for a moment at the foot of the stairs. She could not confront them all at once; the choice was the kitchen or upstairs.

She heard Sarah's screams and the mocking laughter of the soldiers and decided Sarah needed her help to save the baby. She crept quickly up the stairs, full of anger at these brutes daring to molest her daughter. She grabbed the handle of the heavy oak panelled bedroom door, turned the handle slowly and gently opened it just enough to see inside the room. The soldier was pinning Sarah, kicking and grappling, down on the woven brocade covered, four poster bed. Sarah's face was as pale as the white material on the bed, her eyes wide with terror and her cheeks stained from tears. The four other soldiers stood around, in their soiled and torn uniforms, shouting coarse insults, urging their comrade to delay no longer. They did not see Elizabeth as in a rage she dashed forward, holding the dagger in both hands above her head, she plunged it up to the hilt in the back of Sarah's attacker.

The corporal drew his sword. She withdrew the dagger and turned to face him, shaking with anger. 'You brutes,' she yelled, 'leave my daughter alone!'

'No Irish scum kills one of my men and lives, woman or no woman,' he shouted. She advanced towards him and thrust the dagger at his left arm at the same time as he drove his sword into her heart and she collapsed on the floor.

'Mother!' Sarah cried. She struggled off the bed from under the dead soldier and fell on her knees beside her mother. Two soldiers grabbed her arms and she kicked them, but as she had no shoes on it was with little effect. They tore the shift off her and threw her back on the bed. She kicked and scratched with all her strength, but the corporal sat on one leg, nursing the slight wound in his arm, another soldier held her arms above her head, a third held her other leg while the fourth one prepared to rape her.

'Hurry up, man,' they urged him, 'we are all waiting our turn.'

'I'm with child!' she screamed and bit her attacker. He punched her face and covered it with the pillow.

She suffered the rest of her ordeal in silence while she gasped for breath under the pillow, the agony of the savage attack as the soldier thrust himself inside her being unbearable. One after the other the four soldiers raped her, but she had fainted long before they had finished. The corporal then grabbed Lady Elizabeth's dagger and stabbed her through the heart.

The screams in the kitchen had stopped now. There the scene had been the same as in the bedroom above. The half naked, lifeless bodies of the three maids now lay sprawled out on the cold stone floor.

The soldiers searched the house and found no-one else. They stole all the smaller items of jewelry and silver which they could easily carry. They drank the mead from the scullery, wine from the wine store and helped themselves to food. They rested and slept in the drawing room and bedrooms.

'We cannot leave any evidence of this affair,' the corporal said, when he awoke. 'We must set fire to the place. If this is discovered we'll all be in trouble. Go into the rooms downstairs and set the house alight.'

They knew Cromwell had ordered his troops not to do any looting, nor to commit any "cruelties upon the country people." But after the events in Drogheda, where so many of their comrades had died, their feelings towards these "barbarous Irish" had changed. They had no feelings of guilt, rather they felt they had partly repaid the Irish for the loss they had suffered at Drogheda.

They rode away down the drive and stopped, turned and watched the fire destroy the hall, the fierce flames showing as red as the sunset.

CHAPTER 6

THE BLACK BIRD

'Have faith, my son.' William remembered Father O'Neill telling him as the counting got nearer.

'Six...seven...eight...nine,' that was William. He heard the skull of the man next to him split as he was clouted over the head from behind. Tears of relief welled into his eyes.

The survivors were lashed together with ropes, and with their hands tied behind their backs, driven off the wall, along the street and into the stable of the inn William knew so well. An armed guard was posted over them. So ended the barbarous slaughter of Drogheda and William's hopes of victory. The taste of defeat was bitter.

For the rest of that fateful day and during the night, William had plenty of time to think. He had been so confident that they could defend the town and defeat Cromwell, but now here he was trussed up and lying in the straw with all the other prisoners where the horses had stood. He had even had his chance to kill Cromwell himself but he had failed. He knew his brothers were dead; he feared his father was dead; he had seen his girl shot down in the road. All his hopes for a happy married life with Maeve were now gone. Was one blissful afternoon in the hay going to be all he was to know of happiness with a girl? He had no idea how his mother was at home. He knew he was now alone and wondered what his future was to be: he began praying aloud.

'I would keep your prayers to yourself, if I were thee,' one of the prisoners whispered. 'I saw a man's head knocked in for praying. These Roundheads don't like Catholic prayers.'

So William prayed in silence. They cannot stop me praying to myself, he thought.

It was hot and dusty in the stable and he was thirsty. His throat was dry and the ropes hurt his hands and feet. If only he could have a drink!

'Water, water,' he cried out to the guard, 'give us a drink of water for the love of God.'

'Papist blasphemer,' the guard replied. 'Here, take this.' He picked up a bucket of dirty water and threw it all over William, who licked his lips and was thankful for that small mercy, but soon his bonds hurt even more as the wet ropes tightened. Escape! Was there any way he could escape? His bonds were so tight he could see no way he could undo nor cut them. If he could, where could he go? Cromwell's soldiers were all over the place. Perhaps it would be easier to break away later when they were moved from this stable. Imagining what he could do to escape, William gradually fell into a fitful sleep.

His hopes for freedom were finally dashed the next morning when the guards came in with leg-irons and chains. Each of the prisoners was fitted with a leg-iron on both ankles and every batch of ten were connected with a heavy chain. Their bonds were undone and now they had their hands free and sufficient freedom on their legs to walk.

'You first lot of ten men, get up and outside!' They were ordered.

One by one, each batch of ten were ordered outside. When it was William's turn, tired and stiff, he struggled to obey. Outside he took a deep breath of fresh air and looked round to see anyone he knew. There were only Roundhead soldiers standing idly by and jeering at the prisoners in chains. They were lined up facing against the stable wall and told to relieve themselves. William had never been subjected to such an indignity; he nearly cried with shame. How had he come to be so degraded and what did the future hold for him? Even if he could escape, what future was there for him in an Ireland occupied by the Roundheads? "Have Faith", Father O'Neill had told him, but how difficult that was!

Then they were marched back into the stable and given a meal of oat gruel with dry bread and left again to their own thoughts. William realised there was now little chance of escape and wondered what would follow next. He did not think they could keep them here for long, so perhaps they would make them promise to support Cromwell and then release them? That was the only opportunity to escape William could hope for. He saw Father O'Neill on the other side of the stable and waved to him. He acknowledged the wave and put his finger to his mouth, shaking his head signalling to William not to recognise him. He was afraid William would call him "Father".

'What is your name?' William asked the young man next to him. 'I am William Durgy.'

'Thomas O'Leary. Call me Tom. I was learning to be a carpenter. My father was killed on the first day of the siege. I don't know how my mother will live without us.'

'My father was killed too, as far as I know, and I lost two brothers and my girl.'

'At least we are alive,' Tom said, 'but I think we will soon be wishing we were dead too.'

'Recently I was told to have faith,' William replied, 'but I am finding it very hard.'

Turning to an older man chained to William on the other side he asked. 'What is your name?'

'John Flanagan. I don't know how I got into this mess. I never wanted to fight and didn't fire a shot. I don't see why we should not have just accepted Cromwell and his army, what is the point in fighting? Just for doing nothing I nearly got knocked on the head like the man next door to me who had his skull split. Sickening it was.'

'What do you think will happen to us now?' William asked John.

'How do I know, boy? Probably sent over to England and thrown into jail. Terrible places, they are, I'm told.'

William was not pleased to think of such a fate. He silently prayed not to be sent to prison.

They were left to their own thoughts for a whole week with poor food and a twice daily visit to the outside walls of the stable. They had no exercise and after the week the hay and straw bedding was completely flattened and provided no comfort at all.

'How much longer are they going to keep us here?' Tom asked.

'P'raps they've forgotten us,' John suggested hopefully. 'One day the soldiers'll all leave and we'll be left to ourselves.'

One morning, a few days later, a Roundhead officer came in to the stable with another man who was short and fat with a weather-beaten face and piercing blue eyes.

'Get up all of you!' The Roundhead ordered.

'' Ere we go! Summit's happening at last!' John groaned.

They all scrambled up and stood in a rough line.

'Now, Cap'n Short, have a look at this lot and give us your best price,' said the officer.

Captain Short inspected each man thoroughly. He made every one open his mouth and inspected his teeth, like a horse dealer, thought William; he made them drop their trousers and subjected them to a further undignified inspection. He grunted to himself after each examination and after he had finished he went outside with the officer.

William was near the door and could hear Captain Short outside making an offer to buy the prisoners and after some haggling they agreed on a price – a quantity of sugar for each prisoner.

'Get up all of you!' The order was repeated, 'Outside, the lot of you, quickly – outside!'

The hundred prisoners chained together in batches of ten struggled outside, walking awkwardly with the painful leg-irons and chains. They were stiff with lack of exercise and tired from lack of sleep. They shambled out of the courtyard and into St. Peter's street, then down Ship street to the North Quay. William looked for anyone he knew on the way and saw one of the maids from the inn.

'Tell my mother what has happened!' he called out to her.

She turned her back on him. It was dangerous to admit knowing a King's supporter now, she might be arrested herself. No-one wanted to know William, but some of the other prisoners were greeted with cries of anguish as their wives and girl friends recognised them.

'Michael!' one of the women cried out, running towards him, but the guard savagely cracked his whip at her and pushed her away.

'Nora!' the prisoner called back, 'Pray for me!'

At the dock William saw there was a sailing ship with the bow pointing towards the approaching prisoners. He saw the name on the bow, BLACK BIRD. It was well named being black from stem to stern, with a small figurehead under the bowsprit painted yellow, looking like a beak. He could see the furled sails the colour of a female blackbird's wings. It had three masts with crosstrees and he thought it was about 100ft long. A small craft for the hundred prisoners and crew. The prisoners stumbled awkwardly up the gangway, one fell down and caused a hold-up in the proceedings.

'Get up that man, or I'll flog ye to death,' threatened a guard. William sensed he meant it too. He wondered where they were going – he thought it unlikely they would just cross the Irish Sea to England and began to realise that any longer journey was going to cause far more hardship than they had suffered so far.

On the quayside the crowd of women who had followed the prisoners cried out to the men and the Roundheads kept them well back away from the ship, hitting some of them with their muskets.

Once on deck, William took a long look at Drogheda, his beloved Ireland, his home, thinking it would probably be the last time he would see it. Would he ride his beautiful black mare over the green, rolling countryside ever again? Would he see Platten Hall ever again? He wondered what had happened to his mother and his sister, and tears came to his eyes. They were directed to a small opening amidships and told to go below, down a steep companion-way.

It was difficult enough to descend that stairway with the leg-irons and having tears in his eyes made it many times worse. He stumbled halfway down, knocking over three prisoners in front of him and dragging two behind. They landed in a heap on the deck amid howls of painful anger and foul language. When he stood up he hit his skull on the bulkhead.

It was dark in the hold and William now saw it was only a little over five feet high. Most of the prisoners had to stoop when walking down there. They were told to lie down in rows of ten, two rows on the starboard side heads against the ship's side, two rows in the same way on the port side, four rows with their heads amidships, their feet against the first rows and two rows athwart ship in the stern. There was not a lot of room and the crew had to walk down the middle, where three stanchions supporting the upper deck obstructed their passage, or step between the prisoner's feet.

'Now, where you are lying will be your bunk for the voyage. You will always stay in your own place,' the sailor told them.

'Call this a bunk!' the prisoners grumbled.

'Quiet there, or ye'll be whipped!' they were threatened.

William found himself near the middle of the ninth row athwart ship. He discovered this row had more room to manoeuvre than the others and was grateful for that small advantage. He could not see any sign of Father O'Neill.

'Where do you think they are sending us?' asked Tom.

'I do not know, but I fear it must be a long way.' William replied.

'How did I get into this mess?' John moaned, 'I never fired a shot.'

'I'm afraid they're not going to put you ashore just because you did no fighting, you are here now and you will have to stay with me,' William managed a wry smile, 'we are chained together.'

'At least I got away from the wife.'

'Doesn't that make you sad?'

'My son, after you've been married the number of years I have, you'd be glad to get away. Women! They rule your life – do this, do that, don't do that! Your life's not your own. I'm glad for that. I'm on my own now – but I still can't do what I want!'

Soon they heard the crew preparing the ship to put to sea. William had no knowledge of the sea and was puzzled to hear the orders being shouted out overhead.

'Man the top gallant. Cast off the bow line!'

They felt the ship move away from the quayside and knew it was turning round to sail down the river Boyne, then out to sea. After two hours they had a foretaste of what the voyage was going to be like. They could hear the wind blowing hard and the sea was rough. The ship pitched and tossed, and also rolled from side to side. In that dark, practically airless hold, the atmosphere soon became fetid. The prisoners did not feel well.

The crew now appeared with food. Bowls of thin soup with small pieces of salted meat floating in them. One hard biscuit and a small piece of cheese completed the meal. Most of the prisoners did not want to eat anything, but William was determined to keep up his strength as far as he could and ate the distasteful food with apparent eagerness.

' 'Ere, young un,' John said. 'You ate that with relish – I can't stomach mine, you 'ave it. Growing lad like ye ought to eat all ye can get.'

'Thank you, are you sure, John? It's not very nice but it is food. You should eat too y'know.'

Some prisoners began to be seasick. This did not improve the atmosphere and it was not long before they were all very ill.

'I feel I'm dying,' moaned Tom to William.

But William was not seasick. He did not know why, but the motion of the ship came naturally to him and he did not mind it.

'Lie down, Tom, and take deep breaths. Think of something nice – like being at home in your own bed again.'

'You've a wonderful imagination, William. Fancy thinking of being in bed at home in this place!'

On the other hand Captain Short was at home in his own cabin. There was a knock on the door.

'Come.' He shouted shortly. John Mattock, the mate, entered.

'Cap'n,' the mate said, taking his hat off, 'how are we going to treat these prisoners?'

'Same as any other load we've picked up from the East coast.'

'But these are not niggers, Cap'n, these are white men same's you and I.'

'They're prisoners all the same. Irish scum.'

'Are we going to exercise them on deck, Cap'n?'

'Exercise 'em on deck!' Captain Short exploded, 'Exercise 'em on deck! What next will you suggest? We never exercised the niggers, why start now?'

'Well, Cap'n, I think we'll lose fewer if we looked after 'em a bit better. We could let ten at a time on deck for a spell.'

'What do you think this is? A passenger ship? You'll suggest a jig next!'

'I think we should treat them better than we did the niggers. You remember how many we lost last passage.'

'That's true. I think you're crazy, but if you want to do it, be it on your own head. Only ten at a time, mind ye, and don't go taking their chains off. I don't want a mutiny!'

'Aye, aye, Cap'n. I'll organise it.' He backed out of the cabin. 'Good night to ye, Cap'n.'

'And good night to ye, mate.'

The prisoners were left on their own all night. Early next morning one of the crew came down and ordered a group of ten prisoners to get up.

'Get up on deck,' they were told, 'and have a wash. If you jump overboard ye'll have a long swim, I'm telling ye.'

After they had gone, he threw a bucket of sea-water over the patch where they had been lying and swabbed the deck. This happened after each batch of prisoners were sent on deck for a breath of sea air.

When it was William's turn to go on deck he saw Father O'Neill lying near the companionway.

'How are you?' he whispered. He knew he could not call him "Father" or possibly the crew would have him killed.

'Not so bad for an old 'un, my boy. How are you?'

Before William could answer he was prodded in the back to get a move on up the companionway.

On deck he gazed at the endless sea stretching as far as the horizon all round. The waves were not very big, but the small ship pitched and rolled steadily as it ploughed ahead. He looked up at the sails filled out with the breeze and watched the crew going about their work. It was cold and windy, but a relief to be out of that dark hold even for a few minutes. He washed out of a bucket of sea-water and ate his ration of dry biscuit and cheese. He was surprised to be also given a small mug of beer. He exercised his stiff muscles by doing a knees bend and bent down to touch his toes. He was determined to try and keep himself as fit as possible. Some of the other prisoners just sat and moaned with grief.

'Come on, Tom,' he urged his friend. 'Exercise your arms and legs. We must keep ourselves fit.'

'It's all right for you. You don't feel sick. I still feel like dying!'

'Where are we going?' William asked one of the crew as he passed by.

'Never ye mind about that, m'lad. The cap'n knows the way!'

This routine was only done once a day, thus giving the prisoners only half an hour on deck, but it was better than nothing. On returning to their "bunk" the prisoners found the deck swimming with sea water after their patch had been swabbed down. They either had to lie on the wet or stand until it dried. Even when they laid down, they only had the wooden deck and they missed the hay and straw in the stable, as poor as it was.

In the middle of the second night Tom cried out, 'My God! What was that? Something ran over my feet!'

'It's only a rat, boy.' John explained. 'Plenty of them about and they'll be as hungry as you'll be in a few week's time. Just keep your feet moving or they'll chew your legs.'

'Thank's for the advice. When do I sleep?'

On the second night the ship settled down to a more acceptable, regular motion as it approached the open Atlantic and the next morning when William went on deck he found the sun shining and the sea calmer. He took in deep draughts of the fresh air and almost enjoyed the view in sight. He realised his past life was over and felt it was no good grieving for ever. In his prayers he prayed his mother was safe and thanked God for his life. Although he did not know where he was going he almost looked forward to a new life elsewhere. Perhaps one day he would be able to return to Drogheda?

But the voyage was not to be all plain sailing. After two weeks the cheese and the little beer disappeared from the menu. Then they were hit by a bad storm and the crew had their own problems. Captain Short first ordered to reef the upper topsail and after another hour ordered to put a reef in the mainsail.

'We're being blown off course, Cap'n,' the mate reported, 'helmsman can't hold her. We'd better lower the mizzen and take the standing jib off.' The Captain agreed and they struggled on with practically no sail at all.

During the storm William and the prisoners were not allowed on deck. They were confined below, listening to the gale blowing overhead, the creaking of the ship's timbers and the resounding crash of the sea against the hull. As landsmen they did not understand what was going on outside, they feared the ship would sink and they would be drowned like trapped rats.

'Take off our leg-irons,' William beseeched the crew, 'so we can swim.'

'Ye wouldn't swim far in that sea, I'm telling ye. With your chains on ye'll drown that much quicker,' was all the comfort they got.

To keep up the prisoner's spirits Father O'Neill encouraged them to sing a hymn. Soon, most of them joined in and the chorus of voices almost drowned the noise of the storm outside for a while.

After three days the storm abated and Captain Short was able to shoot the sun and find their position.

'We are way off course,' he told the mate, 'this is going to delay us. How are the provisions lasting out?'

'Not too bad now, Cap'n, but if we are going to be an extra week we had better ration the water.'

'Yes, do that now rather than wait for it to run out.'

The prisoners were cut down to one cup of water a day instead of two.

'I bet the crew still get their full ration,' John grumbled.

On the day after the storm they were allowed on deck again. William was glad to get a breath of fresh air at last. He saw the sea was still running with heavy rollers and marvelled at the way the ship rode over them.

After four weeks even the dried biscuits had weevils. The salted meat was varied with dry fish, but otherwise the fare was very monotonous. At night some of them tried to catch the rats to add to their fare.

'A cooked rat tastes like pork I'm told,' John said.

'But we can't cook them here,' William replied, 'I don't fancy eating one raw.'

'First you've got to catch it!' Tom said.

After six weeks several of the prisoners suffered from sore mouths, aching and swollen joints – scurvy! John Flanagan was one.

'You should have eaten more,' William told him, 'and when you went on deck you should have exercised your arms and legs and not just sat and stared.'

'You're young, boy. You can take it, but when you get to my age, you give up. I don't mind if I die. No-one is going to miss me.'

The mate reported the sickness to the Captain.

'So your idea of a jig on the decks did them no good, Mr. Mate.' the

Captain said.

'One of the crew is showing the same illness, Cap'n.'

'Probably caught it from the prisoners. I can't afford to lose any of this cargo. They are worth more per head than the niggers. White slaves fetch a good price. What do you reckon we can do to save them?'

'I'm sure I've no idea, Cap'n. We lost many of the niggers with the same sickness.'

'If we separate the sick perhaps it will not spread to the others. Ye'd better release the sick and allow them on deck. They can sleep in the sail locker on their own.'

'Aye, aye, Cap'n.'

John Flanagan was released from his chains and allowed to stay on deck, and he slept with the other sick prisoners in the dark sail locker up forward.

During the following two weeks, more of the prisoners suffered from scurvy and joined John Flanagan. On the third week John died.

'The first prisoner to be sick died last night, Cap'n,' the mate reported.

'Throw him overboard, then!'

'No burial service, Cap'n?' he asked.

'Burial service? He's Irish Papist scum – not a crew member. Do ye expect me to pray for him? I pray for myself – may no more follow him or I'll make a loss on this trip! Throw him overboard, I say.'

'Aye, aye, Cap'n, as you say.'

John Flanagan was consigned unceremoniously to the sea. Ten died one by one each day and were treated in the same way.

'My God, Tom,' William said, 'I wonder what this sickness is we are dying from?'

'I don't know, but I feel I shall never see land again. I wish I could die quickly and get this over with.'

'Don't say that Tom. Keep up your spirits and pray to God. Try and have faith – that's what I've been told. I know its hard, but I'm determined to live through this.'

'Without your help, I'd have died weeks ago.'

William wondered how many more were to meet this fate. He prayed for land. Captain Short, never before a religious man, was also praying for land.

'Mr Mate, keep a sharp look out. We should have sighted land days ago. If we miss that island we'll be in the Carribees.'

But another week was to go by, William calculated it must be the 22nd or 23rd November, before they heard a welcome cry from the watch on deck.

'Land ahoy, starboard bow!'

When it was William's turn on deck he saw the low, green hills of an island some five miles away. He uttered a prayer of thanks.

'Look at that, Tom!' William cried out. 'Land! I wonder where it is?'

'I don't care,' Tom replied, 'even if it isn't where we are going I hope they find some food and water.'

'What is that land?' William asked one of the sailors.

'Barbados,' was the reply.

'Where's that?' Tom asked, 'I've never heard of it.'

'The other side of the Atlantic, somewhere.' The sailor explained vaguely.

CHAPTER 7

INDIAN BRIDGE

'Black Bird' had sighted the east coast of Barbados, dead ahead. Captain Short knew the only port was on the west side, so he had to steer a course round the northern end of the island.

'Ten points to starboard, Mr Mate,' he ordered.

'Aye, aye, Cap'n.'

'We should reach Indian Bridge by tomorrow,' he added.

William was not to set foot on land until the next day.

Early that morning 'Black Bird' dropped anchor.

'That's a welcome sound,' said Tom, 'the ship'll stop rolling now and we'll soon be ashore, wherever it is. Then we'll get water and better food.'

'Water, yes, better food, I wonder?' William queried.

The prisoners had to wait for a long time before they were ordered on deck. Captain Short went ashore in a row boat and reported to the harbour master.

'I've arrived on the Black Bird with ninety Irish prisoners of war to be sold as slaves. Where do you want me to put them? Same place we put the niggers?'

'Irish prisoners of war? We know nothing of this. We've had a few Scots, but never Irish before. Are they all fit?'

'Yes, all fit.'

'So you didn't lose any on the voyage?'

'A few,' he admitted reluctantly, 'but the rest are fit.'

'Any females?'

'No. All males.'

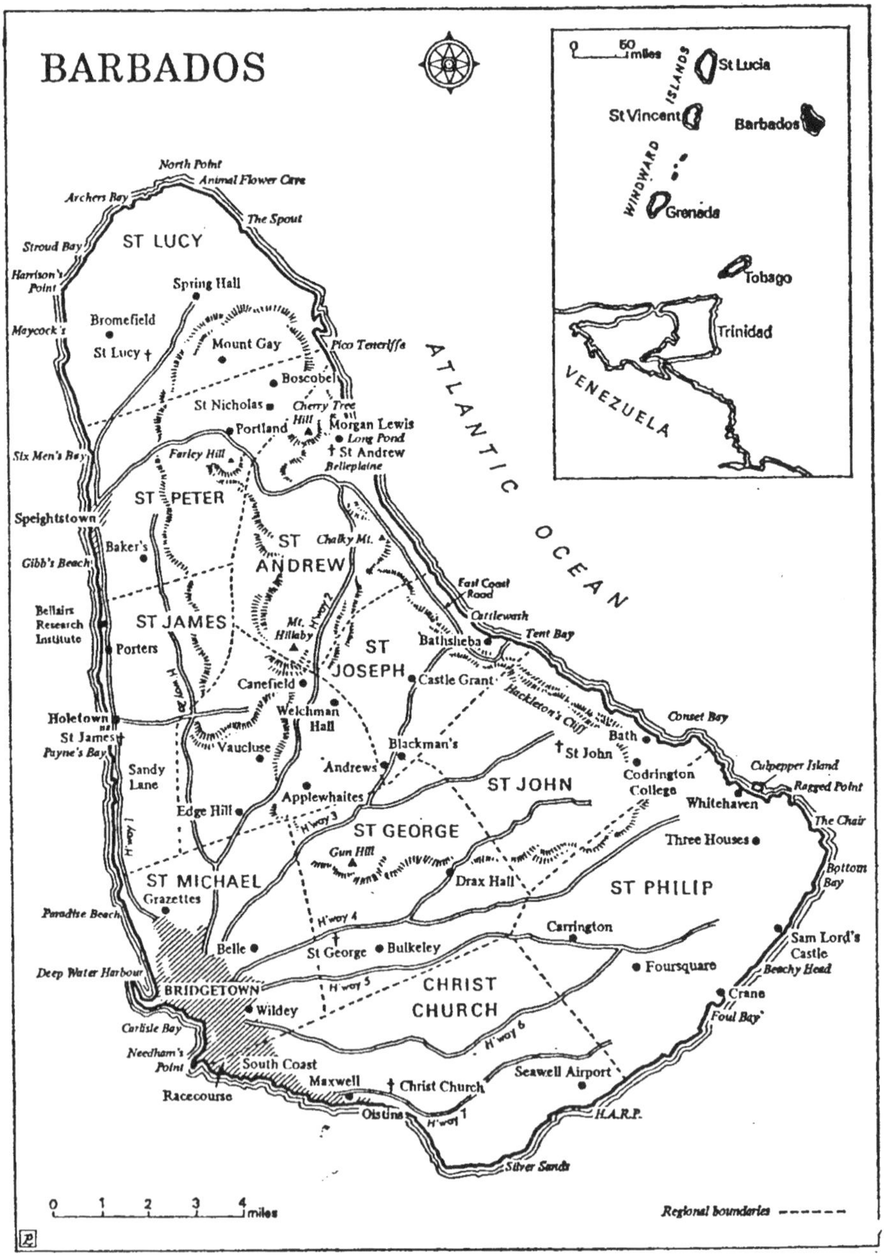
BARBADOS
0 50 miles
St Lucia
WINDWARD ISLANDS
St Vincent
Barbados
Grenada
Tobago
Trinidad
VENEZUELA
ATLANTIC OCEAN
North Point
Animal Flower Cave
Archers Bay
The Spout
Stroud Bay
ST LUCY
Harrison's Point
Spring Hall
Bromefield
Maycock's
St Lucy
Mount Gay
Pico Teneriffe
Boscobel
St Nicholas
Cherry Tree Hill
Morgan Lewis
Portland
Long Pond
St Andrew
Six Men's Bay
Farley Hill
Belleplaine
ST PETER
Speightstown
ST ANDREW
Chalky Mt.
Baker's
Gibb's Beach
East Coast Road
Bellairs Research Institute
ST JAMES
Mt. Hillaby
H'way 2
Cattlewash
Tent Bay
Porters
Bathsheba
ST JOSEPH
Castle Grant
Canefield
Hackleton's Cliff
Holetown
Welchman Hall
Conset Bay
St James
Bath
Payne's Bay
Vaucluse
Blackman's
St John
Sandy Lane
Andrews
Codrington College
Culpepper Island
Ragged Point
ST JOHN
Applewhaites
Whitehaven
Edge Hill
H'way 3
The Chair
ST GEORGE
Three Houses
Gun Hill
Bottom Bay
ST MICHAEL
Drax Hall
ST PHILIP
Grazettes
Paradise Beach
H'way 4
Carrington
Sam Lord's Castle
Belle
St George
Bulkeley
Deep Water Harbour
Foursquare
Beachy Head
BRIDGETOWN
H'way 5
CHRIST CHURCH
Crane
Wildey
Foul Bay
Carlisle Bay
H'way 6
Needham's Point
South Coast
Seawell Airport
Maxwell
Christ Church
Racecourse
Oistins
H'way 1
H.A.R.P.
Silver Sands
0 1 2 3 4 miles
Regional boundaries

'We haven't anywhere we can keep them other than the pound for the niggers. Another batch of 'em arrived yesterday.'

'That'll have to do then. I know where it is, will you supply an escort?'

'I can arrange an escort. We always do with the niggers. Land them about three o'clock and we'll meet them on the jetty.'

Captain Short made his leave and instructed the mate to put the prisoners ashore that afternoon.

The prisoners waited impatiently before the first group of ten was ordered on deck, complete with chains. When it was William's turn he saw many other sailing ships riding at anchor nearby, with their sails furled. It was a clear, sunny day and warm for November. Ashore, he could see a small wooden bridge connecting the mainland with an island. A forest of trees came right down to a group of wooden houses, sheds and a short, wooden jetty built along the water's edge. The sea was clear blue-green and William thought the view was magnificent.

'What is the name of this place?' he asked one of the crew.

'Indian Bridge,'* was the reply.

He was then sent down the steep gangway, which was not secured to the ship's side and swayed with every step, and he found it very difficult being chained to his eight fellow prisoners, but was determined not to fall, as he had when he went below decks on the first day, or they would all be in the water. They reached the foot of the gangway successfully, and one by one scrambled into a waiting row boat.

The boat was rowed to the jetty and the prisoners had to climb a steep ladder to reach the top which the chains made more difficult. Here they waited until all the prisoners landed, they were then marched towards the shore and along a dirt road, escorted by four men carrying muskets, passed a row of wooden houses, stores and sheds. Some of the islanders stood by watching the new arrivals and William felt ashamed to be seen in his dirty clothing with no shoes, the rats had eaten his shoes, and wearing leg-irons. Many of the onlookers seemed well-dressed and he was surprised to see there were some negroes among them.

Most of the buildings were wooden with thatched roofs but a few were built of coral stone with red-tiles. Some of the shops and stores had

---

* Now known as Bridgetown

a veranda in front supported by wooden pillars, giving a covered way on the side walk; a group of niggers were sitting and standing idly in the shade thus provided. The narrow dirt road was crowded with horse drawn carriages, transport for the planters' wives, wearing brightly coloured dresses, wide brimmed hats and parasols. There were many waggons loaded with cotton, tobacco and sugar on their way to the quayside to be loaded onto the ships anchored in the harbour.

William was amazed to see the prosperity of the place, but he also noted that there were many white men who were not so well dressed and seemed to be standing idly around.

The prisoners were driven into a wooden shed and told to lie down. Outside, in a compound, William saw about two hundred black slaves, all naked, with iron shackles on their legs lying on the ground in the hot sun. There were men, women and some children. They looked terrified and stared with wonder at the white newcomers.

After their escort had left the final batch of ten prisoners in the shed, Father O'Neill stood up. 'Now let us thank God for our deliverance,' he announced.

It occurred to William this might be a little premature, after all they did not know what lay in store for them. He had also never seen a priest in such ragged clothing, with irons on his ankles, preaching bare foot before!

'Let us kneel and pray,' Father O'Neill began, going onto his knees. 'Dear God, we give you great and hearty thanks for bringing us safely to this place. We give thanks for saving us from the perils of the sea and the sickness which struck our brothers. We beseech you to forgive us for our sins and we pray for the souls of those of us who died on the journey. We pray for the safety of our loved ones we left behind at home and pray that one day we may rejoin them. In the name of the Father, The Son and The Holy Ghost. Amen.'

He stood up and raised his hands above his head. 'Let us stand now and sing a hymn:

> "Now thank we all our God,
> With heart, and hands, and voices,
> Who wondrous things hath done,

In whom His world rejoices;
Who from our mother's arms
Hath bless'd us on our way
With countless gifts of love,
And still is ours today."

He sang alone, for none of the prisoners knew the words!
'Let us end with Our Father's prayer.."Our Father which art in heaven...".'
When he finished there was a chorus of "amens", some loud, some muttered under their breath.
There was a period of silence while the prisoners were deep in their own thoughts. Not many of them were very religious, but all felt Father O'Neill had given them some comfort.
'Where is this island, Barbados?' William asked Father O'Neill.
'It is on the other side of the Atlantic, near the West Indies. So far as I know, it has only been inhabited about twenty years and they grow tobacco here.'
They were kept in that shed for seven days. The food was not much better than on board the ship but they were given some fruit, including pawpaws and pomegranates which they had not seen before. There were no rats, but many cockroaches, nevertheless they were glad not to have the continuous motion of the ship. There was at least plenty of fresh drinking water but they were still chained and had only a few minutes exercise outside each day, marching with their chains on in a circle among the black slaves.
The black slaves were sold on the third day. There was a small wooden rostrum in the centre of the compound. The planters gathered in front, the slaves were stood on the platform one by one and bids were invited. Unless the bidder was willing to buy husband and wife and children together the families were split and this resulted in many tearful scenes. By the end of the morning the compound was empty and William and his fellow prisoners were on their own.
William managed to move to the door one day and started talking to the guard outside.
'What's this island like?' he asked.

'Not bad. Hot in the summer and a good climate in the winter.'
'Have you been here long?'
'Five years. Two years ago we had the plague and a lot of people died. That was a bad time. Things are better now. Are ye Scotsmen?'
'No, we're from Ireland.'
'We haven't had Irish prisoners here before. A few from Scotland, but mostly niggers.'
'How are the slaves treated here?'
'Quite well. It's the servants who are treated badly.'
'Why is that?'
'They are serving for five years and after that they are free to find work themselves. Ye see many of them looking for work. The niggers belong to their masters until they die.'
'What do they grow here?'
'Mostly tobacco. Some plantations are growing more sugar now and I hear one plantation has built a sugar mill. Here comes the officer, I must stop talking to ye.'

The next day the guard called William to the door.

'Here,' he said, 'this is a copy of a leaflet being posted round the town. Thought ye'd like to see it.'

'Thank you,' said William and read the leaflet:

"SALE OF IRISH PRISONERS OF WAR"

By the instructions of Captain Short of the vessel

BLACK BIRD

a consignment of 88 Irish Catholic Prisoners of War
will be sold by auction at 10 in the forenoon on
NOVEMBER 30th 1649
in the Customs Shed on the Quayside, INDIAN BRIDGE.
All able-bodied men in fit working condition."

He passed the leaflet round to the rest of the prisoners and Father O'Neill read it to those who could not read.

On the day of the sale would-be bidders came into the shed early in the morning and the prisoners had to stand for inspection. One such customer was a man smartly dressed in knee breeches, brass-buttoned coat, yellow waistcoat and a three cornered hat.

'I'll take ten of the strongest men ye have,' he said to Captain Short.

He took his time inspecting all the prisoners. He picked William, Tom O'Leary, Father O'Neill and seven others. Their chains were released and their hands tied with cord behind their backs. They were marched out of the shed and told to get on to a waggon waiting outside. With their hands tied behind their backs William and the other prisoners had to be helped onto the waggon.

The waggoner whipped up the horses and they drove off down the rough, dirt road passing a row of buildings on either side. The people in the street took little notice of them, they were not such an unusual sight as they had been when they trudged along the street from the jetty on their arrival. Soon they were travelling through forest and then the road followed the edge of the cliff and William could see the sea on his left. It looked blue and calm from this view-point, but he was glad he was no longer on it. They drove on for an hour until they arrived at a plantation. They were told to get down and shown into another wooden shed and the door was locked.

Eventually the man in the yellow waistcoat appeared and addressed the prisoners.

'My name is Richard Irwin. I came here from Parracombe in Devon and own this plantation called Sandy Lane. I understand we have an unusual situation here. I have bought you as slaves and as such ye'll have to obey the laws of the island concerning slaves. Ye'll have to work for me and ye'll be arrested and punished if you desert the plantation. In return I will feed and house you. But I understand you were captured whilst fighting for King Charles in Ireland. We support the King on this island, so really we are on the same side. All I can say is that I presume if, and when, Prince Charles is on the throne, ye'll be released from slavery.

'Your immediate task will be to clear ten acres of forest and plant sugar. At present we have two hundred acres of tobacco, one hundred of sugar, fifty of cotton and other plots with food crops. My foreman will be in charge of you, his name is John Huxtable, and he came with me from Devon. If you have any problems you will approach him. Now your bonds will be removed and I trust ye'll work with a will for the benefit of the plantation.'

John Huxtable came into the shed. He was a thick built, stocky man with a weather worn, sun-burnt complexion and piercing blue eyes.

'I will hand these fellows over to you now, John,' Irwin said and walked out of the shed.

'You are lucky,' John Huxtable said as he removed the bonds from each of the prisoners, 'Richard Irwin is a good man to work for, but I warn you, you must obey the laws here for slaves. You stay on the plantation and do not go anywhere without permission. The plantation house grounds are out of bounds, unless you are given work to do there. Under my supervision you will clear an area of trees. It'll be hard work but you will be housed and fed. If you have any problems, come to me. I will now show you your quarters and the mess hut where you will eat with the other workers.'

As he turned to leave the shed he said,'There are a few negro women. Have nothing to do with them, their men are very jealous.' He paused and added with emphasis, 'You can forget any thoughts of women here!'

The prisoners followed Huxtable out of the shed and across a yard to another wooden building with a thatched roof. This was the sleeping quarters for the workers. Down the centre of the room was a line of tables and benches. Along the walls were wooden, double bunk-beds for forty men. The bunks had straw filled palliasses and pillows.

'At least this will be more comfortable than the deck,' said Tom.

'You will find some of these empty. Pick your bed and I will show you the dining hall. Food is being dished up now. Outside you will find a pump if you want a wash.'

They all decided that was essential and queued up to wash.

In the mess hut there were about twenty negro workers waiting for their food. The prisoners were each handed a metal plate, spoon and metal mug as they joined the queue.

The food consisted of pork, sweet potatoes and Indian corn. William and the other newcomers ate with relish, glad to see a change in diet.

'You see, we do have something to be thankful for,' said Father

O'Neill. 'We should say grace but I do not know how our new friends would behave if we did. I suggest we say grace silently.'

William muttered to himself. 'For what we are about to receive may we be truly thankful', but was not sure that many others knew what to say.

After the meal the other workers went to their own tasks on the existing crops. Huxtable took William and his party to see the area of trees they were to clear. The trees were a mixed lot of deciduous varieties, some small and some very large, there were also some palm trees. They were given axes to fell the trees, and shovels and picks to dig out the roots. William and Tom decided to work together and selected one of the smaller trees to start with.

'This should be easy for you, as a carpenter,' William said.

'I have not worked with trees before. I make things with the wood.'

They soon discovered it was hard work and after the life on board ship without exercise, they tired quickly. By the end of the day they could barely summon the strength to lift an axe and were glad when Huxtable told them they could go to the mess hut for supper.

After the meal they were free to sit around outside the mess and talk.

'I propose we get to know each other,' Father O'Neill suggested. 'My name is Patrick O'Neill and this is William Durgy. Who else have we got?'

They each gave their name. Tom O'Leary; Charles Farrell a young man of twenty two; Tim Flaherty a youth of sixteen; Peter Cusack a middle aged man; John More a cook, Mick Newman, Paul Fraser and Tony Chapman were all about thirty and did not say what their occupations were.

'I was given a pike at Drogheda but didn't know what to do with it! I nearly threw it down when we all went up on that wall. I should've done, then I wouldn't be here now. I wonder what my wife is doing now? How can she live without me?' Peter wondered.

'We can only pray for our loved ones and ask God to protect them,' Father O'Neill said. Peter gave him an odd look. William wondered if he was going to ask if he was a priest and what Father O'Neill would have replied.

'I lived with my mother.' Tim announced. 'My father died two years ago and she depended on me. I have two brothers and three sisters, all younger. I don't know how she'll do without me.'

'I was only married six months ago,' Charles said, 'and she is with child.'

'Well, we are here now,' William said, 'there's nothing we can do but make sure we live through this and hope to go back when Prince Charles is restored to his rightful throne.'

'When will that be?' Peter asked. 'Years ahead!'

William slept well that first night and woke the next morning feeling very stiff, with sore, blistered hands.

He saw that only the unattached negroes slept and ate with them. Those negroes with wives had their own quarters with a room each. Not many of them spoke much English, so they were unable to communicate and kept to themselves.

One evening after work, William was sitting outside under the shade of a tree when Huxtable passed by.

'How are you doing?' he asked William.

William stood up and replied. 'Quite well, sir, better than on board the ship! We are finding the work hard but with the better food we should soon be stronger.'

'You were lucky not to have gone to some of the other plantations where the owners support Cromwell. I hear they are treating their Scottish prisoners worse than the negroes.'

'How many plantations are there, sir?'

'Oh, I couldn't be saying. A hundred or more.'

'The population of the island must be quite large then, sir?'

'About twenty-five thousand. It was much higher, but we had the plague two years ago and many died. Then there was a drought and food was short. We do depend on the weather but things are better now and trade is good with the Dutch.'

'Thank you for telling me, sir.'

'Good night to ye.'

'Good night, sir.'

Huxtable walked off with the impression that William Durgy was probably more intelligent than the average prisoner and could be made more use of. He decided to discuss him with Irwin.

This work continued for several weeks. The trees were first cut through about three feet off the ground and when felled, the smaller ones were sawn up into logs for burning; then the roots were dug out. The palm trees were the most difficult to cut through and were later burned.

'Sir,' William suggested to Huxtable, 'I suggest we do not cut through the palm trees, which takes a long time and they are not used, but dig them out by the root.'

'A good idea,' Huxtable agreed, 'I)o that to the palms.'

The larger trees had the branches trimmed off and were cut lengthwise into planks over a saw pit. A double-handed saw was used for this job, one man in the pit and one on the stage above. William and Tom were doing this work.

'Come on Tom, this is more like your work,' William observed.

'Now you should be glad I told you to exercise on the ship. We are in better shape than many of the others.'

'I still find it hard. How many more of these trees have we got to cut up?'

'Don't you despair. There must be a hundred or more yet!'

'I think the negroes should do this work. They look a good bit stronger than us.'

'Yes, I wouldn't want to quarrel with one of them.'

'Some of their women are attractive to look at.'

'You know what Huxtable said. You can forget women here.'

'I wish we had brought some of ours with us.' Tom said.

Although they were told they were better treated than many of the Irish and Scottish prisoners on other plantations, they were always conscious that they were slaves. The work was hard and William wondered how long it would take them to finish felling these tress.

CHAPTER 8
THE JACARANDA TREE

During this period the weather was far hotter than in Ireland. The sun shone every day with a temperature of about 75 degrees Fahrenheit and 60 by night; they had a few light showers of rain and almost every day a cool, nor-easterly wind. Their clothes soon wore out and they were given shorts and cotton shirts, the latter usually discarded while working in the sun. Those prisoners who still had shoes soon wore them out and as there were none to replace them they had to go bare foot. They became very sunburnt and whenever they went with Huxtable to Indian Bridge on the waggon to collect supplies they were taunted by the locals, with shouts of "Red-Legs", derisively referring to their sunburnt condition.

William and Charles Farrell went with Huxtable on one of these trips to Indian Bridge. While Huxtable was in the store, they were left outside on the waggon.

'I am going to that store over there for a drink of mobbie,' said Charles. 'Are you coming with me?'

'Don't be stupid. What is it anyway?'

'The local drink made from yams, I'm told.'

'They won't give it to you. You've no money, anyway.'

Charles jumped down from the waggon.

'Where are yo' goin'?' shouted the negro waggoner.

'To get a drink'.

'They'll throw yo' out!'

Charles crossed the road and entered the shop. All the customers inside turned and stared at him.

'A tankard of mobbie, please,' he asked the shopkeeper.

The man leant over the bar and peered into Charles's eyes.

'You're a red-leg,' he whispered, 'I can't serve you. Ye don't have any money anyway'.

'Why do you call me a red-leg?'

'Because you have red legs,' the shopkeeper grinned, 'and you have no shoes. All my customers wear shoes. If I were you,' he added with a wink, 'I would just quietly leave. There is a law enforcement officer sitting over there and if he suspects anything he'll arrest ye.'

The law officer looked up from his drink.

'Having any trouble?' he called out.

'No, no trouble, this man's just asking the way.'

'Where to? Scotland?' The customers all roared with laughter.

With a sheepish grin Charles did as he was recommended and went out quietly, leaving the customers shaking their heads.

'Nearly got arrested,' he told William as he clambered back on the waggon.

'You were lucky,' said the waggoner, 'If yo'd been arrested yo'd have got ten lashes at least.'

Huxtable came out of the store.

'Right, you two, go into the store and load the goods on the waggon.'

Charles and William went into the store and were shown sacks of flour, a few pick axes and shovels, and a bolt of cotton cloth. They loaded these on the waggon.

The first Christmas in Barbados was celebrated on the Sandy Lane plantation with a day off work. The Catholic priest came and held Mass. The workers were treated with a meal of pork at midday and in the afternoon they gathered round the compound and jigged to music played on home made wooden whistles.

A few days later, in January, some negresses were picking cotton in the plot next to where they were still felling trees.

Time Flaherty called out to the nearest picker, 'Hey there, my beauty, what's your name?'

She looked up and grinned at him.

'Have ye no tongue in your head?'

She shook her head. At that moment a large negro came strolling over.

'What yo done speaking to my woman?' he demanded.
'Just trying to make friends.'
He walked right up to the man. 'Yo no speak with my woman or I knock yo head off!'
'All right, all right, I was just being friendly.'
Father O'Neill and William came over.
'What's going on here?' O'Neill asked.
'Dis man was speaking to my woman.'
'I was only being friendly.'
'Dis man no be speaking with my woman or I knock his head off.'
'I'm sure he'll say he's sorry and then we can forget all about it. Go back to picking cotton,' William ordered.
'No red-leg tells me what to do. I no forget it, and he no say sorry.'
'All right, I say sorry,' and Tim called out to the girl, 'Sorry my beauty!'
The negro raised his fist. William was standing beside him and grabbed his arm.
'Dere he go again, speaking to my woman. I knock his head off!'
'I was only saying sorry.'
'Yo say sorry to me, not to my woman.'
'All right, I say sorry to you,' with that he turned away back to his work.
The negro scowled after him and reluctantly walked slowly back to the cotton.
'That only goes to show how very careful we have to be with these people,' Father O'Neill said. 'That could have been a very nasty affair over such a simple thing.'
Every Sunday morning Irwin insisted that all white workers attended a morning service held on the open space outside the living quarters, conducted by a Roman Catholic priest. The negro slaves were not considered as humans and no-one thought of teaching them any religion.
One Sunday after the service, Irwin called William over to him.
'I have been receiving good reports of you, Durgy,' he said. 'I hear you did not join that fool who tried to get a drink, you helped calm down the affair by the cotton field and you are a good worker. My gardener wants a permanent assistant instead of the extra occasional man. His

name is Mason, report to him tomorrow. This means you have permission to go inside the house boundary. I will tell Huxtable.'

'Thank you, sir. I have never done any gardening but I will do my best. Do you need a carpenter? If so, did you know O'Leary is a carpenter?'

'No, I did not. I will remember it.'

The next day William started his new job. He did not know what it would involve, but reasoned it should be less arduous than felling trees and digging out roots. Mason was an elderly man with a round back, apparently brought about by a life-time of digging. He extended a rough, hard-skinned hand in greeting.

'How do,' he said, 'my name is Josh Mason and I be told ye be sent to work with me.'

'That's right. My name is William Durgy. I've never done any gardening before but I'll do my best to help you.'

'Well, ye won't find it hard. The Good Lord does the hard bit, he makes the plants grow, we just looks after 'em. I'll show ye round.'

He took William to a tool shed, next to the stables at the back of the house and pointed out the spades, forks, trowels and a wooden wheelbarrow, with pride. They were all neatly stacked and as clean as if they were new.

'Mister Irwin is a good man to work for. You are lucky to be with him. There's some on this island, their names won't pass my lips, I could tell stories of that'd make yer 'air curl. But Mister Irwin is a good man. Doan ye let 'im down, mind ye, and he'll see ye'll be awright. I came 'ere with 'im, oh, let me see, some fifteen years back. I knows of 'im way back in Devon.'

He then took William round the garden and showed him the vegetables. There was Indian corn, just beginning to sprout, cassava, pawpaw trees, orange trees, fig trees, carrots, sweet potatoes and onions.

'Figs, oranges, pineapple and water melons grow wild here,' Josh explained. 'The soil is not very deep but things grow well if they are watered. That is the difficulty – shortage of water. Last year everything dried up in the drought and we were short of food.'

He showed William the chicken run, a few ducks and ten goats. This was all at the back of the house. At the front was a large patch of grass with a few trees and a driveway all around leading up to the front door. The house itself was a large building constructed from coral stone with a red tile roof. The front porch had two wooden pillars.

In one far corner was a tree with a few large purple flowers.

'What is that tree over there?' William asked Josh.

'That be a special tree brought from South America called a jacaranda. It usually flowers up to December but this year t'is late. In the summer it's full of large flowers. A beauty of a tree, surely. Now ye've seen the place, we'd better do some work I want ye to dig a patch.'

William worked happily with Josh for several weeks. He learned a lot about gardening from Josh, how and when to sow the vegetables, how to prune the fruit trees as well as how to look after the livestock. One advantage he found with this job were the extra items of food, in the form of fruit and vegetables, he was given to augment his rations.

'We've been told to get the grass in the front cut and the pot-holes in the drive made up,' Josh said one day. 'Mrs Irwin and her daughter are expected in a few days from England.'

The grass had to be cut by hand with a small sickle and other slaves were given this task, with William in charge to see they did the job properly. He also helped Josh repair the drive.

On the day Mrs Irwin and her daughter were due to arrive, the household staff, the groom, William and Josh were lined up by the front door to greet them. The carriage came up the drive and Mr Irwin got out and held out his hand to Mrs Irwin as she alighted. She was a handsome woman dressed in a long purple dress and a large black hat. The daughter then descended from the carriage. William thought she was about seventeen years old, with long black hair and a full, youthful figure, wearing a white silk dress with long sleeves.

'This is my wife, Henrietta, and my daughter, Olive,' Mr Irwin announced.

'Welcome to Sandy Lane, ma'am and missy,' said the majordomo.

They were introduced to all the staff who dutifully bowed and curtsied in turn. William was overawed to shake the daughter by the hand. He was embarrassed by the obvious difference in their status, she in her fine clothes and he standing there in his bare feet, ragged shorts and dirty shirt.

Olive liked riding and every morning the groom took her horse round to the front door. As often as possible William tried to find a job to do in the front of the house at the same time, to catch sight of this beautiful girl as she mounted and rode off down the drive.

On one such morning, a few weeks after her arrival, Olive had just mounted her mare when a mongoose darted out from the bushes across the drive. Josh was in hot pursuit and, on seeing the mongoose cross the grass, fired at it with his musket. The mare reared up in fright and Olive flung herself forward holding on to it's mane. The groom stood by bewildered and did nothing. William ran forward and grabbed the bridle before the mare bolted. He pulled her head down and placed his mouth by her nose. The mare calmed down at once.

'Thank you,' said Olive and rode off.

Later in the morning it rained and on such occasions William and Josh sheltered in the tool shed.

'Those mongooses be a pest,' said Josh, 'they be after my chickens. You were quick to act. I've heard that the Irish were good with horses so I suppose ye know something about them? That nigger groom is useless!'

'Well, I had my own horse at home and trained it from a foal.'

'My father told me the Irish were all poor people who lived in hovels.'

'I lived in a house bigger than Mister Irwin's. My ancestors lived in it for hundreds of years.'

'You must find it hard living this life then. How came you be a slave?'

'I fought the Roundheads at the battle of Drogheda and they defeated us. I was taken prisoner and my two brothers and my father died in the fighting. We were sold as slaves and brought here.'

'We've never had Irish slaves before. Olive is a pretty wench, don't you think? Did ye know a girl like her in Ireland?'

'She reminds me of my sister. I think she is beautiful – I could fall in love with her.'

'Don't ye do no such thing. Mister Irwin would'nt like it, I be telling ye.'

The next morning, when Olive mounted the mare she called out to William.

'Boy, come here!' and when he was close to her she leant down and whispered, 'I want to thank you for what you did yester-day. Meet me by the jacaranda tree tonight at seven,' she rode off without waiting for a reply.

William was amazed. He wondered how he could keep such an assignation without arousing suspicion among the rest of the workers. But he was hiding in the bushes behind the tree at seven. He crouched there for half an hour listening to the crickets and the tree-frogs. He was just about to creep back to his own quarters when he heard footsteps approaching.

'Where are you?' Olive asked. 'What are you doing hiding under the bushes. Stand up boy!'

William stood up and found he was close to her. He was annoyed she had called him "boy" but she was wearing a strong scent and it aroused him. In the half light he could not see her very clearly, but he was aware he was almost touching this beautiful girl. She leant forward suddenly and gave him a quick kiss on his cheek. His annoyance melted away.

'That's my thank you,' she said. 'Where do you come from?'

'I come from Ireland.'

'I come from Devon.' She spoke quickly, without a pause.' We have a farm at Parracombe. I came here with mamma when I was five but there was only a wooden hut to live in then, so we went back to Devon. Now pappa has built this house we are going to live here. The Roundheads were causing trouble in Devon. Did you have anything to do with Roundheads?' she asked, but without waiting for a reply went on talking. 'I had lots of friends in Devon. We used to ride over Exmoor on our ponies. Can you ride? I love riding but I don't like riding here alone. I like a bit of excitement – meeting you like this gives me a thrill – if pappa found out he'd be furious. There is nothing for me to do here, I get bored. Suppose I'll have to make friends on the other plantations, if there is anyone my age there. So far I've only met old men and women.'

William was spellbound by her vivacity, in spite of the fact that he was never given time to say anything himself and was speechless when she suddenly said, 'Must go now, I'll meet you here again tomorrow night. Don't be late!' He had even forgotten that she had been late herself. He wondered what would happen if such clandestine meetings were to be found out? Whilst Irwin would be angry with his daughter the punishment meted out to him would be much more severe.

The next day he did his work in a dream and was back at the jacaranda tree before seven. He waited for an hour but Olive did not come.

The next morning Olive called out, 'Boy, come here,' and again whispered to him, 'see you tonight.'

'Could not come last night,' she explained when she arrived late again. 'Pappa had to go to a meeting and mamma and I went to the governor's house with him. It is exciting what is happening, isn't it?'

'What is happening?' he asked.

'Boy, don't you know? You should know what is happening around you – what other people do affects your life and your future. Colonel Walrond, now that Lord Willoughby is away visiting the other islands in the Caribees, is the governor. He is a friend of pappa's, we knew him in Devon. He held a meeting of the council last night and they declared Charles the second, King of Barbados and the Caribees. There is great rejoicing. Charles is in Holland now and we have been in contact with him. It won't be long before he is back in England and put on the throne.'

'When the king is back,' said William, 'I will be released from slavery. As a free man I will be able to do what I want. I come from a good family in Ireland, my father was Sir William Durgy and we had a large estate.'

'And now you are a slave boy,' she sneered.

'But I am equal to you. My home at Platten Hall was bigger than yours here. When I am free, will you marry me? Olive, dare I say I love you!'

'My name is not Olive, it's Olivia. Only pappa calls me Olive,' she replied haughtily. 'You silly boy, you are pappa's slave and I am his daughter. You must be mad to think we can ever marry! We do not even know one another – and we are never going to. If you behave like this we cannot go on meeting here. Now I must go or I will be missed. I don't know about tomorrow, I'll have to think it over.'

She ran off without another word.

That was foolish of me, William thought, but hearing they had declared Charles as king his thoughts had raced ahead to a possible future.

'Where do you go at night?' Tom asked.

'We are having trouble with slugs and they only come out at night.'

'Oh, yes?' Tom said unbelievingly, 'one night I'll come with you to help!'

'I told Mister Irwin what ye did to that mare of Miss Olive's the other day,' said Josh a few days later, 'and he asked me if I thought ye'd be a good groom and could I spare ye.'

'Oh, thank you. I would love to look after the horses. I know more about them than I do about weeds!'

'Well, I expect he'll be telling ye himself.'

The next day Irwin came to see William while he was sowing some carrot seeds.

'Durgy,' he said, 'I understand you are good with horses.'

William stood up, 'Yes, sir, I had my own foal at home which I trained and I have worked with horses on my father's estate.'

'That negro groom is no good. I want you to take over the horses and stable. Teach him how to look after the horses. At present I have to keep an eye on supplies of food. I want you to do that.'

'Very well, sir. I'll do that.'

William started work as a groom in June 1650. He moved his sleeping quarters to the hayloft over the stable but still had his meals with the other workers. He had to exercise the horses not used in the day; there was Olive's mare, Richard Irwin's horse and the one used for the waggon or the carriage. Olive, or Olivia as she wished to be called, usually rode every day and Irwin rode his own horse around the plantation, so William sometimes had only one horse to exercise. Apart from grooming, feeding the horses and repairing the saddlery he had to keep the stables tidy and order the feed as required.

He enjoyed this work and still had Josh for company when not working, or on wet days. He sat under the jacaranda tree on two nights and waited, listening to the chorus of frogs and crickets for an hour but he did not have to listen to Olivia. Now that he slept in the hayloft it was easier for him to do this than when he had to slip out of the slaves' dormitory. Olivia never kept the tryst again; she barely even thanked

William when he took the mare for her morning ride. No-one would guess that anything had passed between them.

He longed for female company, especially Olivia's, but as time went by realised he had been foolish and that she was merely a flippant, young girl who enjoyed teasing him and craved for younger company which presumably she had now found elsewhere. He saw Richard Irwin more often now and grew to like him. Richard explained to him what was happening on the island.

'Last month, the elected members of the Council proclaimed Charles II King of England, Scotland, Ireland, Wales, Barbados and all other plantations. Lord Willoughby has been appointed as Governor. Governor Bell has retired to St. Christopher.'

William could not tell him his daughter had already told him this.

'Will this have any effect on our status as prisoners, sir?' William asked, hopefully.

'Possibly, but the status of all the prisoners cannot be altered until Charles II issues the necessary edict. As we have proclaimed him King, we believe he may order the release of all Scottish and Irish prisoners of war. But I expect the Commonwealth will act when they hear this news. Probably, they may send troops to take the island by force, so the Council have decided to train an army to defend the island. You fought at Drogheda, didn't you?'

'Yes, sir. That was where I was taken prisoner.'

'You would be required to join this army. You would continue to work for me and spend some time training. I will talk to all the prisoners and workers.'

'Yes, sir, I'll join,' William assured him, 'and I'll talk to the others as well if you wish.'

When he next saw Father O'Neill and Tom he told them the news.

'I'll join,' said Tom. 'I've news for you too. Mr Irwin has made me assistant carpenter, so if you want anything done in the stables you know who to ask!'

'I don't think I can fight,' said Father O'Neill. 'This puts me in an awkward situation.'

'Why don't you tell the priest or Mr Irwin who you are?'

'No I don't think I will just yet. Later, maybe. If Cromwell's men take over here and they know I'm a Catholic priest I will be killed for certain.'

The next day the priest, Father Sullivan, came to William with his horse.

'I hear you are good with horses. Mine has gone lame, could you look at it for me?'

'Walk it round, Father, and I'll have a look. Ah! I see, it's the left fore-leg.'

He lifted the horses hoof and inspected it.

'It's just a stone that's got stuck. I'll soon get it out for you.'

After he had treated the horse the priest asked, 'Are you a Catholic my son?'

'Yes, Father.'

'I hope you use your rosary every day.'

'No, Father, I lost it at Drogheda in the battle.'

'Well, in that case I will bring you another. It will be a present from me with my blessing, for seeing to my horse. Thank you, my son!'

After the morning service on the following Sunday, the priest came over to William

'Here, my son, here is the rosary I promised to give you.'

'Thank you, Father.'

'Mind you use it every day as a good Catholic should do.'

'Yes, Father, I will. And I'll try not to lose this one!'

'You take good care of it, my son,'

On two afternoons every week, William and six of the other workers went on the waggon to the plantation next door, about a mile away, for military training. They spent most of their time learning to march and drill with staves. As they had no firearms William thought it was a waste of time, he wanted to learn to use a firearm more efficiently and practice firing. He could not forget the last time he fired in Drogheda and missed Cromwell! On the other hand, now that they were drilling, they were issued with shoes which was a great advantage!

During another Sunday morning service, while they were lustily singing a hymn, there was an interruption. Colonel Drax, from the neighbouring plantation, rode up on his horse.

'Stop that singing!' He shouted. 'You know the Commonwealth forbids the singing of hymns!'

'We are Royalists and as such are permitted to sing,' Irwin replied.

'I will bring this matter to the Council, damn you! You'll see then what will happen.' They continued singing with even more vigour. Colonel Drax rode off.

Chapter 9
PREPARING FOR INVASION

William thought Olivia was right when she said the actions of other people affect their lives. He realised he did not live in a bubble on his own, he had to follow the stream wherever it took him.

Lord Willoughby, the Governor General of the Caribees, had left Colonel Walrond to administer the affairs of Barbados. On the 3rd May 1650, Walrond and his brother persuaded the Assembly to pass the resolution to declare Charles II as King; but not all the Assembly were in favour.

At the next meeting of the Assembly, Colonel Drax stood and addressed the chairman, Colonel Walrond.

'Mister chairman and members of the Assembly, I have to report that last Sunday at Sandy Lane plantation, I heard the Catholic priest, mister Irwin, and all his workers and Irish slaves singing hymns at Sunday mass. As members of this Assembly are aware, such actions are forbidden by the Commonwealth.'

'Colonel Drax, I must remind you that the majority of this Assembly agreed to declare loyalty to King Charles II. As Royalists we are permitted to hold Mass and sing at Mass. I see nothing wrong in Mass being performed at Sandy Lane.'

'I support Cromwell and many of my fellow members in this Assembly also support Cromwell. We insist the planters follow the laws made by the Parliament in England.' Drax protested.

'This island stayed neutral throughout the Civil War,' Bedford declared, 'I do not see why we must commit ourselves to either side. We never belonged to England, we belonged to the King. Now the King is no more, we can trade profitably with the Dutch and declare ourselves independent. We can encourage the other islands in the Caribees to follow our example and declare a New England state.'

'That proposal is preposterous! If we did that we would have no support from either Cromwell or the King.' Irwin said. 'Cromwell would quickly send troops to invade us and that would be disastrous to our trade. By supporting the King, at least Prince Rupert may send his fleet to help us.'

'The London merchants hove ordered us to trade only with them if we are to look to Cromwell for protection.' Nicholas Foster said.

'We do not need Cromwell's protection,' Walrond insisted, 'We have already declared our loyalty to our King. We are free to trade with the London merchants or the Dutch as we wish. I see no reason why this Assembly should deal with a crowd of rebels who will not bow a knee to the King. I propose we remove all planters who are Commonwealth supporters from the island.'

This proposal was greeted with many cries of disapproval, but many more shouts of agreement.

Eventually the proposal was put to the vote and passed with a majority. The assembly then discussed a list of names of those who should be banished from the island. It was decided every planter should be requested to declare allegiance to the King within seven days or leave the island and be relieved of his plantation.

'If we insist on this matter,' Colonel Alleyne stated, 'We put a lot of planters in a difficult situation. If Cromwell decides to take action after our declaration of loyalty to the King, and he invades Barbados – then will the Commonwealth banish all those planters who supported the King as we propose to banish those who do not? I propose we should leave the planters their freedom of choice without the threat of banishment and loss of property.'

'I agree the planters should be given freedom of choice,' Walrond decided, 'We will only banish those who openly refuse to declare loyalty to the King, and accept those who wish to support the King or abstain from declaring for either side '

After much further discussion and heated argument this was agreed. It was decided that all planters should be given the seven days to make their minds up whether to support the King, or the Commonwealth, or to stay neutral. Once again Walrond had imposed his will on the Assembly.

Later, when Irwin came to the stable William asked what had happened at the Assembly.

'The Assembly agreed that as declared Royalists singing is permitted.' Irwin told him 'also, they insisted that all the planters must swear allegiance to the King. Those that refused would be expelled from the island and they were given seven days to make up their minds.'

'Do you think many planters will refuse to swear allegiance, Sir?' William asked.

'It is hard to say. No doubt those members of the Assembly who are in support of the Commonwealth will refuse, but I think the majority of the other planters will not wish to give up their plantation and will either support the King or wish to stay neutral.'

That evening after work William told told Josh and Father O'Neill the news.

'I think this means Cromwell will send troops to Barbados,' Father O'Neill said.

'That means we will have to fight,' Tom said, 'Although I am now training for it, I don't want to fight again.'

'I'm too old for fighting,' Josh declared, 'I'll leave that to you young 'uns.'

'I must admit I don't like the idea of fighting either,' William said, 'but if it means holding the island for the King we have no choice.'

A week later, Irwin called all his white slaves together in the compound.

'I have to tell you,' he announced, 'that Colonels Drax, Alleyne and Foster and about a hundred other planters have refused to swear allegiance to the King and they are being banished from the island. Tomorrow, six of the men training will be issued with muskets and go with me to Colonel Drax's plantation, which is next to ours, and escort him and his family to Indian Bridge.'

William and his "troop" of six trainees had their first military duty the next day. They marched to Colonel Drax's plantation at Ridge Hill with their muskets, unloaded. There they found two waggons loaded with the family possessions and a carriage waiting by the front door.

'Colonel Drax!' Irwin called out, 'Are you ready to go?'

A servant came to the door. 'The master is not ready yet, sir. He will be here soon.'

While they were waiting for the Colonel, William saw among the slaves, who were gathered watching, a few of the prisoners who came on the *Black Bird* with him. He spoke to one of them, Jack Dickens.

'How are you doing?' William asked.

'We are not sorry,' was the reply, 'our conditions here have been as bad as on the ship. One of our men, Pat Flanagan, do you remember him?'

'No, I don't remember him.'

'Well, Pat Flanagan died after being flogged for not working hard enough when he was ill. What ever happens next could not be worse than what we have been suffering. Hard work, floggings and bad food.'

'I'm sorry to hear that. We have had to work hard but we've had no floggings.' William felt grateful he had been bought by Irwin and not Drax.

The Colonel came to the door, his wife and two children just behind him.

'Aye, damn you, we are ready! But ye'll regret this day, my good Mister Irwin. We'll be back and we'll not forget this ignominy.'

'It is not my decision. It is by the order of the Assembly.'

'Aye, but ye did not keep your mouth shut. You spoke up for this. I'll not be forgetting that.'

He then helped his wife and children mount the waiting carriage. He ignored the servants, lined up by the door, who were all crying – they had lost their jobs and did not know what was going to happen next.

The coach and waggons were escorted down the hill to Indian Bridge at a walking pace with three armed escorts on either side. As they approached the buildings of the town the local populace, lining the sides of the track, shouted abuse.

'Rebels! Get ye going out of here. God save the King!'

Eggs and fruit were thrown at the coach, one egg missed its target and hit William in the face. Everyone cheered and William laughed.

When they arrived at the dock, Drax and his family were escorted along the jetty and put aboard the waiting row boat. The waggons were unloaded and all the luggage rowed out to the ship riding at anchor in the harbour.

Irwin and his party then returned to the Drax plantation in one of Drax's waggons. He called the servants and slaves together.

'Now listen to me,' he said, 'your master has been exiled because he refused to declare allegiance to the King, Charles II, God bless him. I am now taking over management of this plantation and you will all work as before but under my direction. Your foreman will carry out my orders and this plantation will be run in the same manner as mine.'

'Things will be better now,' William told Dickens. 'Irwin is a good man to work for.'

'Yes, I see you look well enough and you are wearing shoes! Where did you get them?'

'That is because we have volunteered to train as soldiers. But also we are well fed. I have a job as groom and do you remember Tom O'Leary? He's working as a carpenter. The others have been felling trees and are now planting sugar-cane.'

When they returned to *Sandy Lane* Irwin sought William out at the stables.

'Durgy,' he said, 'I am not happy with the state of that plantation. I would like you to go and inspect the stable there and see how the horses are.'

William was now free to ride outside the plantation unescorted. His extra responsibility filled him with pride and helped him to forget Olivia and the constant thought that he was only a slave. He was now a man in charge of the horses for two plantations and overseeing the work of other men, this made him feel that the future held some prospect for him.

He found the horses at Ridge Hill were poorly cared for, two had saddle sores and others were unfit through lack of exercise. He was happy to see them improve during the following weeks.

But as time went by he was more unhappy with the military training. They did little more than march up and down and drill with their staves. He asked Irwin if he could be excused this duty, as the work with the two stables took up all his time.

'I agree for the time being,' Irwin told him 'but later, if we hear the Commonwealth are going to invade, you will have to start training again. By then we should have some firearms to practice with.'

During the months ahead, William saw and heard about the preparations being made to defend the island against possible invasion. Every day he had to take the waggon with several negro slaves to the harbours on the west coast such as Indian Bridge, Holetown or Speightstown, where new defensive forts were being built. He met many of the prisoners who had arrived with him on *Black Bird* and found that they, like most of the islanders, were filled with feverish excitement at the prospect of fighting the Roundheads. Tom's ability as a carpenter meant he had work to do on these undertakings.

In the evenings, after work, William, Tom, Josh and one or two of the other slaves used to sit outside the stable talking. Josh smoked an old, well-worn clay pipe.

'I wish you'd sit downwind of me,' Tom said, 'that pipe of yours smells!'

'Ye'd better move and sit upwind then,' Josh replied, 'I be an old man and I be comfortable 'ere.'

'Tom, what do you think of these forts they're building?' William asked. 'I saw the siege guns at Drogheda destroy the walls of the town in one day. Surely these wooden forts are not going to stand any such bombardment?'

'I don't suppose the guns on the ships will do as much damage as the siege guns at Drogheda. These wooden forts will be enough to protect us against musket fire.' Tom replied.

'As I told ye before, I be too old to do any fighting,' Josh declared. 'I hope I don't have to be in one of your forts to find out how good they are! I'd rather be in charge of the rations.' Tom picked up his fiddle, which he had made, and starting playing a tune. The others sat quietly and listened.

Huxtable walked round on his evening's inspection.

'Well, I see we have a happy little party here!' he greeted them. 'How's the fort building going?'

The little group stood up and Tom replied, 'Quite well, sir.'

'I was wondering what use they will be, sir' William said. 'I was at Drogheda and saw what the siege guns could do to thick stone walls. I don't think these wooden forts will stand up to any bombardment.'

'Let's hope it will never happen. I don't look forward to any fighting,' Huxtable said. 'I must be on my way, good night to you all.'

Irwin often explained to William what was happening and so he learned that as well as confiscating the plantations belonging to the banished planters, the Governor, Anthony Walrond, imposed a levy on all goods exported to raise funds for arms. This levy on exports was not popular with many of the planters, who had never had to contribute to the island's needs before.

The arms were bought from Holland where Charles II was in exile with Prince Rupert, who had left the Scilly Isles and gone to Holland for his own safety. He was invited to come to Barbados with a fleet of ships to help defend the island and encourage the other islands in the Carribean to fight for the Royalist cause, but the invitation had not yet been accepted.

Lord Willoughby returned from his visit to the Caribees and Walrond went on board his ship to welcome him home.

'I trust you had a good voyage, sir,' Walrond asked.

'Very interesting, Anthony. Most of the islands support the King, very encouraging. How are the affairs in Barbados?'

'We had trouble in the Assembly. Drax and his followers did not want to support the King and once again tried to impose the laws of Parliament on the island. There was a heated discussion in June and eventually I persuaded the majority to declare that all planters who refused to swear allegiance to the King should be exiled from the island. The only exception we made was to allow those who wished to remain neutral to stay. We banished Drax, Alleyne and a hundred or so others.'

'God's teeth, that was severe! I'm not sure I like that. They'll go home and persuade Cromwell into action. He'll invade us. Have we been in touch with Prince Rupert? Is there any chance he will bring his fleet to defend us?'

'We have asked him but had no reply as yet.'

'What action have you taken to defend the island?'

'We have a volunteer force training. We have put in hand the building of forts at Holetown, Speightstown and St. Oistins.'

'Good. Hopefully we can buy arms from Holland.'
'I have declared a levy on all exports to raise the necessary funds.'
'I don't suppose that is popular, but very wise. Well, I'll get ready to go ashore now. We'll meet tomorrow and have a further discussion. Thank you for meeting me.'
'Glad to see you back, sir.'

Meanwhile, in England, as soon as Colonels Drax and Alleyne arrived with their families and the other exiled planters, they appealed to the Committee for Trade and Plantations, who exercised power on behalf of the Rump Parliament's "Assembly of State", to invade Barbados and restore them to their plantations.

Oliver Cromwell had always been in favour of establishing strong support for the Commonwealth in the 'Caribees' and also wanted to defeat the Spanish forces in the area. Barbados was the most prosperous island in the area and so he supported a proposal to invade the island and use it as a base for further operations.

On the 1st February 1651, a warrant was issued to Sir George Ayscue instructing him to: *"reduce Barbados to the obedience of the Commonwealth, to force the inhabitants to submission, to land men, surprise their forts, beat down their castles and places of strength, and to seize all vessels belonging to them or any others trading there."*

To safeguard the property of the republicans, two commissioners were to be sent with Ayscue, who had to obtain their permission before launching operations against plantations on the island.

Chapter 10
THE INVASION

The King has defeated Cromwell at Worcester! The splendid news spread like wildfire over the island after the arrival of a ship from England on the 12th October, 1651. They heard that Charles II and his army had marched from Scotland down to Worcester, where they had defeated the Commonwealth army.

The next day, there was great rejoicing at Sandy Lane where Irwin organised a party with a feast of pork, vegetables and the inevitable mobbie. The servants and slaves danced and celebrated late into the night. Tom played his fiddle and was accompanied by three others on wooden whistles.

'You will soon have your freedom now,' Irwin told William, 'I hope you will stay with me as my groom.'

'Yes, sir, thank you I will be glad to.'

William was delighted, as his days of slavery were hopefully at an end. He would be a free man to work for whoever he wished and perhaps to return to Ireland. Olivia was not at the party, she had gone to a neighbouring plantation to celebrate with them. William missed her presence but did not think he would have had an opportunity to talk to her.

'Now is the time you should tell Mister Irwin that you are a priest,' he told Father O'Neill.

'Yes, maybe you are right, my son,' he replied. He spent some time thinking the matter over; he knew he should admit his transgression in denying his cloth but wondered what the reaction of his priest would be. He decided to see Irwin.

'Sir, now that it appears the king will be restored to the throne and the Commonwealth is at an end I should tell you that I am a Catholic priest.'

'Indeed, O'Neill. I cannot say I am at all surprised. You have obviously shown yourself as more intelligent than most of the prisoners. How did you become a prisoner then?'

'At the battle of Drogheda I discarded my cloth and took up arms to help defend the town. I was among the last defenders who were rounded up on the town wall with William and the rest of the Irish here. Every tenth man had his skull smashed. it was sickening. The rest of us were taken prisoner and sold as slaves.'

'I suggest you go and see Father Sullivan. He will tell you what to do.'

'Thank you. May I go tomorrow?'

'Certainly. I will tell Huxtable to give you a day off work.'

He went to see Father Sullivan and after he had explained what had happened at Drogheda and doing penance for the cloth, he was appointed lay priest.

On the 15th October, the look out at St. Oistins Bay sighted seven warships which were identified as English and the news was carried to Lord Francis Willoughby.

Sir George Ayscue, in charge of the fleet, landed at St. Oistins Bay and was taken to see Willoughby.

Willoughby stood and held out his hand to greet Ayscue.

'Sir,' Ayscue said, ignoring the proferred hand, 'I have been sent by the Parliament of England with a fleet to demand the surrender of Barbados.'

'I think you are mistaken, sir,' Willoughby said. 'We had news last week from England that Charles had defeated Cromwell at the battle of Worcester. We have been celebrating this victory.'

'I have to tell you, sir, that you are mistaken. Charles was defeated, his army completely routed and when we left England the Roundheads were searching the country for him. No doubt he has been found and is probably now in the Tower of London.'

Willoughby sat down in amazement and held his head in his hands. 'This is bad news indeed,' he replied, looking up at Ayscue, 'and now you seek our surrender?'

'That is so, sir. We have two thousand troops on board the fleet and are prepared to invade if necessary. But we would prefer to negotiate a peaceful surrender. My instructions from Cromwell are to negotiate a surrender. We do not wish to invade the island and cause destruction of property and loss of life and trade. We are prepared to offer reasonable terms, but if they are declined I will have no alternative but to order an invasion. You have usurped power and expelled those planters who did not support you'

'That is not correct. We have the same Government here that has always been approved of by England. I will have to call the Assembly together and we will discuss this matter. What are the terms you are offering?'

'Royalist planters may retain their plantations. You will govern with your present Assembly providing a proportion of members are Commonwealth supporters. You will only trade with London and not allow any Dutch ships to trade. You may even elect a member of the Assembly to sit in the Parliament of England.'

'We will never agree to forbid freedom of commerce, but as I say, I will have to consult the Assembly. Go back to your ship, sir, and we will be in touch tomorrow '

'I need supplies. Food and water. We will need to garrison two thousand troops ashore which will have to be provided for.'

'We will consider all these points. I bid you good day for now, sir.'

Ayscue departed and returned to his ship.

The Assembly met the next day end Willoughby outlined the terms for surrender.

'The planters will never agree to restrict trading with London alone,' Walrond said, 'We have always been free to trade where we like. I do not trust these terms. What guarantee have we got that Royalist supporters will be allowed to stay?'

'We can only insist on that being one of the terms of the Treaty to be agreed and trust they will abide by it.'

'I think we have no alternative,' Modyford said. 'We do not want the island invaded. Think of the loss of life and the damage to the plantations!'

'With all the defences we have built,' Bedford declared, 'I think the

English will get no further than the beaches. We are King's men, let us defend the island in the King's name!'

The discussion went on for two hours and at the end a vote was taken to decline to surrender and a declaration was drawn up which stated:

"We find these Acts of the English Parliament to oppose the freedom safety and well-being of this island. We, the present inhabitants of Barbados, with great danger to our persons, and with great charge and trouble, have settled this island in its condition and inhabited the same, and shall we therefore be subjected to the will and command of those who stay at home? Shall we be bound to the government and lordship of a Parliament in which we have no representatives or persons chosen by us?

"It is alleged that the inhabitants of this island have, by cunning and force, usurped a power and forced an independent government. In truth the Government now used among us is the same that hath always been ratified, and doth everyway agree with the first settlement and Government in this place.

"Furthermore, by the above said Act, all foreign nations are forbidden to hold any correspondency or traffick with the inhabitants of this island; although all the inhabitants know very well how greatly we have been obliged to the Dutch for our subsistence, and how difficult it would have been for us, without their assistance, ever to have inhabited these places in the Americas, or to have brought them into order. We are still daily aware what necessary comfort they bring us, and that they do sell us their commodities a great deal cheaper than our own nation will do. But this comfort would be taken from us by those whose Will would be a Law unto us, However, we declare that we will never be so unthankful to the Netherlanders for their former help and assistance as to deny or forbid them or any other nation, the freedom of our harbours, and the protection of our Laws, by which they may continue, if they please, all freedom of commerce with us.

"Therefore, we declare that whereas we would not be wanting to use all honest means for obtaining a continuance of commerce, trade and good correspondence with our country, so we will not alienate ourselves from those old heroic virtues of true Englishmen, to prostitute our freedom and privileges, to which we are born, to the will and opinion of anyone; we can not think that there are any amongst us who are so simple, or so unworthily minded, that they would not rather choose a noble death, than forsake their liberties.

The General Assembly of Barbados."

William was in the stable when Irwin came in early the next morning the day after the Assembly meeting.

'Afraid I have bad news for you, Durgy,' he said, 'we now hear that Charles was defeated at Worcester and the Roundheads are searching the country to take him prisoner.'

'Oh, God, sir! Does that mean those ships that arrived yesterday are going to invade us?' William did his best to hide his feelings

'We are negotiating with Admiral Ayscue; and have declined to surrender. This means you will have to go back to training again. We hear Dutch ships arrived this morning with, we hope, arms; but I believe Ayscue is now attacking them. We do not know what the outcome will be.'

'I am bitterly disappointed to hear this, sir But I will do my best to help defend the island.' After Irwin left William went to the hayloft, got out his rosary and prayed. He was afraid of what the future held for him. He did not want to fight, but felt he had no alternative.

The declaration from the General Assembly was sent to Admiral Ayscue by a messenger. At the same time as he arrived on board the Rainbowe, seven Dutch ships were sighted and action stations were called. The messenger was unwillingly trapped on board the Rainbowe, the flagship of the fleet, while Ayscue attacked the Dutch ships and captured them. He stripped the captured ships of all the food, water and cargos for his own fleet of seven, placed a prize crew on board and sent them off to neighbouring islands for supplies.

In reply to the refusal to surrender, Ayscue issued a proclamation telling the colonists that the Governor had refused to submit to Parliament. Appealing to them over Willoughby's head he called the planters' attention to the danger of resistance. By opposing Parliament, he told them, the island would be transformed from its flourishing condition into a "seat of war."

"Whatever the specious pretences of any amongst you are," he mockingly wrote, "you cannot be ignorant, but that they are altogether unable to give you protection without which this island can no way subsist".

When the General Assembly met to discuss this latest ploy by Ayscue, Lord Willoughby had an important announcement to make.

'Gentlemen,' he addressed the Assembly, 'when Ayscue's fleet was approaching our island they fell on some Dutch traders and captured them, as you know. One of the Dutch sailors managed to escape from his ship at night and came ashore requesting to be taken to me. He had been entrusted by his captain to bring me a message from Prince Rupert in Holland. Gentlemen, I am pleased to tell you that Prince Rupert is on his way here with his fleet and they will attack Ayscue and send him scurrying back to England.'

This speech was greeted with acclamation.

'Gentlemen,' Willoughby proceeded, 'all we have to do is resist Ayscue as long as possible. He will be short of victuals and water, his troops will be dying of scurvy. I propose we tell Ayscue we intend to risk our lives and fortunes to defend His Majesty's interest and lawful power in and to this island.'

The Assembly agreed to this proposal and also added to the message that they "would risk their lives to defend the person of the Right Honourable Francis Lord Willoughby."

Irwin told William and the other Irish slaves they would have to help defend the island. When William rejoined the small band of volunteers for training he was given a wheel-lock musket which was the latest firearm from Holland and was able to practise with it. The situation looked grim as the islanders expected the troops to land from the fleet immediately.

Lord Willoughby, who commanded the defending forces, inspected the volunteer force of about a hundred men under Irwin's command.

'Remember how you felt when you arrived after the voyage from England,' he told them. 'You are now in better fighting condition than they will be. You know the land, whereas they are strange to it; you are fit and well-fed but they are seasick and will be hungry. They will not be in good fighting condition.'

They spent a lot of time going to various positions on the west coast and practising defensive manoeuvres. William, Tom, Josh and a small detachment of men were detailed to take up position at Denmark Fort, near Speightstown, where a constant watch was kept in case of attack from the north. It was an uncomfortable place to be as at night they were plagued by gnats and the land crabs swarmed inshore and bit their legs.

Meanwhile, on the Rainbowe, Ayscue was having his problems.

'We should invade immediately,' he told Farrell and Burton, the two commissioners appointed by Cromwell.

'We will not give you permission to invade until every effort has been made to negotiate a peaceful surrender.'

'But the Assembly has already said they will not surrender. You've read the declaration we've just received in reply to the proclamation I sent. What point is there in continuing negotiations? My crews and the troops are short of provisions and water. We must land at least a small force to secure essential supplies immediately.'

'First we must find out where they are lightly defended. Give me a day or two to send some good men ashore to find out the strength of their defences.'

'So long as they do it quickly, I can only agree. Arrange for your spies to go to work at once.'

Ayscue then sent small raiding parties every day to various landing beaches along the coast, taking any livestock they could find and replenishing their water supplies.

Two men who were landed by night at a deserted cove near Holetown returned to report that Speightstown and Holetown were both lightly defended.

'Then I propose sending two ships to cruise off that coastline to land a small party for supplies.' Ayscue declared.

In the meantime the islanders were given every chance to continue to prepare their defences. Willoughby expected the main attack to be near St. Oistins or Indian Bridge.

Prince Rupert, King Charles's nephew, was a great strategist and gallant cavalier, but Willoughby had privately said he was, "on a horse, a genius; on a ship, in charge of a dozen other ships, a complete ass."

Prince Rupert was indeed sailing his fleet across the Atlantic to the rescue of Barbados, but he ran into minor troubles, as his navigator reported later.

'When we were about fifty leagues east of Barbados, on what I took to be a perfect heading, some outlook spied a small ship which looked as if she might be Dutch and richly laden, so we set sail after her, but she proved faster and we never caught her. During said chase Admiral Rupert's ship sprang such a great leak that we had sore trouble trying to keep her afloat, and when the chase ended we found we had overrun our reckonings and had passed Barbados in the night without seeing it. We doubled back but never did find it, and the troops we carried for the island's defence were wasted.'

What was worse, whilst searching for Barbados, Prince Rupert sailed his squadron straight into the teeth of a hurricane, where he lost many of his ships, including one commanded by his brother, Maurice. Shamefully, he then sailed back to Holland with the remainder of his fleet.

It was not until late in November that the commissioners finally agreed to allow Ayscue to send a small force of two hundred men, under Captain Morris, which landed near Holetown. Most of the fleet was still further south and there were few defenders at Holetown to meet them. After a small skirmish Morris's force captured thirty prisoners, some planters among them, and secured some livestock and refilled their water butts.

The desultory raids on the island continued and Ayscue made no attempt to make a major invasion until a Parliamentarian fleet arrived bound for Virginia. Feeling that this extra force would intimidate Willoughby he sent another summons which was again turned down.

Ayscue urgently needed more water and provisions, so on the seventh of December another force was landed at Speightstown.

Denmark Fort was a small square, wooden block-house built on a low cliff overlooking an inlet to defend Speightstown and had four cannons, two pointing out to sea and two across the small inlet. It was capable of holding fifty defenders, William, Josh and Tom were among them, and they had been told that if a landing was attempted it would only be a small party. Behind the fort Modyford had a force of twelve hundred pikes and cavalry; they were confident they could deal with any landing force.

Two ships of Ayscue's fleet had been standing offshore for three weeks, the rest of the fleet was in Carlisle Bay.

The defenders had been on watch for a week and were bored with looking at the two ships sailing up and down and sometimes dropping anchor. Then one night they could just see in the moonlight a few small ship's boats appear round the stern and bow of the two warships as the clouds cleared. As they approached, the moon was obscured again and they could not see how many boats were coming.

'Look at that!' William cried out. 'I saw rowboats, but now the moon has gone and I can't see them.'

'Everybody stand to,' the sergeant in charge ordered, 'It looks like a small landing party coming.'

For William and many of the others, this sight brought back stirring memories of Drogheda. as once again they were faced with battle.

As soon as the flotilla was within sight, the cannons opened fire. William saw the opening volley splashing in the water around the small craft. On the second round, one boat was hit and smashed to pieces, the men flung into the water, but now the defenders could see it was not a small party but some twenty or thirty boats all full of soldiers which were soon pouring across the foreshore. They were only a hundred yards from the fort, about four hundred of them led by men wearing kilts and some playing bagpipes. The sight and sound of these fighters, marching quickly with an unfaltering step directly towards the fort, struck William and his company of volunteers with dismay.

'Hold your fire until they are really close,' they were ordered.

William waited with his matchlock ready, determined not to miss this time! The attackers outnumbered the defenders in the fort three to one, but the defenders had larger reserves in the rear. William fired his first shot and saw one of the soldiers fall. He reloaded and took aim again, but by now some of the invaders were in part of the fort, and Josh had been hit in the shoulder. William fired again, but did not see any result. It was plain they could not defend the place and many of the Barbadians in the fort threw down their arms and fled.

Colonel Modyford, in command of the large force behind the fort, had no wish to fight the Commonwealth army; he wanted to support Ayscue, but was unwilling to openly defy Willoughby. At this stage be was running with the hare and hunting with the hounds. As soon as the landing began he withdrew his men.

'We must get Josh out of this,' William shouted to Tom; they lifted Josh up to carry him away.

'Leave me be, you're hurting me,' Josh cried out. 'Save yourselves and get out.' But they persisted, managing to leave through the back of the fort they struggled into the trees and undergrowth beyond. They hid in a thick copse while the invaders passed close by, foraging for any animals or defenders they could find. William held his hand over Josh's mouth to stifle his groans.

The fort had now been taken. Colonel Alleyne, who led the landing party, had been killed, but they captured the four guns, fifty arms and powder, together with many prisoners. The invaders then withdrew before there was a counter-attack.

Peter Cusack went to find a waggon and William tried to console Josh. The waggon appeared after two hours with twenty more casualties moaning and groaning in the back. They lifted Josh, now unconscious, onto the waggon and it left on its way to Speightstown.

'I hope he'll be all right,' said William 'He's an old man and has been a good friend to me.'

There was no more fighting that night and the islanders reinforced the fort. The next day William was given permission to go to Speightstown to see Josh. The building where the injured were being cared for was a long, log hut with straw laid down for bedding. There were four women in charge, doing what little they could for the wounded. Medical facilities were pitifully inadequate for casualties of this scale and the hot, airless building smelt of human sweat and excrement, but the injured had at least been washed and were as comfortable as they could possibly be. He found Josh, looking drawn and deathly pale.

'How are you, my old friend?' he greeted him.

Josh opened his eyes and peered up at William 'M'boy,' he answered faintly, 'I be dying!'

'You can't do that – there's the garden to dig!'

'I'll no be digging a garden again. My arm's dead – but my fingers still itch.' He paused to take a deep breath. 'William, I never was a man of prayer, but 1 did thank God for His work in my garden. D'ye think 'e'll let me into heaven?'

'Do you believe in heaven, Josh?'

'I believe.'

'I think that will be enough, my friend.'

'You're a good man, William. Take care and ye'll go far.'

'I'll pray for you, Josh. I'll pray to God that you'll be back at Sandy Lane soon.'

'Thank ye, m'boy. Now I want to sleep.'

'I'll be back tomorrow if I can. Sleep well.'

Josh tried to smile and William took his leave. He was worried about Josh, he looked so ill. The next day, William heard that he had died in the night with a smiling face. *Perhaps*, William thought, *he had found his garden in heaven after all?*

For William his third taste of battle was as acrimonious as the previous ones. Once again, he had been defeated by Cromwell's men and lost the life of someone close to him. First he assumed, his father, and he knew his brothers and his darling Maeve, now Josh who had become his close companion over the many months they had worked together. Although he still tried to have faith, it was very hard to believe that God was on his side!

William and Tom were sitting outside the stable that night.

'I miss old Josh's pipe!' said Tom.

'Poor old Josh. He was a good friend to me,' William replied, 'I shall miss him as well as his pipe. I wonder what will happen now. it doesn't look as though we've enough trained soldiers to defeat the roundheads if they land in force.'

Father O'Neill rode up on his horse, alighted and sat down to join them.

'I've just heard about Josh. I'm sorry, he was a good friend, wasn't he?'

'Yes, Father. We were just saying how we missed his foul pipe. As bad as the smell was, we wish he were with us!' William replied.

'It is hard to see how God's Will works; but we must trust that things happen for the best. Josh had lived a good life and we must be thankful for the friendship and help he gave us. We lost many men at Denmark Fort; it is very sad.'

'Do you think we should surrender, Father?' Tom asked.

'We must always fight for what is right. I said this to William before the battle at Drogheda. I cannot believe it is right to give way to these men responsible for the death of our king. We must fight them and with God's help we shall defeat them.'

'I hope you're right, Father,' William replied.

'I must be on my way now,' Father O'Neill said, 'I came to say how worried I was about Josh. Good night to you both. God go with you!'

'Good night, Father,' they chorused.

'I suppose we're not going to solve the problem of defending the island by sitting here all night, so we'd better go to our beds. Good night, Tom.'

'Good night, William. Are you going slug watching?'

'Not tonight"

After the landing at Denmark Fort Lord Willoughby called the General Assembly to a meeting.

'I do not understand how a force of a few hundred seasoned soldiers can defeat a regiment of one thousand pikes, muskets and cavalry,' he asked the Assembly.

'Sir,' said Irwin, 'I am informed that Colonel Modyford's men turned tail as soon as the fort, which was only held by some fifty defenders, was attacked. Had they counter attacked it would have been a very different story.'

'How say you sir?' Willoughby asked Modyford.

'We thought it was a much larger landing force and the wooded nature of the area was not the best place to fight them. We expected them to advance inland to open country where we were prepared to meet and do battle.'

'I think this only goes to show,' said Hawley, 'that we are not strong enough to meet the Commonwealth troops. Seasick or not they are trained soldiers and we only have untrained volunteer bondsmen and white slaves. We should negotiate to surrender. Ayscue must be short of supplies by now and should be more reasonable to offering us terms acceptable to us.'

'I have further bad news to tell you,' Lord Willoughby said. 'I have heard from the captain of one of the traders from Jamestown that Prince Rupert's fleet hit a hurricane and lost many ships. The remainder returned to Holland. So I see no other course than to negotiate a peaceful settlement.'

The Assembly discussed the matter at length and finally decided to draw up a proposition to send to Ayscue.

Among the prisoners taken at Denmark Fort were some planters who were taken into Ayscue's cabin.

'I want you to go back ashore and persuade your fellow planters to press Willoughby to surrender. Who do you think can be persuaded to support the Commonwealth?'

'I know Henry Hawley, who was governor from 1630 to 38,' said William Morgan, 'he has a plantation of a thousand acres and is not a supporter of Willoughby. He is against the levies Willoughby has imposed on exports. I could see him.'

'And I know Colonel Modyford, he commands a regiment,' Charles Taylor said, 'I'm sure he would support the Commonwealth. But what terms for surrender can we offer them?'

'Good. Do any more of you know who you could see?'

There was a general muttering of denial. They all wanted to return to their plantations, but none of them would commit themselves to act as traitors to the King.

'Very well. Morgan and Taylor go back to the island and see Hawley and Modyford. Impress upon them the strength of our forces. We have two thousand trained soldiers, your volunteers are no match to them. We do not wish to invade and cause loss of life and damage to property if we can avoid it. If you can convince Hawley and Modyford to change sides, Willoughby will be forced to surrender. Tell them that their plantations will be safe and the Commonwealth will not impose levies on exports. To show our good faith I will release all prisoners we took at Denmark Fort. That should convince everybody on the island of our good intentions.'

So all the prisoners were put ashore by night and the next day Morgan went to see Henry Hawley.

'I was taken prisoner at Denmark Fort,' he explained, 'and Admiral Ayscue has sent me to ask you to support him and the Commonwealth forces by persuading Willoughby to accept surrender.'

'That would be very difficult,' Hawley said, 'I am among the minority on the Assembly who were in favour of accepting surrender. I could not openly attack Willoughby's forces, it would be futile. But if Ayscue invades, then I will side with his forces. That is the best I can offer. How will you be in touch with Ayscue again to tell him?'

'That I do not know. No arrangement was made to communicate. I am certainly not going to row out and tell him myself!' He now realised he had been so anxious to be released and return to the island he had not given sufficient thought as to how he could complete his mission successfully. He was conscious of his inadequacy.

'Well, perhaps he will send someone ashore to see you. We'll leave it at that, shall we? But I trust this conversation between us will be treated as secret. I do not want the whole island to know what I have said I would do if there is an invasion.'

'Of course, sir, you can trust me.' Morgan bade Hawley farewell and returned to his plantation to await further action.

Taylor went to see Colonel Modyford who had come to Barbados in 1645 declaring he would not return to England until he had amassed a fortune of one hundred thousand pounds. He had the largest sugar plantation and had built a sugar mill. He had no desire to see the island invaded and his crops destroyed. After Taylor told him what had happened to him Modyford said, 'I would attack Willoughby tomorrow if I thought it would change his mind, but I'm afraid his forces are too strong. It would be much better if I supported Ayscue once he has landed his troops, as I did at Denmark Fort. I withdrew my force as soon as the landing began.'

As neither Taylor nor Morgan had made any arrangement to be in further communication with Ayscue there was nothing further they could do.

There was an outbreak of scurvy on board the fifteen ships recently arrived, so before these forces could be properly deployed, and all the supplies they had secured on the raid on Speightstown were not as much as they had hoped, they sailed on to Virginia leaving Ayscue with his seven ships to continue the blockade. The Commonwealth commissioners still wary of a full-scale attack, decided to bide their time and wait for insurrection inside the Council to settle the siege.

Willoughby's proposition from the General assembly was sent to Ayscue. Of the eleven articles, the first was the one to emerge as critical to both sides. it stated that, "The legal and rightful government of this island remains it is now by law and our own consent established."

A peaceful month followed during which time Ayscue made no attempt to communicate with Morgan or Taylor. Christmas Day was celebrated at *Sandy Lane* with a church service in the morning and a dinner of chicken, sweet-potatoes and onions. At least the defenders still had the luxury of fresh food and vegetables.

After dinner William noticed that the African, native slave-drums were more active than usual. He decided to investigate. Walking down to the native lines he met one of the slaves.

'What's all the drumming about?' he asked.

'Can you keep a secret? If so, I can take you to our chief and he will tell you.'

'I can keep a secret,' William replied, intrigued.

He was led to the hut where the drumming sounded. Inside were a crowd of half-naked black slaves lined against the walls, clapping and stamping their feet to the beat of a drum. The hut was dark and hot, the air filled with dust from the earth floor. In the middle a female slave, wearing only a skirt, was dancing. When they saw William, they stopped drumming and the native he had spoken to on the day by the cotton fields, came up to him. He now recognised the girl as the same one spoken to that day.

'I am the son of the Oni of Ife, and I will lead our people to freedom. You red-legs are slaves like us and you should join us. Can I trust you to help us?'

'It depends on what you want me to do,' William said doubtfully.

'Let de white man fight among themselves, and after de fighting is over we will kill those that remain. Together, we can rule this island on our own. Now that you know this, you are one of us and we expect you to get the other white slaves to join us. We will watch you day and night to see you do not betray us.'

'How do you plan to defeat the white soldiers?'

'You have been told enough. Will you join us? If not we will have to kill you now.'

William was astounded. This was the first time he had known the black slaves had any intention to rebel and he realised he would have to be very careful. He was trapped so had no alternative but to agree.

'I will do everything I can to defeat the Commonwealth soldiers and if you have a plan to do this, I will help.'

'Don't forget, we will be watching you.'

He was very relieved to get out of that hut alive and he returned to his quarters but did not tell anyone what he had heard, as he could not see how the slaves could achieve anything significant.

Ayscue replied to the General Assembly propositions by drafting fourteen articles of his own. He promised free trade with foreigners, no taxation without the consent of the people of Barbados, no garrisoning of English troops in the island, but he demanded the removal of Lord Willoughby and reformation of the General Assembly with two members from each of the eleven districts. On December 29 the Council and Assembly rejected Ayscue's articles answering that "we do unanimously adhere to the first article in our proposition... and until a grant first to that, we shall not yield to allow further treaty."

In the new year, on the 3rd January 1652, Colonel Modyford succeeded to persuade five hundred infantry and about one hundred cavalry to change sides and openly support the Commonwealth with his regiment. Willoughby tried to win these forces back by negotiation, but failed.

This situation demanded instant retaliation, so on the 5th January, Willoughby and the planters who supported him including Irwin, as a senior officer, planned an attack on Colonel Modyford's forces. William was among the men who were put into position around the camp during the night, intending to attack at first light. They were hiding in a small copse on some high ground and the sky was overcast, unusual for that time of year. They could see very little and could hear nothing as the wind was blowing hard from behind them. Every man was wide awake, peering into the darkness for any movement from the other camp.

William found his eyes closing, his head nodding forward and had difficulty in forcing himself to stay awake. Then he saw a small light in the distance and as he watched it grew bigger, while other lights started nearer.

'Look over there. The sugar is on fire!' He exclaimed.

William went over to Irwin. 'Sir, the sugar field over there is on fire. I think I know what it is. The black slaves have been planning something so that they can take over control.'

'That is Drax's plantation over there. We cannot spare any men to fight the fire or we will not have enough to defeat Modyford. We must carry out our attack as planned.'

The fires grew bigger and spread rapidly. Then nature took a hand – there was a flash of lightning and a roll of thunder, followed quickly by a heavy downpour of rain. They never had rain in January on Barbados, but they had plenty of it that night. It was a very mixed blessing, it dampened the fires but it also dampened the morale of the men, who were not equipped for rain, and the ground soon turned to thick mud, making movement of the cavalry and men difficult.

They attacked at dawn, struggling through deep mud, only to be met by heavy musket fire and they were soon driven back. Willoughby's cavalry were unable to move effectively on the muddy ground. The rain lasted for seven days and Willoughby's men were eventually defeated by Modyford's forces and the weather.

William now assumed that defeat was inevitable, but the Commonwealth forces still refused to follow up Modyford's success and during the months ahead both sides had long negotiations; it was not until the 11th June, that articles of agreement were signed to end the war at the Mermaid's Tavern in St. Oistin's Bay.

Praised as the *Charter of Barbados,* these articles of agreement gave all the planters a general indemnity and at the time was greeted by them with much satisfaction. However, as soon as the republicans gained control of the General Assembly, they set the agreement aside and ordered Willoughby and his main supporters, to be banished from the island.

'We have lost the battle for freedom,' Irwin told William in the stable, later in June. 'My family and I will have to leave and the plantation will be taken over by Colonel Drax.'

William did his best to hide his tears as he fondled one of the horses. 'What will happen to me? Will I continue to look after the horses?'

'I cannot say. But I wish ye God speed, and thank ye for all the work you have done for me. There is nothing else I can say, except that one day we shall be back when Charles II is on the throne.'

A few days later, Colonel Drax appeared at *Sandy Lane* with an armed party to escort Richard Irwin, his wife and Olivia along with their possessions, down to the quay at Indian Bridge and the ship to England.

'Irwin, I prayed to God for this day and he has answered my prayers. I told you I'd be back and ye'd regret the day you sent us away. Are you ready?'

'We are ready, but God willing, one day we shall be back!'

Before leaving he shook hands with all his servants, including William, Huxtable, Tom and Father O'Neill and wished them God speed.

The Irwin family mounted the carriage, but before driving off Olivia called out to William. 'Good Bye Durgy. Good luck.'

With his eyes full of tears, William watched the carriage and two carts of possessions disappear down the dirt track. For over two years he had worked for the Irwin family and had grown to respect them. He had been doing the work he loved, caring for horses; he had found a good friend in Josh, but now he had lost him. William turned away and climbed to his loft over the stables, where he found his rosary and said his prayers. He knew that the relative happiness that he had enjoyed over the past two years was going to change dramatically. He recalled Father O'Neill's advice, "Have faith, my son!" *Surely*, he thought, *I must have been saved so far for some destination? I believe my life must have a purpose which I have not yet fulfilled.*

Chapter 11
CANE-CUTTING

Early the next day, William was in the stables at Ridge Hill doing his routine work looking after the horses when a large, dark shadow of a man blocked the light from the doorway. He looked up and saw the tall figure of Colonel Drax wearing a black leather hat with a wide brim, a sleeveless leather jerkin over a white shirt. His woollen stockings covered the bottom of his calf-length trousers and the square buckles on his shoes glinted in the sun.

'Who the hell are you?' Drax demanded.

'Durgy, sir.'

'What the hell are you doing here?'

'Looking after your horses, sir.'

'Who gave you permission?'

'Mister Irwin asked me to do this and I've been looking after the horses here for over a year now. I think you'll find them in good condition, sir'

'But you're an Irish prisoner, aren't you?' His normal florid complexion was going redder every minute.

'Yes, sir.'

'Well get the hell out of here back to Sandy Lane. I'll not have a bloody red-leg in my stables; and who gave you those shoes?'

'Mister Irwin, sir.'

'You can damn well take them off right now and leave them here. Now be off with you! Don't let me see you here again!'

William bent down and took off his shoes. While Colonel Drax glowered at him he patted each of the horses he had grown to love. He mounted his horse from the Sandy Lane stable and rode away full of foreboding; things were going to change, he could sense that. He went slowly back to Sandy Lane, taking in the view, thinking it would probably be the last time he would see it. He had made this ride every day for many months and had never ceased to enjoy it. Now he was going to be confined to one plantation, like all the slaves, unless he was escorted outside.

At Sandy Lane he found Tom repairing one of the stalls in the stable.

'I've been thrown out of Ridge Hill by Colonel Drax.'

'Doesn't he want you for his groom then?'

'No. He made me leave my shoes behind, as well.'

'Sounds like he's going to be a tyrant.'

'Yes. He swears well too. I think he's a bad-tempered man and we are going to have a tough time if he takes over here.'

'You're damn right, you are going to have a tough time!' Drax was standing in the doorway and his loud voice made William and Tom jump with surprise. 'What are you two doing here?'

'Well sir, I am the groom here and this is Tom O'Leary, the carpenter.'

'Two bloody Irish red-legs! Time you damn well did some real work. Get to hell out of it, both of you. Go to MacGregor in the cane field and sweat your guts out. And you there, O'Leary, what're you wearing those shoes for? Get 'em off. Slaves wearing shoes. By Gad whatever next! Get on now – you're cane cutting from now on until the devil prays to God or you drop dead!"

While Tom took his shoes off, William went up to the hayloft and collected his belongings; he came down with them stowed in a sack and they went over to the sleeping quarters of the slaves. They found Father O'Neill there.

'Hullo William, my son, and Tom I was coming over to the stables to see you and say goodbye.'

'Goodbye, Father? Why, where are you going?'

'Back to England. All the Catholic priests have been given two days to pack up and leave.'

'I'm sorry to hear that, Father. We shall miss you. What will you do in England, do you know?'

'Probably be thrown into prison, if we are not killed.'
'I hope not, Father.'
'The best I can hope for is prison, my son, these Roundheads don't like Catholic priests. Father Sullivan is coming with me but I am sure I would be better off staying here with you.'
'I don't know, Father. We've lost our jobs and been told to work on the sugar cane. The future looks grim.'

Father O'Neill said a short prayer, shook hands with them, then mounted his horse.

'God be with you!' he shouted as he rode away.
'I'm afraid that is the last time we'll see him," said Tom.
'Yes, I'm sorry to see him go,' William replied, 'I've known him many years and he has been a great help to me; I shall miss him. I'm very sorry I persuaded him to talk to Mister Irwin, if he had kept quiet he would still be with us!'
'That was his own decision, I don't think you need be sorry.'

Drax strode over to them.

'I thought I told you two to go bloody cane cutting,' he shouted, 'what are you doing here?'
'Just going, sir. I brought my things over from the stables.'

The two left Drax spluttering and swearing to himself and went down to the sugar field where they found the slaves busy cutting the cane with long bladed knives and stacking it in piles. Huxtable was working with them like a slave.

'What are doing?' William asked.
'Don't ye dare ask me,' he replied. 'Another foreman has been put over me and now I'm working like the rest of them. I dare not stop to talk for fear of the lash, I'll talk to you later.'

The new foreman, Jock MacGregor, a tall man with a red face and ginger hair, walked over to them with a swaggering gait, holding a long leather whip. He seemed to have a cruel twist of a grin permanently chiselled into his features and he raised the whip high in the air bringing it down with a crack on William's back. William fell to the ground groaning with pain.

'Stop talking! Get back to your work!'
'We haven't been told what to do yet,' Tom said nervously. 'We've

been sent down here by Colonel Drax. I was the carpenter and Durgy here was the groom.'

'Get up, you!' The foreman ordered William. 'Go to the store and draw your blades. Get back here double-quick and start cutting cane. Mind you cut close to the ground and don't stand around talking, or ye'll feel the cut of my whip again!'

He strode off to berate another slave further down the field.

'That took me by surprise,' William said on the way to the store, 'I didn't see him coming up behind me. That whip hurts and I don't know how I'm going to cut cane, but I shall have to try, as I don't want to be whipped like that too often! I think I'd be more comfortable without my shirt.'

They collected their knives and returned to the sugar field. They cut the canes and stacked them in a heap, finding it was harder than it looked. Some of the canes were thicker than others and they had to judge the amount of swing required to cut with one sweep. They were not allowed to take two cuts at any cane as this damaged the plant and it would not regrow. It was back-breaking work and soon their arms and legs were covered with deep wounds from the sharp cane leaves.

At sundown they returned to the slave quarters for a meal. They found the quality of the food was not as good as it had been before. It was mostly vegetable soup with very little meat, dry bread and no fruit. William and Tom were so exhausted they did not finish their meal. William was glad to collapse onto his bed, face down, the livid gash across his back glistening in the flickering candlelight.

'I know what to do to that back of yours, William,' Huxtable decided. 'Salt and vinegar will soon make it better.' He found the necessary ingredients and poured the mixture over the weal. William screamed out with the pain, praying to himself for the strength to survive this latest ordeal.

The next morning William was stiff from the unaccustomed heavy work of the previous day and his back was still very painful. He got up and struggled down to the cane field and did his best to do as little as possible without attracting the attention of MacGregor's whip.

Peter Cusack found the hard work and heat unbearable. He was also trying to do as little as possible but as he was sitting down behind a bundle of cane, mopping his brow with his hand, he was spotted by MacGregor.

'Get up there, you lazy bugger!' The whip came down with a searing blow on his back.

'Go to hell! I can't get up!' he lay sprawled on the ground. The whip came down again, once, twice, three times. Peter groaned and did not move. The slaves stopped work and watched in horror. They dared not raise a finger to help.

'You, there,' MacGregor pointed to William and Paul Fraser standing nearby, 'pick this man up and take him to his quarters. I'll finish dealing with him tonight. And you get back double quick!'

They lifted Peter and together carried him to the mess. They laid him face down on his bed.

'Leave me be!' he pleaded. 'I'll rest here.'

'I wonder what will happen to him tonight?' Paul said on the way back to the cane field.

'I hate to think.' William replied.

After supper that night MacGregor came into the mess and asked, 'Where's that lazy swine?'

'He's in a bad way, lying on his bed,' Huxtable said, 'His back should be treated.'

'I'll treat his back for him. Get him outside.'

John Moore and Huxtable carefully lifted Peter up and carried him outside. There was a post in the middle of the yard and George, the barber's assistant, was standing by with a whip. He had a darker skin than most of the negroes, was six foot tall and sixteen stone.

'Tie him up there,' MacGregor ordered, 'and bring all of you red legs outside. You've got to see what happens if one of you refuses to work. No one tells me to go to hell!'

George ripped Peter's shirt off his back and then he was stood up facing the post with his hands tied above his head.

'Now,' said MacGregor, 'how many shall we give him? Can you count to ten, you black bastard?'

'Yes, sir!' George gladly replied with a grin.

'Then, go ahead. I'll be counting too, so don't give short measure.'

The white slaves stood around and watched with repugnance,

wincing as each lash of the whip descended on Peter's bare back. Peter groaned as each of the first four lashes hit him and then he was silent. After the tenth lash descended his back was a mass of long bleeding scars.

Everyone stood around deadly silent, the only sound came from Tim Flaherty as he was being sick in the back row.

'Leave him there to cool off. ' MacGregor ordered. 'Not one of you is to touch him. Now get back inside and in future I don't want any more lazy workers.' He strode off without a backward glance. George grinned at the white slaves and walked off to the married slave's huts.

During the night, William crept out of the sleeping quarters with a mug of water. He looked around to see no one was watching and went up to the post.

'Here, Peter, a sip of water,' he held the cup to Peter's lips. Peter opened his mouth and William tipped the water gradually until it was empty.

'I'm dying,' Peter groaned, 'but thanks.'

'No, you're not going to die. We'll have you down in the morning and treat your wounds.'

The next morning Huxtable was up at first light and went to see Peter. He came back to the quarters looking very glum.

'He's dead,' he said, 'It was too much for his old body. He died in the night.'

Peter was buried in a grave outside the yard with no burial service – no one knew what to say. They put a crude wooden cross on top of the grave and walked silently to the sugar canes.

A few days later, William saw one of the negro slaves secretly eating a pawpaw while MacGregor was out of sight.

'Where did you get that?' he asked.

'Oranyan,' he replied.

That evening after work he went to see Oranyan, the son of the Oni of Ife, the negro who had set the sugar fields ablaze.

'Oranyan, I hear you have some pawpaws. Can you give me one or two? Our food is so poor, now that Colonel Drax is in charge.'

'I wanted to see you. What happened when we lit the sugar cane? It was de signal for all slaves to rebel and fight de white men.'

'How was I to know that? You never told me what your plan was. I had to do my duty fighting the invaders; but I kept my word to you, I did not tell any of the white men about your plan.'

'I believe you. But we all in a bad way now. One of our tribe was beaten to death on a plantation up north for not working hard enough, like your brother the other day.'

'I hadn't heard of that. I am sorry.'

'What happened to your brother white man slave was bad. What happened to my brother was worse. He was beaten on the post for eight whole days and then they cut his ear off!'

'How terrible!'

'That's not all. They roasted his ear and made him eat it, then left him to die.'

'Oranyan, these Commonwealth people are not good men. That's why we had to fight them and try to stop them taking the island. They are not good masters like Mister Irwin was.'

'That is right. Now you ask for pawpaw? We do not have much pawpaw, but I'll see if we have any I can spare.'

He went to the back of his hut and returned with two pawpaws.

'Don't you let anyone else know where you got 'em, or they'll come and destroy our crop.'

'Thank you, Oranyan, you know you can trust me.'

William hid the fruit under his shirt and returned to his quarters.

'Tom, I have a pawpaw here for you. Don't let anyone else see it and don't ask me where I got it.'

'Thanks, William I have not eaten one for ages.'

A few weeks later, William woke up with a bad toothache. He still had to go to work but by midday the pain was so bad he approached Jock MacGregor.

'I have a very bad toothache and cannot work. I must get it seen to.'

'Distemper of the mouth doesn't stop you from working, ye lazy beggar. Go and see the barber after sunset.'

William seldom cleaned his teeth, although occasionally he might rub them with a piece of cloth or use a stick to extract bits of food stuck in the crevices. In the evening William went to see the barber, who also attended to any dental or medical problems. He operated in a small mud hut with a thatched roof, an earth floor, no windows and was furnished with an old wooden chair and small wooden table which looked as if it had never been cleaned.

'Distemper of the mouth? It'll probably go after a day or two,' he was told, 'but I'll give ye a mouth wash of vinegar and water'.

He prepared the mixture in the shell of a gourd and William swilled it round in his mouth, grimacing at the unpleasant flavour, he spat it out.

'Here, take some aniseeds and suck them. If it is not better in a couple of days, come back and I'll pull the tooth out. But I warn ye, that'll hurt ye more than your distemper!' The barber laughed at William's worried expression.

William suffered with that tooth for a week. He had a swelling on his jaw and obviously there was an infection; diluted vinegar and aniseeds were doing no good. Reluctantly he went back to the barber.

'Still got distemper?' The barber greeted William with a cruel grin. 'Well, it'll have to come out! Sit in that chair.'

William looked at the barber's chair, a broken mirror propped up on the table in front of it, with dismay. To sit there to have his hair cut was one thing, but now it looked like a seat of torture.

'George, come and give a hand here,' the barber called to his assistant, the tall, fat negro who had administered the whippings to Peter and was now sweeping up the last customer's hair from the dirt floor. George approached the chair grinning at William; he was going to enjoy this!

'Stand behind the chair and grab 'is 'ead,' the barber ordered. William smelt George's sweaty, dirty hands as he took a tight grip of his head. 'Open your mouth, young feller, which tooth is it?' The barber asked.

William pointed with his finger and saw the barber was now holding a rusty pair of pliers. He closed his eyes as the tooth was gripped with the pliers.

'Is it that 'un?'

William nodded assent as best as he could, belatedly wondering whether this had been a good idea after all.

'Right, first of all I've got to loosen it sideways. Hold 'is 'ead steady!' He struggled and grunted with the effort.

'It doesn't want to move. We'll 'ave to use another tool. I'll try the pelican.'

He produced a tool like a pair of pliers with long handles but the end was shaped like a pelican's beak and the two jaws fitted on both sides of the tooth by the gum. William had never felt pain like this before and did not care what the barber did with this awesome implement, as long as the pain would be stopped. Using the long handle as a lever and with one hand on the bottom jaw, the barber gave a sudden wrench. William felt a searing pain as the tooth shot out of it's cavity. His mouth filled with blood.

'There ye are! Not too bad, Was it? A nice big 'un'.

William got shakily to his feet, his eyes moving from the bloodied tooth lying forlornly in the dirty, cracked china dish, to the barber's and George's broad grins. He staggered outside as quickly as he could. It was several days before he felt any better. It did not pay to have any sickness in this place!

A week later Jock Macgregor came to William and Tim Flaherty while they were cutting canes.

'You two are to go tomorrow to Colonel Drax's plantation to work in the sugar mill. You pack your things and go first thing in the morning. There'll be a waggon to take you.'

'Yes, sir,' they replied.

'I'm being sent to the sugar mill tomorrow, Tom,' William told him that evening, 'Tim is coming with me. I don't know how long we shall be there, but keep away from MacGregor's whip while I'm away.'

'I'll try. Sorry to see you go, hope you'll soon be back.'

The next morning William and Tim mounted the waggon with their sacks of possessions and were driven to Drax's plantation, which was only three miles away.

This was a much bigger plantation than Sandy Lane. On arrival they were met by the foreman.

'So you are the two new men for the mills, eh?' he asked.

'Yes, sir. My name is William Durgy and this is Tim Flaherty.'

'My name is Kennedy, just sir, to you. Stow your things in the dormitory, you'll find a couple of empty bunks, and I'll show you the mill.'

They found the dormitory was much larger than their's and they chose two bunks.

On the way to the mill, William said, 'This is a large place here, sir. How many acres are there?

'Oh, over eight hundred or so. We have about a hundred slaves but no red legs like you. I want you to learn the work in the mill and see the slaves do their job.'

They arrived at the mill which was a large wooden shed with several cart loads of sugar cane standing at the entrance.

'The cane is off loaded and first of all the leaves are stripped off by the women and children,' Kennedy explained. 'The stalks are then chopped into small lengths and fed into the mill.'

He took them inside the building where they saw a large metal chute where the chopped cane was being placed. Over the chute was a metal roller with a handle at each end being turned by two slaves. A trickle of water flowed onto the roller.

'Now,' said Kennedy, 'after it has been crushed and the water added, the chute drops into a bin at the end. You see it is a dark green liquid and is acid to taste. We then add milk of lime, stir it up and pour the bin into the boiler, here.' He walked on and showed them several boilers, some of them with a fire lit underneath. 'When the juice has boiled it is left to settle. We then run the clear juice off the top and this is taken to the next machine.' William and Tim somewhat bemused by now and feeling the heat inside the building oppressive, followed Kennedy.

'Here we have the machine which separates the molasses from the sugar. Then we have sugar inside and liquid outside at the bottom. The sugar is then emptied and poured into sacks.' William gazed in amazement at the quantity of brown sugar pouring from the machine.

'Now your job is to see that the water is always running over those rollers we saw at the beginning, that the right amount of lime is added, I'll show you how to measure it, and above all to see that none of the slaves steal the final product. Anyone caught stealing sugar is flogged.'

William saw that this job was going to be very different from cutting cane. He realised that it carried some responsibility and was going to be difficult to carry out.

'If you have any problems, come and see me. We have no one

reliable to oversee this work and it is too much for me as well as supervising the cane cutting. This work goes on for about three months when the cane cutting season finishes.'

'We'll do our best, sir.' Tim said.

William and Tim worked together quite happily on this job for ten weeks. It was hot work, but interesting and they had few problems. The greatest problem was shortage of water as the summer advanced. When the water run out they had to stop the rollers, hold up the whole procedure, until more water arrived. It was brought in drums, carried to the top of the building and poured into containers over the rollers. Primitive, but effective.

At the end of their service here they were returned to Sandy Lane and given more work felling trees.

Meanwhile, in England, decisions were being taken which were to affect William's future. In June 1654, Cromwell outlined in Council the plan for his Western Design; it was his intention to capture the colonies of the West Indies held by the Spanish. He had complained to the Spanish Ambassador that the English traders there were not being treated fairly and were being persecuted for their religion, being Protestants among the Spanish Catholics. He had stated that England could only remain on friendly terms with Spain providing all the English traders in their territories were granted freedom of conscience in their religion and given the right to free-trade. The Spanish would give no such undertaking.

So the plans for the Western Design were initiated. Thomas Gage, a Dominican monk, had spent some years in the West Indies and had written a book on his experiences. In his opinion the Spanish colonies could be taken easily and when Cromwell consulted him, he advised Cromwell that the Spanish were weak enough to collapse with the minimum assault.

General Robert Venables was appointed in charge of the army and Admiral William Penn was in charge of the fleet. John Desborough, Cromwell's brother-in-law, in overall control of organising supplies. Two civilian commissioners were appointed; Edward Winslow, who had sailed in the Mayflower and had been Governor of New Plymouth, and Gregory Butler, who was from Bermuda. They were to be responsible for the setting up of the colonies after their capture.

The expedition arrived in Carlisle Bay on the 28th January 1655. The next day General Venables landed and went to see Governor Searle, who had replaced Willoughby.

'Welcome to Barbados, sir,' Governor Searle greeted the admiral with a warm hand shake, 'I trust you had a pleasant voyage.'

'Thank you, sir. Nothing is pleasant about the sea as far as I'm concerned. My digestion and stomach has been upset since I walked on board.'

'I am sorry to hear that, sir. And where are you going?'

'Admiral Penn and I have brought a fleet to capture the Spanish colonies in the Caribees. Colonel Modyford has told Cromwell you can provide us with four thousand fighting men and while you are recruiting these you will have to find billets for two thousand five hundred of my troops. They will pay for what they take.'

'That will take some tine, sir. I do not know how we are going to find four thousand fighting men.' Searle was an ardent Commonwealth supporter, but he had his limitations.

'You'll have to round up all the unemployed men free from indenture and get volunteers from the servants and white slaves.'

'We will do our best, but it will take time. Can we offer the white slaves their freedom if they volunteer?'

'You can offer it, sir, but I cannot see Cromwell agreeing to ratify the promise. We can deal with that when they come back – those that do, that is!'

'I will call a meeting of the General Assembly tomorrow. Would you wish to address them?'

'That would be a privilege, sir, and I'm sure will expedite the operation. In the meantime may I call on your hospitality – I crave a few nights away from that accursed ship.'

'You will be most welcome, sir.'

The General Assembly met the next day and General Venables and Admiral Penn, who came ashore especially for the occasion, addressed the members. They pointed out the advantages of their mission, should it succeed; and to ensure that success they called for four thousand recruits, including members of the island's militia. Venables added, 'We require a list of all the freemen on the island, so as to avoid enlistment of servants. All white slaves will volunteer.'

The Assembly greeted this announcement with an uproar.

'We cannot possibly spare four thousand men. Without our militia we would be defenceless against an uprising by the black slaves.'

'I entreat the Assembly to support Cromwell in this mission,' Thomas Modyford said. But the majority of the members did not listen to him, particularly as they had heard he had, without consulting them, promised Cromwell Barbados would supply what he wanted. They complained about having to house troops in their households, and the meeting broke up without a decision.

The news of the fleet's arrival spread round the island very quickly and William wondered what it was all about. He was soon to learn.

Colonel Drax arrived at the plantation one morning early in February and called all the Irish prisoners to gather outside their quarters.

'A fleet has arrived from England with troops to sail to the Caribees and capture the Spanish colonies. We have to recruit four thousand men to go with them. All Irish red-legs will go and I regret to say some of my own servants will have to go as well. You will be told when you are required to go, in the meanwhile carry on with your work.'

William, Huxtable and the other six fellow white prisoners all looked at each other.

'Now what are we being sent to do?' Huxtable asked.

'Fight for Cromwell!' William said with astonishment. 'I'd rather fight against him! But what choice have we got?"

'We've no choice,' said Mick Newman, 'we've just got to do what we are told. But if it comes to fighting, I'm going to make sure I do as little of it as possible.'

'I'm sure we all agree to that,' Charles Farrell agreed.

'I don't see why I have to go,' said Huxtable, 'I'm not a red-leg and I'm too old to do any fighting!'

'Come and keep us company,' said William smiling, 'we'll show you how to keep your head down when the shooting starts."

All through February and March they continued to work on the plantation each day expecting to be told to pack up and leave.

'I hear they should ask for volunteers among the white slaves,' Huxtable said one evening while they sat around outside their sleeping quarters.

'We weren't asked to volunteer,' William said. 'Colonel Drax told us we would have to go whether we liked it or not."

'That's right. Perhaps we'll be better off away from this eternal sugar cane and tree felling, anyway,' Tom said.

'I don't like the idea of being cooped up again in the hold of a ship, to be landed God knows where, to fight the Spanish. I don't want to do any fighting for the Commonwealth.' William declared.

'Nor do we,' the others chorused. 'but what choice have we got? None! We will just have to do as little fighting as we can'.

'But if we do not fight,' Huxtable said, 'our forces will be defeated and we will be killed or taken prisoner by the Spanish!'

'What a horrible thought,' William said.

It was not until the 30th March they had their orders to leave.

'Pack as few things as possible and go to the harbour at Indian Bridge,' Jock MacGregor told them, 'an escort of soldiers will see you get there safely. Anyone trying to escape will be shot.'

'I wonder how many trunks I can fill?' William asked. 'One torn shirt, one pair of shorts, and my rosary – I don't think they could say that is taking too much!"

'Volunteers, did someone say?' Huxtable asked, 'Volunteers being driven aboard at the point of a musket. I'm sorry MacGregor is not coming. He is the first one I'd shoot if I had the chance!'

They collected their belongings in sacks and were marched off to Indian Bridge, eight of them escorted by two soldiers. They were not being offered a ride to the town in a waggon!

When they reached the harbour they found a large crowd of Irish and Scottish prisoners, as well as hundreds of white servants and a group of women.

'Have you come to see us off?' William asked one of the women. The first woman he had spoken to for ages! Her red cotton dress was dirty, with holes at the elbows, and her hair was unkempt.

'No,' she replied, 'we are going with you as nurses. God help you if you require our services though, we know nothing about nursing! But I expect we'll be able to serve you in other ways!' She laughed, showing several front teeth missing and poked him in the ribs. William looked at her with distaste; he needed a woman but not one like that!

He gazed with amazement at the fleet in the harbour. There were dozens of ships lying at anchor.

'We are not going alone, I see,' he said.

'They say there are sixty ships out there,' the "nurse" replied, 'and they have seven thousand men and seven hundred or so women from here to join them. It's going to be very crowded on board and we're going to be busy,' she added with a wink at William.

'At least we won't be in chains,' William observed.

'Come on, don't stand around, get into that row boat,' an officer wearing a three-cornered hat ordered.

They walked along the wooden jetty and scrambled into a small boat with their sacks of belongings. As soon as it was full, with the water nearly coming over the sides, they pushed off and were rowed out into the harbour. There was no room for Huxtable and they waved farewell to him as he was taken away by another rowing boat to a different ship.

'That was a pity,' William said, 'no room for Huxtable; we've got to show him how to keep his head down when the fighting starts!'

'I expect we'll find him again,' Tom replied.

As they approached one of the ships William saw the name *Falmouth* on the bow. It was smaller than the *Black Bird* and he could see a row of guns poking out through the port side. They came alongside and climbed up the gangway to the deck. The ship seemed full already, soldiers, seamen and some women crowding around.

'Get down below and find yourself a space,' ordered one of the seamen.

It was dark down below and they had to stoop to avoid hitting their heads on the deck above. It took them several seconds to adjust their eyes to the gloom and then they found there were rows of wooden bunks filling the hold. They found some bunks apparently without any owners, left their belongings and went back on deck.

William thought that the sea-legs he had found on the *Black Bird* were to be put to the test once more. He looked back to the shore and wondered whether he would ever see Barbados again. He was not sure if he wanted to, but he hoped that wherever he was taken he would be alive and well. At least, it should be better than cane-cutting!

CHAPTER 12
JAMAICA

The fleet sailed the next day on the 31st March. William and Tom had time to rest and to discuss their future.

'I wonder where we are going?' Tom asked.

'One of the sailors told me we are going to Hispaniola*, but now we are sailing north and I thought Hispaniola was to the west.' William replied.

A soldier was standing nearby and William turned to him.

'Do you know where we are going?' he asked.

'To an island called St. Kitts where we will pick up more men, nurses and supplies.'

'I don't like the idea of fighting for the Commonwealth,' said Tom. 'In Drogheda we fought against these men, now we are bound to fight on their side.'

'If you don't fight, my Irish papist, ye'll be shot,' said the soldier. 'So ye'd better watch yer tongue.'

'We are going to fight against the Spaniards,' William observed. 'If we win and capture the island, when Charles comes back to the throne he'll have another settlement. That is the only way I can see it. We don't have any choice in the matter.'

'Ye'll never see Charles on the throne, I'm telling ye,' the soldier said. 'We've had enough of royalty and their evil rule.'

William made no reply. On the journey to St. Kitts the sunshine of Barbados gave way to strong winds, heavy rain and rough seas; soon the

---

* Note. Now known as Dominica and Haiti.

overcrowded ship was full of sick men and women, again Tom was seasick but William was not.

The ship's galley could not cope with cooking for all the troops, slaves and women. The galley cooked for the crew and each batch of forty soldiers were issued with a daily ration of one pint of water per head for drinking, washing and cooking; a week's ration of two pounds of salt beef; and four pounds of flour. The women took turns cooking on little fires in sandboxes on the deck. The water was only sufficient for each man to drink half a cup a day and they washed with sea water.

The *Falmouth*, being smaller than most of the ships in the fleet, took four days to reach St. Kitts, a day longer than the rest. When they arrived William saw that the harbour was smaller than Indian Bridge and there were fewer houses, but the land looked fresh with plenty of green trees round the town and harbour.

When the main fleet had dropped anchor, General Venables went ashore to see the Governor. General Robert Venables, aged forty-three, was an ardent Commonwealth supporter and had fought at Drogheda and later secured Carlingford, Newry and Belfast for Cromwell. Whilst he had proved his ability in the army, Venables was not a happy man at sea; at the start of the voyage to Barbados he was very seasick for several days. He had hoped, when he left Barbados, the same feeling would not return but instead he was just as bad again.

'I would be obliged if you would see the Governor and make known our requirements,' he asked Admiral Penn. William Penn was ten years younger than Venables. He was an experienced sailor who had been Blake's Vice-Admiral in 1652, but had recently, unbeknown to Cromwell, offered his services to King Charles in Holland. He had been told to await a more favourable time.

'I consider that is your duty, sir. I have no business dealing with your troops and their needs.'

'But I am not in good health after this sea passage.'

'Sir, I consider then you will recover more speedily if you go ashore.'

When Venables landed at St. Kitts he was feeling very ill and in a bad temper.

'I have been appointed by Cromwell with a special commission as Overlord in the Caribees to demand that you supply my force with two thousand men to secure the Spanish settlements in the Caribees.' he bluntly informed the Governor. St. Kitts was a smaller colony than Barbados and not as prosperous.

'That is impossible, sir,' the Governor replied.

'Nevertheless, sir, you must find some way of complying, or the Council will replace you as Governor. Also, whilst we are at anchor, you will supply us with victuals, so the quicker you perform your duty the sooner we will be at sea again.'

'I will have to discuss this with the Council.'

'You can inform your Council that John Desborough, Cromwell's son-in-law, is in charge of supplies. These should have arrived by now, but are delayed. When they do arrive you will be reimbursed your victuals. In the meantime I would be obliged if you would provide me with accommodation ashore as I am very unwell at sea.'

It took six days to try and fulfil these demands, during which time Venables recovered from his malaise. But his ill temper was not diminished when he was told by the Governor that the island could only muster five hundred men.

Nevertheless, Penn and Venables had no choice but to proceed and the fleet sailed on April 8th.

The supplies supposed to be sent from England had still not arrived, so after the fleet had taken on these extra five hundred men rations had to be cut down and the situation was becoming desperate.

Six days later the *Falmouth* reached Hispaniola, where the fleet had stood off shore for two days, waiting again for the slower ships to arrive.

On board the flagship Venables and Penn were in disagreement. The main cause was in the orders given by Cromwell to each of the officers giving each the impression he was in sole command.

'I propose we sail at night straight into the harbour of St. Domingo and take the Spaniards by surprise.' Venables explained to Penn, Winslow, Butler and Gage who were all gathered together in the Admiral's cabin.

Cromwell had appointed Edward Winslow and Butler as his Agents to establish the colony after capture from the Spanish. Winslow was over sixty years old, not a good sailor and a very sick man, suffering from the early effects of scurvy. He had sailed with the Mayflower thirty years before and had been Governor of New Plymouth. Gregory Butler had been Governor of Bermuda and knew the Caribees well.

'I agree,' Gage concurred, 'I believe the town should only be lightly held'.

'Absolutely impossible,' Penn declared. 'We'll be shot out of the sea by the fire from the forts before we reach any landing. I propose we land here,' he pointed at the chart spread out on the table, 'Point Nizao. It is flat there, good landing beaches and far from any Spanish force. This will give you time to muster your forces and then march on St. Domingo.'

Venables disagreed and they continued to discuss the matter until the rest of the fleet arrived. Meanwhile, ashore, the Spaniards sighted the huge fleet and realised they were going to be invaded.

It took two days for the rest of the fleet to arrive, during which time the fleet rode at anchor. Most of the troops had been seasick on the voyage and now that the ships were stationary the seasickness increased.

'I think I'm going to die,' moaned Tom.

'Keep on deck as much as you can and walk about,' William advised him.

'But the sun is hot up there and it is so crowded.'

'Better than staying down here in this airless hold.'

On the 17th April, Admiral Penn had his way and sailed the fleet to Point Nizao. William watched the small boats being lowered from the ship's sides, they filled with troops and rowed towards the beach. It took two days to land the seven thousand men. William and the others from the Sandy Lane plantation were among those landed on the morning of the second day. The sun beat down from a cloudless sky and it was getting hot.

'We must find Huxtable,' William suggested.

'How do we do that in all this crowd?' Tom wondered.

They had no time to look for Huxtable. They were ordered to fall in line and commence marching. They were equipped with eight foot long pikes but were not organised into groups under any special command. All the slaves were bare foot but the regular soldiers from England had shoes and were armed with muskets; the pike men were supposed to defend them whilst they re-loaded. They proceeded along the flat foreshore for three miles, with open country on their right, until they reached a thick wooded area. They were led into the wood and carried on for two miles. It was cooler among the trees, but their view was restricted. They were halted in the wood, within sight of Port Jeronimo, at night fall and a cup of water and dry biscuits were distributed.

At dawn the next morning they heard firing ahead of them.

'Can you see anything?' William asked.

'I don't want to see anything,' the slave next to him replied. 'I didn't volunteer for this and I'm not doing any fighting. I'm going back.'

'You'll get shot if you desert.'

'Who by? Can you see any sergeant or officer here? No, son, they're all at the back!'

'Come on men, about turn!' he shouted to the rest of the men nearby. They all obeyed and started to go back.

The sound of firing increased and seemed to be getting nearer.

'No point in staying here alone,' William decided. He and his party joined the others. After four hours they were back at the beach head, part of a disorganised rabble. Later in the afternoon they were joined by Venables himself and the remainder of the force. Venables went back to the flagship but the troops were left ashore to look after themselves. William and Tom searched for Huxtable but without success.

'An absolute shambles,' Venables complained to Penn, 'I haven't got an army, I've got a band of thieves and vagrants! They can't even understand an order. They do not know who their officers are and at the first sound of shot they turn tail and run!'

The next day he went ashore again and gathered all the officers together, most of whom had been on different ships from their men for the whole voyage, and instructed them to select their men and give some rudimentary training. They were given two days to 'Knock this rabble into something like a fighting force.'

In fact Venables was right. These were not the same calibre of men Cromwell had taken to Ireland. When the force was formed in England, units were asked to supply a number of their men. The Commanders had selected the worst of their unit, men they were glad to see go. Furthermore, they had not been paid and a soldier likes to be paid, even if he has no chance to spend it. The men picked up in St. Kitts and

Barbados, like William, had no desire to fight. Whilst the orders given in Barbados was to call for volunteers, in fact the army had picked up any freeman they could get hold of, drunk or sober, and forced them on board. Those planters with Commonwealth sympathies had sent all their Irish and Scottish slaves whether they wanted to go or not. No promise of their freedom had been given in return for their services. All these latter had not been allocated to any officer nor organised into any formation.

On the 24th April, one week after the first assault, the force had been re-organised. Each company had been allotted an officer and some practice firing had been given. Once again they marched off along the foreshore, through the woodland and by the end of two days were within sight of St. Domingo.

They were ordered to halt and group themselves ready to attack the city at dawn the next day. They spent an uncomfortable night being pestered by mosquitoes and were given very little food.

At dawn the Spanish forces attacked them on both flanks and opened fire with canons and muskets from the city. William and his "platoon" were in the rear of the force and could not see any enemy to fire at. Some of the invading force at the front advanced and met the enemy, but they were not supported from the rear who turned tail and withdrew, ignoring their officer's orders to stand and fight. The result was once again a complete rout.

The whole force returned to the beach head and Venables went aboard the flagship. That evening, in the Admiral's cabin, with one oil lamp hanging from the bulkhead swinging as the ship rolled, he discussed the situation with Penn, Winslow, Butler and Gage.

'We should have sailed straight in to Santo Domingo harbour at night as I proposed,' Venables complained to Penn.

'No sir, the trouble is you have not an efficient army,' Penn replied.

'I have to agree with you, there. This miserable lot turned and ran again when they heard the first shot. I have now lost over a thousand men, not only in the fighting but also from scurvy and dysentery. The fact is they do not have enough to eat, your sailors are taking the best rations!'

'That is not true. I have had losses from scurvy among my crew, as you have among your soldiers.'

'Gentlemen, gentlemen, this is not the time for argument,' Winslow beseeched them. 'We have to decide what to do next and decide quickly. Cromwell has not lost a battle yet; this little foray will not please him. I recommend you find another target without delay, while you still have enough men left to fight with.'

'Where can we go within short sailing distance? We have neither the food nor water to go far,' Venables asked.

'I understand Jamaica, not too far from here, is lightly held,' Gage suggested. 'You could consider sailing on to there. It is a big island with much potential, we could establish a settlement there far easier than here. The Spaniards only use it as a staging post to the settlements further West.'

'I will consider the possibility,' Venables pondered.

'We should not stay here long or we run the risk of being attacked at sea,' Admiral Penn observed.

Meanwhile, ashore, William and the others spent their time looking for Huxtable without success.

'He could have been killed by the Spaniards,' Charles said.

'He could die of scurvy aboard,' John More suggested, 'I don't think we are going to see him again.'

'I hope you are all mistaken,' William replied, 'We must continue to look for him.'

The next day orders were given to return to the fleet. It took two days to bring the army off the beaches back onto the ships. William and Tom were glad to be back again, on the second day, not having used their pikes.

'That's one in the eye for that tyrant Cromwell!' William gloated happily, once aboard.

'I wonder what will happen next?' Tom asked.

'I don't know.'

'I'm not sure whether I would rather be ashore and run the risk of being shot, or stay on board and continue to feel I'm dying from sea-sickness!'

'Come on, cheer up, Tom; there are not so many of us on board now, thanks to the Spaniards and the scurvy, so maybe our rations will improve!' William tried to comfort him.

'Don't you believe it! If there are any extra rations the sailors will make sure we don't get them!'

'Well anyway, I don't think we'll stay here long,' William said.

But the fleet rode at anchor for another two days while the commanders decided on their future action and the "nurses" entertained the soldiers; so it was not until the 28th April before the fleet sailed again.

'Where are we going now?' William asked one of the sailors.

'Jamaica,' he was told. 'I have been there before. It is the poorest of the Spanish colonies. They have occupied it for many years but never developed it. It's a miserable place, nothing but trees and mosquitoes!'

They reached Jamaica on the 9th May, with fair weather and no storms. By now the food supplies on board were so desperate some of the men were dying from starvation as well as scurvy, including Edward Winslow, who was buried at sea within sight of land.

On the morning of the 10th May, William and his friends were the first to be landed with a small force at Cagways within sight of the fort. They were met with some musket fire from the fort and took cover in a ditch until more troops were landed. They were then ordered by an officer to advance to the fort.

'Keep your head down, Tom, and take as much cover as you can,' William advised as they crawled along the ditch towards the fort.

Suddenly the firing from the fort ceased. Apart from a few of the invaders firing their muskets towards the fort, at no visible target, there was comparative silence.

The soldiers in front had now entered the fort and found it deserted. They hoisted their puritan banners with "*God with Us*" emblazoned on them. Venables landed with extra troops and decided to camp at the fort for the night. The occupying force spent a miserable night being plagued by the mosquitoes and land crabs.

William and Tom were glad to be ashore again and delighted they did not have to do any fighting to capture the fort; but their efforts did not earn them any better food, they had to survive on dry biscuits and water.

They waited two days for all the men to be put ashore. Venables was not going to take any risks by advancing with only a small force. On the third day Venables and a squadron of men, including William and the "Sandy Lane platoon", advanced cautiously towards the town of Villa de la Vega, about two miles away. Venables was determined not to be ambushed again, like at Hispaniola. He cautiously sent scouts ahead to find any of the Spaniards, which delayed his advance, but proved that the way ahead was clear.

When the Spanish deserted the fort they retreated to Villa de la Vega and reported the invasion to the Governor. He was a fat, paralytic, old man who had been in Jamaica many years. He suffered from gout and was resting in a hammock – a wonderful innovation invented by the Arswak Indians – under the shade of a large tree in the palace gardens, a native girl by his side fanning off the flies.

'Senor, we are being invaded!' the Captain from the fort reported to him breathlessly.

'Rubbish, it can only be a few French buccaneers,' the Governor declared. 'Buenos Dios, who on earth would want to take this mosquito ridden, hell-hole?'

'But Senor, there are dozens of ships lying off the shore and they are landing thousands of soldiers! They have captured the fort and killed many of our men!' He exaggerated.

'I don't believe it. We have had small raids by pirates, the English and the French, but none of them stay – no one wants this plague ridden swamp. They'll take on water, steal a few pigs and go away. Leave me in peace!'

The Spanish soldiers and most of the population decided to evacuate the town and proceeded over the mountains to the north coast, taking their cattle and livestock with them. The Jewish Portuguese shop-keepers were the only residents to stay – to protect their own property. The Governor was left to sleep peacefully in his hammock.

William was with the small force, accompanying Venables, when he marched into the grounds of the Governor's palace, late in the afternoon on the third day. They found the Governor still in his hammock, fast asleep, with the native servant by his side still fanning the flies off his face.

'Senor, I demand your surrender,' Venables shouted.

The Governor awoke and stared with disbelief at his visitors.

'Pardone? What do you say?' he asked.
'Senor, I demand your surrender,' Venables repeated.
'No entiendo, I do not understand. Surrender? Who to?'
'I am General Venables in command of Cromwell's army, sent to take Jamaica for the Commonwealth.'
'Buenos Dios! You must be mad! What do you want Jamaica for?'
'Your sword, Senor, if you please. And I demand your soldiers lay down their arms!'
'As you see, General, I am unarmed and alone.'

In fact, Venables was soon to find the demand was an empty one when he discovered all the soldiers and most of the population of the town had evacuated, apart from the few Jewish Portuguese traders.

Venables and Penn made the Governor's house their headquarters. With Gage and Butler they drew up the surrender terms to present to the Governor. These laid down that all those who wished to stay in the town could do so and keep their property, except their slaves. Those who did not wish to stay would be sent to the nearest Spanish territory with only their clothes and books. The Spanish army had to lay down their arms. After five days the Governor signed the surrender terms.

In fact, the terms were meaningless, as all the army had evacuated to the North of the island. Only the shop keepers were left in the town and they decided to stay.

Being dismissed from the party at the Governor's house, William with a dozen other soldiers went to look at the town. They found it had about three hundred buildings, mostly small wooden houses in narrow, dirty lanes. There were a few pigs and some chickens but not a cow nor a horse in sight. They had captured Jamaica without firing a shot, but their victory was somewhat hollow.

Villa de la Vega was inadequate to accommodate the force of six thousand men and women. The women and the officers were given the houses and the men had to fend for themselves in the open. They were plagued by the continuous attention of the mosquitoes.

It was soon apparent to William and Tom that they would have to look seek their own accommodation. The officers were not organising the food nor where they should sleep.

'Let's catch a chicken,' William suggested, 'it will give us a good meal.'

'They're not easy to catch,' John More said, 'but if we wait until night we can grab one while it is asleep.'

That night they found a house where there were chickens in the back yard. They could hear the women entertaining soldiers inside the house. They soon grabbed a chicken, wrung its neck and plucked it. They lit a fire in the corner of the yard, John More rigged up a spit and soon had the chicken cooked. They were enjoying the best supper they had had for weeks when one of the women came out of the house.

'What are you doing?' she asked.

'Eating our supper,' William replied.

'What is it?'

'A chicken.'

'Where did you get that?'

'In the hen house there.'

'That's a good idea. Would you get us one?'

'Help yourself,' he recommended.

'Why don't you come in and join our party? We have plenty of wine and rum.'

'No thanks, we are quite happy here. We'll sleep in the chicken house and guard tomorrow's meal!'

William saw that the troops helped themselves to the few chickens and pigs and after a few days there were no animals left. Some even broke into the wine shops and helped themselves to rum and brandy; as a result there were many drunken brawls and complete disorder. The officers had no interest in enforcing any sort of order.

Foraging parties were quickly ordered to seek out cattle and wild hogs for food.

William and Mick Newman and John More were among a squad of twelve men led by a sergeant and ordered to follow the river upstream. It was very hot, with no wind, as they marched along a narrow, beaten track with the river on their right and dense forest and undergrowth on their left.

'This is very different from Barbados,' remarked John, perspiring from the humidity and heat of the day.

'Stop talking along there,' the sergeant hissed urgently.

They trudged along for two hours without seeing or hearing any signs of life, apart from the birds in the trees.

'It would probably be better to fish in the river,' William whispered.

They reached a piece of open ground when the silence was suddenly broken by the loud reports of several firearms, apparently coming from a bend in the river a short distance upstream. The party fell to the ground in some undergrowth.

'See anything?' someone asked quietly.

'Nothing,' William answered.

'About-turn" the sergeant ordered. 'Keep your heads down, we'll withdraw to those trees.'

They retreated about a hundred yards and halted in the forest for consultation.

'I was told there were no Spaniards left on the south coast,' the sergeant explained. 'This must be either a small party just looking for food, or maybe they are planning to attack the town and recapture it. There is nothing we can do, we will have to go back and report.' This brought a smile to the faces of the Irish "soldiers"!

Next door to William's chicken house, which they had made their living quarters, was Juan da Silva, a Jewish Portuguese, who owned a wine shop.

'Buenos Dios,' Juan greeted William one day.

'Good day to you. Do you speak English?'

'A little. You like some wine?'

'Thank you, but we have no money.'

'All soldiers, you have no money. Here, take a bottle. I give you and you see no soldier steals my wine.'

'Thank you. Where are all the Spanish soldiers?'

'They do not fight. They run away, up across the hills. They take their wives, children, cattle, they take everything.'

'Do you think they will come back?'

'No. They will attack in small numbers where they can. They live in the woods. They have their buccan with them.'

'Buccan? What's that?'

'Dried meat. They smoke the meat over a fire until it is hard like leather. Then it keeps long time. They chew it when they want it.'

'That's a good idea. We should try that. Now we have to eat it as soon as it is cooked or it goes bad in this heat.'

'You soldiers got a lot to learn. You eating chickens?'

'Yes. We are getting tired of them, but the eggs are good.'

'Spanish soldier's chickens, they are. Why not you come and have supper with my family tonight?'

'Thank you. That would be nice.'

'I can't feed you all, but you can bring one other if you like. Eight o'clock. Buenos Dias.'

That evening William took Tom with him for supper with Juan da Silva. His house was built of timber, with a small shop at the entrance. The walls of the shop were lined with shelves where the wine, rum and brandy was stocked. A door led to a living room behind. There was a round mahogany table in the centre of the room, and several upholstered chairs, a large sideboard with pewter plates and mugs displayed and in the centre a wooden Bible box and candle stick with seven candle holders. A flight of stairs led to bedrooms above.

'Meet my wife, Maria,' Juan introduced her to William and Tom.

'Buenos noches, senora,' they said and shook her hand as she sat in the chair. She was very fat and William thought she looked as though she was unable to rise.

'Mucho gusto, senor,' she replied.

'I'm afraid Maria does not speak any English. And this is my daughter Theresa,' Juan added as a young girl of twenty with long black hair entered from the kitchen at the back. She was wearing a long blue dress with a white apron.

'Buenos noches, senorita,' William and Tom greeted her.

'Mucho gusto, senores,' she replied.

'Theresa speaks no English, too,' Juan explained.

'What a pity,' William thought.

'Theresa has prepared the meal,' Juan added, 'and if you would care to sit at the table she will serve it.'

They sat at the table and Juan helped Maria up from her chair. She walked with difficulty the few steps to the table and lowered herself onto a small wooden chair. William wondered if the fragile looking seat could bear her weight.

'My wife suffers from the gout,' Juan told William and Tom, 'she drinks too much of my wine!' he laughed.

Theresa brought the meal in on pewter plates. It was fish with cassava, carrots and bread. When everyone had been served Theresa joined them at the table. Juan produced five pewter goblets and poured out some red wine.

Juan said grace in Spanish which the two visitors did not understand. They then began their meal using knives and spoons, there were no forks.

'Usted gusto?' Theresa asked.

'Theresa asks, do you like it?' Juan translated.

'Yes, thank you, it is very good.' Tom answered.

'Where did you learn to speak English, senor?' Tom asked.

'In England. We had a little shop in London.' After each sentence Maria grinned and nodded even though she did not know what her husband was saying. 'When Cromwell came to power we sold the shop and came here. We were frightened as we thought the Commonwealth people would persecute the Catholics, and especially Jews.' Maria grinned and nodded again. Juan explained to her in Spanish what they were talking about and she nodded even more vigorously.

'Yes, we fought against the Commonwealth army in Ireland,' William said, 'and when we lost the battle we were taken prisoner and sent to Barbados. Now we are being made to fight with them and we are not happy about it, but we have no choice.'

'Well, all I ask you to do, while you are living in the chicken house next door, is to guard my shop so your soldiers don't steal my wine. I'll give you a bottle each day. This is not a bad wine, is it?'

'Thank you, senor. It is a very good wine, and we will watch your shop for you.'

'Theresa is very sad,' Juan said, 'she is engaged to one of the Spanish soldiers, but when your fleet arrived he left with the rest of them without even saying adios.'

'That is sad,' Tom said, 'I doubt he will ever come back.'

William and Tom were enjoying their meal – the first one they had had sitting with a family for many years and after all the hardships they had suffered it was a very welcome treat.

After the fish, Theresa brought a bowl of fruit, oranges and pawpaws and served coffee.

When the meal was finished they said their thanks and left wishing their hosts good night.

The Spaniards had not planned to attack Villa de la Vega, as they did not have enough manpower. They had decided on guerrilla warfare, in the form of harrying the foraging parties and occasionally even burning some of the buildings on the edge of the town. They had the advantage of knowing the country and how to live in the climate which was so foreign to their invaders. They knew how to dry and preserve their meat supplies, producing what they called their "buccan". The English had not yet learned this procedure; they had not even been provided with water bottles, which restricted the distance they could go on these foraging trips.

The next day, William and Tom were detailed to help with unloading supplies from the fleet. Dry biscuits, arms, powder and tools were stacked on the foreshore in the open.

'These should be stored in the buildings and guarded,' William observed.

'We've been told to just leave them here,' Tom replied,

'But I don't think it will be long before the men help themselves!'

'I do not see why there is all this food stored here and yet soldiers are starving in the town,' Mick Newman observed, 'It is like starving in a cookhouse!'

'We should try to buccan our meat,' William suggested.

'Buccan? What is that?' Tom asked.

'I was talking to Juan the other day. He says the Spanish and the Arawaks buccan their meat by drying it over smoke. Let us try it tonight. We'll get a piece of beef in exchange for a chicken.'

'If we kill many more chickens we'll have no eggs,' John More remonstrated. 'We should keep some of them.'

'We can spare one more.'

That night they exchanged a chicken for some beef, cut the meat into slices, strung it up on a spit over the fire and sat watching it cook. Juan came from next door to see how his friends were faring.

'Buenas noches,' he greeted them, 'what are you doing?'

'Trying to buccan our meat,' William replied.

'Buenas Dios, you'll cook it that way. You have to have a lot of small, slow burning fires in a small room and hang the meat well over the smoke. The room fills with smoke and it takes many days to smoke the meat. The wood you use alters the flavour. Fir and pine are no good. Chicory is best. But you'll never do it like that,' pointing at their fire and laughing.

'We'd better cook it in the usual way and eat it,' Tom said.

'I wonder where Huxtable is?' William asked as they ate their beef.

'Surely, you don't think it is going to be possible to find him among all the thousands of men and women here, do you?'

'I'd just like to know if he is still alive or not; as for the women they aren't much good, are they? I'm surprised we brought them with us,' William said.

'I heard one of the soldiers say they have a good time with them in their houses at night. With plenty of wine from the stores too.'

'They're welcome; from what I've seen of them I wouldn't want to touch them, as much as I long for a woman.'

There was little conflict over the next few weeks and the invaders were beginning to appreciate they had merely occupied a swampy, plague ridden island. The soldiers raided the liquor stores and spent the nights drinking with the "nurses".

William and his party heard that many soldiers were dying from "marsh fever", dysentery and starvation. As the weeks went by all the troops were getting weaker and less inclined to go foraging for food. Many were drunk every night.

Admiral Penn saw little point in keeping the fleet here and wished to separate his seamen from the soldiers, so on the 25th June he sailed with part of the fleet for England, maintaining he had completed his part of the campaign.

Shortly afterwards, Venables, who complained he had not been in good health since he left Barbados, departed with the rest of the fleet, leaving a small, token force to maintain order on the island. He took with him the Irish slaves and bondsmen from Barbados, to return them to their masters – at least, those left alive. William and the others said goodbye to Juan and his family.

William was glad to leave Jamaica and delighted to see Barbados again. The weather on the journey back was better than the outward trip and he and his friends quite enjoyed it. He thanked God for delivering him safely through this terrible experience.

The Irish slaves and bondsmen were landed at Bridgetown and shut up in the same hut William knew from his first landing. Notices were sent round to the planters to collect their slaves, if they wanted them. Colonel Drax had never liked the red-legs so he ignored the notice and William, and those who had been with Drax, were left to languish until someone came to collect them.

Chapter 13
FARLEY HILL

Every day planters came to look over the slaves available, Mick Newman and John More had left, but no one had selected William. After a week, one afternoon a tall man with a friendly expression, wearing a long leather jacket, breeches and knee-high boots arrived and spoke to William.

'What do you do?' he asked.

'I like looking after horses, sir. I've worked with them all my life and trained my own mare in Ireland.'

'By Gad! I need a good groom. I'll take ye.'

'My friend here, Tom, is a good carpenter.'

'Another useful man to have. I'll take ye too.'

While the planter was dealing with the purchase of these two they said 'Good bye' to their other friends left behind.

'Try and keep in touch,' William said, 'and I hope we all find good masters. Preferably with no sugar cane!'

'At least it looks as though Drax doesn't want to see us again,' Paul Fraser said, 'and I don't want to see him or MacGregor!'

They shook hands all round and were told to go outside and get on to the waggon waiting there. The driver was a black slave. He whipped up the horse and they drove off. The planter followed on his own mount.

They drove North along the coast, passed Sandy Lane Plantation, passed Hole Town and as far as Speightstown where they turned inland and climbed a hill for another two miles.

They arrived at a plantation and alighted from the waggon. The planter handed his horse to a slave and walked over to William and Tom.

'My name is Job Bishop,' he explained. 'This is *Farley Hill* plantation and our main crop is tobacco. Which one of you said you were good with horses?'

'I did, sir,' William answered, 'my name is William Durgy and I come from Ireland, where I worked as an ostler in Drogheda.'

'Good. I'll show you the stables tomorrow. I want you to look after the horses and work on the tobacco when required. And you,' he added turning to Tom, 'are the carpenter?'

'Yes, sir. I'm Tom O'Leary, also from Ireland.'

'Good. My foreman will show you your duties tomorrow. You'll also work on the tobacco. I'll show you your quarters and then you can go and have your supper.'

The quarters were similar to Sandy Lane, but smaller. There was room for seven black slaves and William and Tom. The supper was very welcome, better than Drax's fare. They had a meat broth, bread and plenty of fruit.

Farley Hill plantation stood much higher than Sandy Lane. That evening, after supper, William stood outside the slaves' quarters and took in the magnificent view looking North over valleys and green trees stretching for several miles. While he was admiring the view the foreman came by.

'So you are one of the new men?' he asked. 'I'm the foreman and my name is John Harper.'

'How do you do, sir,' William replied, 'I'm William Durgy and I'm going to be the groom.'

'I hope you know something about horses. Our present stable boy isn't much good. I know more about horses than he does, but I suppose he didn't have horses in Africa, I don't know.'

'I trained my own mare in Ireland.'

'So you must know something about horses then. Where were you before you went to Jamaica?'

'On Colonel Drax's plantation at Sandy Lane, sir.'

'Drax, eh? What was that like?'

'Mostly sugar cane. We did not like the foreman, MacGregor.'

'I've heard of him. We have one hundred acres of tobacco here, fifty acres of cotton, five acres of pawpaw, oranges and pomegranate and five acres of vegetables. There are ten slaves, three of them have wives. We are small compared with some plantations but we do well when the weather is good. We supply the town with our fruit and vegetables. Job's brother buys the tobacco and cotton'.

'I'm glad you have no sugar, sir.'

'That's where the money is, but we've not the acreage to make it worth our while. Work well, Durgy, and you'll be all right here. Get any problems, come and see me. Mind you don't leave the plantation without permission. Slaves are not allowed to wander about, as you know; but really you should consider yourself as an unpaid servant rather than a slave here.'

'I felt like that under Mister Irwin before he was sent to England. Then Drax took over and things changed.'

'So you had a tough time there. How did you like Jamaica?'

'Not much. It was very hot and a lot of marsh fever. Many of us died there.'

'Glad I didn't have to go! I'll wish ye good night then.'

'Goad night, sir.'

William saw that Bishop's house was built of wood but not as grand as Irwin's. William and Tom were the only white slaves, which was to bring them together and bond their friendship more than ever.

The nest day, Harper took William to the stables and showed him the four horses and introduced the West African slave who looked after them.

'This is Oduduwa.' He turned to the negro. 'Now Oduduwa, I'm putting William Durgy in charge of these horses and you must help him and do what he tells you. I'll leave you two to get to know one another.'

'Oduduwa,' said William, 'what are the horse's names?'

'Names, sah? Dey got no names. Just 'orses''

'Oh, I see. Well, we'll have to give them names. And what does your name mean?'

'I'm named after de second son of Olorun, who was the creator of de earth and god of the sky. Oduduwa was de first king of the earth.'

'Was he? Do you know Oranyan, son of the Oni of Ife?'

'Hush, sah! Do yo no say his name. He was hanged two moons ago for stirring up trouble.'

'I knew him before I went to Jamaica. I'm sorry to hear he was hanged. He used to give me pawpaws when I was hungry.'

'We grow our own and pomegranates, yo'll have no trouble getting as many as yo like. Bishop, sah, is a good master, feeds us well and dere's no beatings and no hangings here.'

'I'm glad to hear it. Now let me see these horses. Ah, I see this first one is crib-biting.'

'Dat's de lazy one. Never wants to go out.'

'He must be given good exercise and tethered outside on the grass. He'll soon stop crib-biting, that wastes his energy. Now this next one is in better shape; I'll call this one "Black Bess."'

He soon knew the four horses and was pleased to be able to ride again. A few days later, after asking Harper permission, he went to the grave yard of All Saints Church, a mile away, where Josh was buried. He alighted from his horse and stood by the simple grave with a small, wooden cross.

'Hullo, Josh, my old friend,' he said aloud. 'You see I'm back again. God has been good to me, I have a new master who seems to be fair and I've been to Jamaica and back. I've seen men die in battle and die of scurvy, but God has spared me. Do you think there is some reason? Has He spared me for some purpose? What is my fate? Will I ever go back to my home at Platten Hall? I know you cannot tell me, my old friend, can you?' He crossed himself and turned to see Bishop riding up towards him.

'Friend of yours Durgy?' he asked.

'Yes, sir. Josh was the gardener on Irwin's plantation at Sandy Lane. He was killed at Denmark Fort when the Commonwealth troops landed.'

'You fought there did you?'

'Yes, sir, and I fought at the battle of Drogheda, in Ireland, where I was taken prisoner. All of family supported the King, but they were killed at Drogheda.'

'I'm sorry to hear it. So you're a King's man. I don't say I support King or Cromwell, I keep my opinions to myself and keep my mouth shut. That way I keep my plantation whoever rules; but between you and me, and these two nags, I'll be glad when Charle's comes to the throne.'

'Who is the Governor of the island now, sir?'

'Daniel Searle. Are you interested in the affairs of the island, then?'
'I like to know what is happening, sir. It affects all our lives.'
'Yes. I suppose you are right. Tomorrow, after you've seen to the horses, I want you to work on the tobacco. We're planting out the seedlings and that needs all the hands we can spare. I'll leave you to pay your respects to your friend.'

William watched Bishop ride away, happy to realise that he seemed a kind man, of good heart. Certainly an improvement on Colonel Drax! He thanked God for his good fortune.

The next day he went with Tom to work on the tobacco. There was a large wooden shed with a thatched roof. Inside were rows of small wooden trays laid on the floor containing the tobacco seedlings, each about four inches high.

'Now take a tray of seedlings,' Harper instructed, 'and plant them in straight rows nine inches apart. There are a supply of dibbers in the corner over there, use them to make the hole, and press the earth firmly after planting. Watch the blacks and see how they do it. The black children will keep you supplied with trays of seedlings.'

William picked up a tray of seedlings, collected his dibber which he thought looked like a foot long piece of old spade handle, rounded off at the end, and walked to the tobacco field. Here he found the straight lines marked out with rope. He started sowing the seedlings by bending down to plant each one and was thinking that this was going to be back breaking work, when he noticed the slaves were kneeling down to the job. They made four holes with their dibbers and planted four seedlings, then moved on down the line.

'This is easier than cane cutting, Tom.'

'That it is,' he said, 'but I think I can improve on these dibbers. I'll make some with handles, that'll be better.'

'A hundred acres to plant, did Harper say? I wonder how long this will take?'

'There are fifteen of us here, with the wives, that means five acres each.'

'Nearer seven, Tom, you're arithmetic isn't very good.'

'It never was.'

It took them three days to do that job. The black slaves were quicker, but with practice William and Tom did not do badly.

William's daily work in the stable was comparatively easy, certainly better and less arduous than cane cutting! He had plenty of opportunity to exercise the horses and went with Bishop to Speightstown to purchase supplies and deliver produce from the plantation. He was treated more as an unpaid servant than a slave, as Harper said he would be.

Speightstown was smaller than Indian Bridge, but there was a harbour with a few ships, loading and unloading, and one street of stores and shops. He was glad to have the opportunity to see other planters and their wives and the general activity of the town. He felt almost a freeman again and wished he could own a store himself.

Communication between the plantations, apart from the one next door, was difficult, but William wanted to find out if John Huxtable had returned to Sandy Lane.

'Do you ever go to Indian Bridge, sir?' he asked Job Bishop one day while driving the waggon from Speightstown.

'Not very often, Durgy. Why do you ask?'

'On your next visit I would like to go with you if possible to see Sandy Lane and find out if one of my friends returned safely from Jamaica. John Huxtable was Irwin's foreman and was separated from us when we boarded the ships and we never saw him in Jamaica. He could be dead for all I know.'

'I'll be going next week on business. Colonel Drax has Sandy Lane, I'm not too keen on meeting him but you could come with me on the waggon, if ye wish,' Bishop agreed.

'Thank you, sir.'

They left early one morning to go to Indian Bridge, about fourteen miles away, calling at Sandy Lane on the way. They drove up the drive to the house and William was sorry to see the whole place had deteriorated; the garden was full of weeds, the grass in front of the house was knee-high and the house itself was empty with the windows boarded up. The jacaranda tree was not in bloom and looked uncared for. *Josh would be sad to see this*, William thought.

They drove round the back of the house to the stables and, as they approached Jock MacGregor came out of one of the stalls. He was pulling up his trousers and was followed by a young, naked slave girl, who looked as though she was crying. He slapped her behind and shouted, 'Now get back to work!' She ran round the corner of the stable, down the track to the native quarters, wrapping a piece of coloured material round her loins.

'What do ye want?' he asked, striding aggressively towards the waggon. William and Job stayed where they were.

'I wanted to see Huxtable, sir,' William said.

'Huxtable? I don't know him. Ye've come to the wrong place, now get off this plantation, it's private property!'

'Huxtable was the foreman here in Mister Irwin's time. You took over from him sir.'

'Oh, yes,' MacGregor scratched his unshaven chin, 'now I remember the man. He went to Jamaica.'

'Do you know where he is now, sir?' William asked.

'Probably buried in a bog! I heard the old bastard died of marsh fever!'

'Oh, I'm sorry to hear that,' William said as his eyes caught sight of a negro running round the corner of the stable, brandishing a cane blade in the air.

'Look out!' He cried a warning to MacGregor, who turned to face his assailant.

'Yo no take my woman!' the negro shouted, bringing the blade down onto MacGregor's shoulder. He was defenceless without his whip and as he ducked he tried to punch the negro in his stomach. The blade came down again, striking him heavily across his back, opening a deep cut from shoulder to shoulder; MacGregor slumped onto the ground, groaning, blood pouring from his wounds. Job and William were horrified at what they saw.

'We must get out of here!' Job said in alarm. 'I do not want to get involved in this!' Turning the waggon, he whipped up the horse and they sped down the drive. William looked back and saw the negro hacking at the prone body of MacGregor.

'Friendly lot,' Bishop said, 'I'm glad Drax wasn't about, he'll hang that negro for sure!'

'I'm sorry to hear Huxtable died in Jamaica, he was a good man and did not want to go, but like me, he had no choice. I'm not sorry to see

MacGregor meet his well-deserved end. I still have a weal on my back from his whip.'

'Yes, I have no sympathy for a man who treats his negroes like that. There are too many planters on this island who think of their black slaves as animals; in my opinion they are just as human as we are and we should set them a good example. I have come across Colonel Drax before and I don't like the man. I have no wish to see him now, especially after that incident.'

They went on to Indian Bridge and William sat in the waggon while Job Bishop attended to his business. William saw little change in the town apart from the fact that it did not seem so busy.

Back at Farley Hill, William saw Tom.

'I went to Indian Bridge today with Mister Bishop and we visited Sandy Lane. You will be sorry to hear Jock MacGregor told us Huxtable died of marsh fever in Jamaica.'

'Poor old Huxtable, he didn't even want to go. What is Sandy Lane like now?'

'The garden was full of weeds, the grass uncut and the house was empty and boarded up. But the good news is, while we were there a negro slave attacked MacGregor. It all happened so quickly, the negro came running round the corner of the stable, waving his cane blade in the air and shouting. He hit MacGregor on the shoulder as he turned to face him and then again on his back. MacGregor fell to the ground with blood pouring everywhere; it was a terrible sight. Mister Bishop drove off quickly, but I glanced back and from what I could see it looked as though the slave was killing MacGregor!'

'I'm glad to hear it.' said Tom. 'He got what he fully deserved. I'm very glad we didn't have to go back there.'

'So am I,' William agreed.

It was a very hot night in June and William tossed and turned, unable to sleep. He had moved out of the slaves quarters and his bed was at the end of the stable, near the stalls. He could hear the horses were equally restless, moving about. He rose from his bed and went outside, it was cooler there and a full moon shone in a cloudless sky. He walked over to the nearest tree to relieve himself.

He heard a movement near the tobacco shed and quietly stole over, curious to see what it was. Two black figures lay on the ground, the moonlight glistening on their naked, sweating bodies. They were talking in their native tongue, which he did not understand, but by the low tones he could tell, in any language, that they were making love. Fascinated, he quietly moved closer and watched them.

He was still a young man and often the desire for a woman stirred in his body; but he had no chance here. The planters could bed any woman they wanted and the black slaves had their own women, but the Irish slaves had no chance with any woman on the island. As Huxtable had said years before when they arrived; *You can forget any thoughts of women here.*

Eventually the two figures stood up and he recognised Oduduwa and his girl, Eshu. They walked off hand in hand back to their quarters, not seeing William.

The next day, William was grooming the horses and Oduduwa was giving them their oats.

'It was hot last night, Oduduwa, wasn't it?'

'Yes, sar, it was.'

'I could not sleep and went outside where it was cooler.'

'Yes, sar?'

'I saw you and Eshu. I stood watching you together, wishing I could have a woman.'

'Yes, sar. Yo be unlucky with no womens. We've our women, and white "boss men" have their women or any of ours they want. But yo've no one.'

'No, I've no one. Only these horses to love.'

That night, William woke with the feeling someone was standing near him. Perhaps he was dreaming, but he thought he could see a black girl outlined against the moonlight outside, standing in the stable doorway, quite still and proudly upright. Eshu unwrapped her robe and let it drop to the ground, her young, beautifully formed figure clearly visible. She knelt down, lifted his sheet and lay down beside him. He took her in his arms and kissed her. They lay for a long time just fondling each other. William thought of Maeve and the last time he had made love in the hayloft. He closed his eyes and finally knew another girl.

Afterwards, she rose, wrapped her robe around her and walked away. Not a word had been said and he lay there and wondered if he had had a dream.

William kept his experience to himself. He knew that if Bishop found out he would be very annoyed. He said nothing to Oduduwa about it, although he knew Eshu must have been sent by him. She would not have come on her own, as he had nothing to do with her in the course of his work. He wondered how she had felt and whether she would come again.

Later in the season William and Tom had to help harvesting the tobacco leaves to be dried in the tobacco shed. Another white slave arrived from the next door plantation.

'You're from the next plantation, aren't you?' William asked.

'Yes, I've been sent over to help.'

'I'm William Durgy. What's your name?'

'Mike O'Connor. I know your name, you're from Platten Hall, aren't you?'

'That's so. You were not at Drogheda and sent here on the *Black Bird* were you?'

'No, I was taken prisoner at Trim and came here two months after Drogheda.'

'But you knew Platten Hall?'

'Oh, yes, I knew all about your family and Platten.'

'What happened there, do you know?'

'Haven't you heard? After the battle of Drogheda the Commonwealth soldiers broke into Platten Hall and they killed everyone there, including your mother and your sister and they set fire to the place.'

'Oh my God! No! Are you sure?' William was stunned by the news.

'Yes, I'm sure. I heard of it in Trim.'

'Do you know if my father is still alive? We were separated in the battle and I assume he was killed but do not know for certain.

'Yes, he was killed at Mill Mount with Aston and the others'.

'I was afraid of that. I suppose I always knew he was killed, but never heard for certain. That means I've lost all my family.'

'I'm sorry to tell you such news. I would've thought ye knew. You went to Jamaica with the rest of us, didn't you?'

'Yes, I went to Jamaica.'

'Did you hear what happened to Penn and Venables when they reached England?'

'No.'

'They were both put in the Tower for failing. Serve 'em right, I say. They lost over a thousand men, many of them my friends. I hope they rot in the dungeons!'

William went back to the stable and fondled Black Bess.

'I am really all alone now,' he whispered to the mare, 'I've no family left.' He had now heard what he had feared was the truth – all his family were dead. Was there now any reason for him to return to Ireland, if he ever was released from slavery? Could he reclaim possession of Platten Hall, which was now presumably a ruin? His heart felt heavy as he thought of his loss and silently he cried.

After work the next day he visited Josh's grave again.

'Hullo, Josh, old man.' he whispered, 'I've now heard my mother and sister were killed by Cromwell's men. I have no one left. I cannot even see their grave, so I come to yours instead.' He knelt and prayed by the grave.

'Dear God. Why? Why have you taken all my family? What am I to do? Where am I to go? Guide me, help me, dear God, I put my trust in thee.'

Whilst he was praying he heard footsteps behind him. He looked round, stood up and faced an elderly man wearing a black cloak and wide brimmed black hat, his long grey hair reaching his shoulders.

'Sorry if I disturbed you,' the man said.

'Not at all.'

'Friend of yours?'

'Yes. He died after the fighting at Denmark Fort.'

'I'm sorry. I'm the parish priest of All Saints. I do not recall seeing you before.'

'No, sir. Are you Catholic, Father?' William was not sure how to address him.

'Oh, no. They were all banished years ago.'

'So they were. One of them gave me my rosary.'

'I see.'

'Another Catholic Father told me I must have faith. I have just heard my mother and my sister were killed by the Roundheads. I find it very difficult to have faith.'

'Do you think you are confusing faith with hope? You can hope bad things will not happen, but they do. That should not destroy your faith in the Almighty. Yes, have faith at all times, but do not abandon it when your hopes do not come true. God works in mysterious ways and it is often hard for us to see any reason to them. But He knows what is best for us. Your undying faith will bring you through.'

'I have not thought of it like that before.'

'Have you a bible?'

'No, sir. I don't have a bible.'

'Would you like one? I assume you can read?'

'Yes, sir. That would be very helpful.'

'Come then. Come to my house and I'll give you a bible.'

'Thank you, sir,' William walked with the priest, leading his horse beside him and came to the priest's house, which was next to the church. He tethered the horse to a tree and followed the priest inside.

'Come in. I'm sure I have a spare bible somewhere here.'

The room was well furnished with a large, round mahogany table, four mahogany dining chairs, several leather covered comfortable armchairs and the walls were lined with shelves full of books. The priest searched along the shelves and found a bible, rather an old one with well worn, leather binding.

'Here you are. You're welcome to have that.'

'Thank you, sir. I will treasure it, you're very kind.'

'Not at all. I presume you are a servant from one of the plantations?' William assumed he thought this as he was wearing shoes. Slaves did not usually wear shoes, but Job had given William and Tom a pair each.

'Not a servant, sir, a slave, but I'm treated like an unpaid servant. Mister Bishop is very good to me, that is why I'm allowed away from the plantation.' He wondered whether, had the priest known he was a slave, he would have given him the bible?

'I see.' The priest pointedly looked down at William's shoes – he had never seen a slave with shoes before.

'Yes, you see he even gave me shoes to wear.'
'Well I hope the bible will give you some comfort.'
'Thank you, sir. Now I must be on my way back.'
'Good night to you, then.'
'Good night, sir, and thank you.'

William rode back with his bible which he was to read on many nights to come.

One day in September, Job Bishop came to the stables with a stranger, leading a horse which was limping.

'Durgy,' Job said, 'this is my brother Thomas, come to visit us.' William could see the likeness; he was a tall man with a pleasant, kindly smile. 'He hired a horse which has gone lame. I've told Thomas you are good with horses – have a look at it for him.'

William took the bridle and led the horse round watching how it walked. He stroked the horse's head then his hand went down to feel the left fore-leg.

'He's sprained a tendon down here, Mister Bishop, sir. He'll need rest and then I can treat it for you, but it'll take a few days. You could ride one from the stable here, sir.'

'Thank you, Durgy. I'll leave the horse with you.'

The next day, Job came to the stable. 'How is my brother's horse?'

'I've put on a poultice, sir, and we can only hope that in a few days it will be better.'

'My brother comes from Ipswich, New England. He has a ship and takes my tobacco and cotton from here to Boston. He'll be here for a week or two. He heard that Cromwell was asked to be King of England, but he refused. He is now called the Lord Protector.'

'Thank you for telling me, sir, Mister Irwin used to tell me what was happening. I have heard that my father's house in Ireland, Platten Hall, was burnt down by Cromwell's men and my mother and sister were killed. My family name is descended from the D'Arcy's of England and hundreds of years ago I believe they were given lands belonging to Cromwell's ancestors. That is why, when they came to Ireland, I think Cromwell sought out my family and had his revenge. At the battle of Drogheda my father and two brothers were killed.'

'So you told me before, Durgy. I am very sorry to hear about your mother and sister. When Prince Charles comes to the throne, perhaps you will be released and I will see what I can do for you. Thomas sometimes sails to England, maybe he would take you back if you wanted to go.'

'Thank you, sir. If that ever happens I would consider your offer, but while Cromwell rules England, I seem to have little future.'

At night, William spent many long hours thinking about his future; how much longer did he have to wait for freedom? He spent as much time as he could reading his bible when the light was good. He had no candle nor oil lamp.

One late afternoon, a month later, Bishop came running out to the stables calling for William. 'Durgy, get the waggon hitched up at once and call as many men as you can find. There's a big fire at St. Michael's and they want help!'

William alerted Tom and they hitched the waggon up. Oduduwa collected half a dozen slaves and they gathered up as many sacks and leather buckets as they could find. They all clambered onto the waggon, while Job took the reins and drove the horse as fast as he could. It was early evening when they reached St. Michael's, about six miles away. As they neared the settlement they could see the glow of the fire in the fading light.

When they arrived they saw that many of the wooden houses were beyond saving. Together, with a large crowd of slaves and villagers, they formed a chain from a nearby stream to the house nearest the fire, throwing water on the walls to stop the fire spreading. The heat was intense and they threw bucket after bucket of water, but it was all in vain. Cinders from the burning houses blew onto the thatched roof and soon the house they tried to save was ablaze. They had no means of reaching the roof to save it. They could only salvage some of the furniture from inside, before the fire took too much of a hold on the roof and it collapsed.

They then started trying to save the next building and so they worked through the night. By morning they were all exhausted and the fire had burned itself out. Over three quarters of the buildings had been destroyed.

Unable to help any further, they wearily clambered back onto the waggon and returned at a slower pace to Farley Hill.

'A tragedy like that is disastrous to the villagers,' Bishop explained while he drove. 'All those who lived in the burned buildings lost all they possessed and there is no way they can gain any recompense. They rely on the kindness of sympathetic merchants, planters and neighbours.'

A few days later, William took the waggon with Bishop into Holetown for supplies and he was amazed to see in the town square an iron cage suspended high in the air from a tall post. Inside the cage was a naked white man.

'Mr.Bishop, sir, who is that?' William asked.

'That is one of the Scottish slaves. He has been found guilty of starting the fire at St. Michael's. This is a common form of punishment.'

'I have never seen it before, sir! I think it is terrible.'

'These Commonwealth planters and rulers are very strict, it is their way. I pray God none of my slaves will ever suffer thus.'

Some bystanders were throwing eggs and fruit at the cage, but the man was obviously close to death and could not be aware of this further indignity.

In October 1658, Job came looking for William. 'Durgy,' he called out, 'I've news I think will please you.'

'Yes, sir?' William paused from his work in the stable.

'We've just heard, Cromwell is dead. His son has taken over, so maybe you will soon have your freedom.'

'Thank you, sir. That's great news, but I've a feeling one Cromwell could be as bad as another. I wonder how long it will be before Charles is made king?'

'That is hard to say. It may depend on how strong a leader Richard Cromwell proves to be.'

William was to wait until 1660 before Charles II came to the throne.

Chapter 14
LAND OF THE EAGLE

Five years later, on the 3rd September 1663, one of Bishop's servants came to the stables calling for William.

'Sah, Mister Bishop, sah, wants to see you at the house.'

William had never been called to the house before, so he realised that what Job Bishop had to tell him must be important. He wondered what it could possibly be, whilst he hurriedly washed his hands and face and tidied himself up.

At the house he found the front door open and he knocked with his clenched fist. Bishop called to him from a room on the right.

'Is that you, Durgy?'

'Yes, sir.' He entered the hall nervously. The wooden floor was bare and the only furniture was a chair and a sea-chest.

'Come in, come in!' William entered the room and found Job sitting at a table covered with papers. The room was as barely furnished as the hall with no floor covering, two chairs at the table, one wooden armchair in the corner and an oak dresser displaying pewter mugs and plates.

'I've great news for you!' Bishop announced with a broad smile. 'I've just heard that the King has, at last, granted all Irish prisoners their freedom. From today Durgy, you are a freedman.'

'Thank God, sir!' William said with relief, 'I've waited five years for this news, since Oliver Cromwell died. Thank you for telling me, sir.'

'I hope you will stay with me; or later you may wish to join my brother when he next visits. I know he would like to have you as a servant and he could take you to America, or possibly even to Ireland if you wanted to go.'

'I'll be happy to stay with you, sir. I don't know about going back to Ireland; all my family are dead and I've been told my home at Platten Hall is in ruins. I would like to see America, but I wouldn't want to let you down, sir. I appreciate you have been very good to me for many years.'

'You won't be letting me down, Durgy. I've already discussed this possibility with my brother and he will be pleased to have you, on a five year indenture. You are free to do as you wish.'

'Thank you, sir,' William replied, 'I think there will be more opportunities in America than in Barbados.'

'You're probably right. You'll be all right with Thomas.'

During the past five years William had met Job's brother, Thomas, several times when he came from Boston. He felt he knew him well and liked him. He thought he would be a good master.

'From today you are my groom and I will pay you five shillings a month with keep. We'll leave it like that until my brother arrives in a few weeks time. We'll see what he says.'

'Thank you, sir.'

'Will you ask Tom O'Leary to come and see me?'

'Yes, sir.' William backed out of the room in a deferential manner, as was befitting a slave. Outside, he exclaimed, 'Free! I am a free man at last!' He was overcome with excitement. He cried with tears of joy. He ran over to see Tom in his workshop.

'Tom! I've great news for you!' William shouted excitedly.

'Oh? What's happened?'

'We are free! Tom from today we are free men! King Charles has given us our freedom at last.'

'God! Isn't that marvellous!' He grabbed William and they danced around, hugging each other with delight.

'Mister Bishop wants to see you up at the house. You'd better go quickly.'

'Up at the house? I've only been there once to do some work,' Tom said with surprise.

'Yes, well I expect he will be offering you a job as carpenter, not as a slave!'

Tom went to see Job Bishop and later returned to William in the stables.

'You're right, William. He has offered me a five year indenture at five shillings a month with food. After that I will be free to set up on my own on the island. Isn't it marvellous! What are you going to do now?'

'I'll stay here for the present. Thomas Bishop is coming in a few weeks and I may join him. What will you do?'

'I'd like to get back to Ireland. Maybe my mother is still alive. I asked Mister Bishop if he would release me if I could find a way of returning and he said he would.'

'Perhaps you could work your way back on a ship? They always want carpenters.'

'Yes, that's a good idea.'

As freedmen and servants of Job Bishop's, William and Tom could leave the plantation without permission, when their work was done. So once a week they rode down to Speightstown for a drink. Here they met the sailors off the ships that had arrived from Jamestown, Boston and England.

'The colonies in New England are developing fast,' they were told, 'a young man has plenty of opportunities, providing he is prepared to work hard and accept rough conditions.'

'How about a job as carpenter on a ship to Ireland or England?' Tom asked.

'That should be easy, carpenters are scarce but there is a greater demand for them in the new colonies.'

'I want to go back to Ireland,' Ton insisted.

'Why don't ye see the mate of my ship? He's over there, go and ask him.'

Tom went over to the mate and returned after a few minutes.

'He'll take me on when Mr. Bishop releases me. They sail next week to Liverpool. I'll get a passage to Ireland easily from there.'

Job agreed to let Tom go and on the day of sailing William went down to Speightstown to see Tom off.

'I'm sorry to see you go, Tom we've been through a lot together. You've taught me carpentry and I know that will be useful.'

'Yes, and you've taught me to ride. I'm disappointed you'll not be coming with me, William. We've been good friends and you have helped me. Without you on the *Black Bird* I think I'd have died.'

'God go with you, my friend, and have a safe passage.'

'When I get to Ireland I'll find out about your home. You know I can't write but I'll find someone who can and try to let you know what has happened there.'

They embraced and Tom boarded the row boat that was to take him to his ship. William gave a final wave and wondered if he should have gone too. Should he go back to Ireland, or should he go to America? Perhaps the opportunities there would be better than in Ireland? He felt that destiny was drawing him in that direction; surely he had been saved from all the perils he had faced for some purpose? Perhaps his destiny was in America?

For another month life continued as usual for William at Farley Hill. He missed Tom and felt lonely, Odudawa was his only daily companion. Eshu had never visited him again and he had no contact with her. John Harper, the foreman, was friendly but distant; he never conversed with William more than the work demanded. He was not as close to Harper as he was with Huxtable. He did see the parish priest fairly frequently and had some discussions with him but he had no other, real close friend like Tom.

At the end of the month Thomas Bishop arrived and sought William out.

'Job tells me you would like to come to Ipswich with me, Durgy.'

'Yes please, sir. I can look after your horse and be your servant, sir.'

'I would be glad to have you. I will take you on for five years with eighteen meals a week, a bed and five shillings a month. You can look after my animals; I do have one horse but I have more sheep, pigs and chickens. You can help Mistress Bishop with the heavier housework. I have two sons and they work the land. My ship is being unloaded and then I'll be taking on a cargo of tobacco, sugar and cotton. We should sail for Boston in about a week, be ready then.'

'Thank you, sir. I'll be ready.'

William was overjoyed; at last he would leave this island and see America. He imagined all the things he would do there and could hardly sleep at night with all the wild fancies in his mind.

A week later, Thomas Bishop came to the stables and found William grooming a horse as usual.

'Durgy,' he said, 'time to pack your bags and come aboard.'

'That won't take me long, sir,' William laughed. 'The little I have will go in a small gunny sack and take one minute to pack!'

He patted each of the horses he had cared for over the past years and put his scant belongings in a sack.

'Odudawa, get the horse and cart ready. Mr Thomas and I are going to Speightstown.'

He went down to the tobacco shed to find Harper.

'I'm off now to America with Thomas Bishop.' He told him.

'Sorry to see you go, Durgy. I wish you God speed.'

'Thank you. Good bye.'

He went up to the house to say farewell to Job Bishop. He found Job standing at the front porch talking to Thomas, the horse and waggon were waiting in the drive ready to depart.

'Good bye, sir,' William said, 'and thank you for your kindness. I'm glad I did not have to go back to Colonel Drax.'

'His loss was my gain, Durgy. Good bye, I'm sorry to see you go but I wish you God speed. You'll be all right with Thomas, but don't forget the settlers you are going to live with are ardent Protestants and they don't take to Catholics.'

A warning William was going to have to remember. He had not thought about the different religions and recalled the animosity the Protestants had shown to the Catholics in Ireland. He did not know Thomas's religious leanings and had not given it any consideration. Job Bishop had not held prayer meetings on Sundays; William had had to be satisfied with reading his bible and using his rosary.

Thomas mounted the cart while Odudawa took the reins sitting by his side. William climbed onto the back and as they drove off he gave a final wave. Good bye, Farley Hill! He had spent seven years here, seven comparatively easy years, but he was not sorry to leave. He had learned how to sow and care for tobacco and cotton, as well as the various fruits and vegetables. Tom had taught him all he knew about carpentry. He hoped that was going to be useful in the future.

At Speightstown there were several ships at anchor in the harbour and he wondered which one was Thomas Bishop's. He jumped off the cart and lifted down Thomas's trunk, while Thomas alighted and came round the back of the cart.

'Good man,' said Thomas, 'the small boat will soon be here and we can go straight aboard.'

'Good bye, Odudawa,' he said, 'Look after the horses well. I hope I have taught you something.'

'Yes, sar. You've taught me a lot and I'm sorry to see you go. I hope you like where you are going.'

'I'm sure I shall, Odudawa.'

Odudawo drove the cart back to Farley Hill and they were left standing on the quay among a crowd of sailors and local people. Thomas took his hat off and waved it in the air. On board the ship they must have been waiting for the signal, for immediately a small rowing boat left the side and proceeded to the quay. When it arrived they clambered aboard with Thomas's trunk and William's gunny sack.

They rowed out into the harbour and approached the ship. It was a two masted brig about eighty feet long and had the name *Redemtioneer* boldly painted on the bow. Thomas climbed up the short Jacob's-ladder and William followed. A line was attached to the trunk and it was heaved on board. The captain greeted Thomas.

'We are all ready to sail, sir,' he said.

'Then go ahead, George,' Thomas replied. 'Durgy, they'll show you where to stow my trunk and that sack of yours.'

One of the seamen led William carrying the heavy trunk, to Bishop's cabin, then up forward and showed him a bunk in the crew's quarters. William went back on deck and watched the activity as they raised anchor, set the sails and departed. It was the 13th October 1663 and he took his last look at Barbados. He had a new job; although only a servant to his master, he was a free man and on his way to a new life in a new country. His heart was filled with the anticipation of a great new adventure.

He went to Bishop's cabin and knocked on the door.

'Come in.'

'Is there anything I can do for you, sir?' William asked.

'Yes, you can unpack my trunk.'

On the way to Boston William got to know several of the crew. This was a different experience than he had had on the way to Barbados and to and from Jamaica. The crew were friendly and treated him as an equal.

'Mr Bishop doesn't live in Boston, does he?' he asked.

'No. he has a house in Ipswich, just a few miles north of Boston. That's where the ship lays to waiting for the next voyage.'

'Have you been with Mr Bishop long?'

'Oh, let me see, five years now. He's a good owner, but of course we have more to do with the master. But Bishop keeps his ship in good order. Many owners don't bother so much.'

After a calm voyage they called in at St. Kitts. William was able to go ashore and see more of this island which he had called on before, some years ago, but had been unable to land.

Although he had been a free man for five weeks, he still had a wonderful new feeling of freedom as he walked the streets. Like a man released from prison, he thought. And he had money in his pocket – four whole shillings! He had spent one shilling with Tom.

He found the island was very similar to Barbados. Narrow, dirt roads with wooden houses, stores and shops, planters and their wives going about their business, white servants and men hanging about with apparently nothing to do. It did not seem as prosperous as Bridgetown. He spent another shilling, to buy a hat. Slaves never wore hats and he decided to stop looking like one. He chose a black hat with an eight inch crown and wide brim.

They took on board some more sugar and rum before sailing on to Boston.

The *Redemtioneer* docked at Boston on the 9th November. It was a grey, misty day and colder than Barbados. William was amazed at the size of the port, it was far larger than Bridgetown and there were a great number of ships. He went ashore and found it was a large town, consisting of a mixture of wooden and stone buildings built alongside earthen thoroughfares with an open drain running down the middle. The town was crowded with sailors from the ships and the local people busy shopping, buying and selling, in the various trading stores. He went into an inn for a rum which was better than the mobbie in Barbados.

'This is a busy town,' William said to the innkeeper.

'Yes, it has grown quickly in the thirty odd years since the first settlement. Lots of smaller places around too. Where are you from then?'

'Barbados. Going to Ipswich.'

'Ah, yes, that's just up the coast. A small place.'

He went back on board and watched the cargo being unloaded. They were three days in Boston and then sailed on to Ipswich. As they entered the mouth of the river, William saw a small group of houses on the right bank, behind trees growing at the water side. The *Redemtioneer* dropped anchor and the rowing boat was lowered. William with his gunny sack of possessions went down the Jacob's ladder into the row boat. Thomas Bishop's trunk was sent down on a rope which William unhitched. Thomas then came down himself and they rowed to a small, wooden, landing jetty by a stream which ran down from the valley. They walked up a dirt path alongside the stream, William carrying Thomas's heavy trunk. Two hundred yards up the stream they cleared the trees and came to some twenty houses scattered about. Each house had an enclosure for animals and crops.

'This is called Heard's Brook and that's my house,' Thomas said as they walked up the path, pointing to the back of a timber frame building, with clapboarding on the walls. Margaret Bishop, his wife, came running out of the house.

'Thomas,' she cried, 'how lovely to see you! How are you?'

'Fit enough, my good woman,' he replied, embracing her. 'This is William Durgy. I've brought him to lend a hand.'

'Welcome, William ' Margaret Bishop held out her hand.

'Thank you,' he said, putting down the trunk and shaking her hand, 'I'll serve you as well as I can.'

'He's good with horses,' Thomas went on as they entered the house, 'but I don't know how he will cope with sheep, eh?'

William lifted the trunk up again and followed Thomas into the house.

'No, sir, I've not looked after any sheep before.'

The house had a small porch inside the doorway with steep, narrow stairs leading to the floor above. They went into a room on the right and William saw this was the living-room. It had low timber beams on the ceiling, wattle walls between the timber frames, one small, leaded

166 FROM THE HARP TO THE EAGLE

This seventeenth-century room, with its hand-hewn beams and huge fireplace, was the centre of family activities, including meals and the daily Bible reading

window on the right-hand wall and a welcome log fire in a large brick fireplace on the left. In the centre of the room was a long table with stools around it and a "Betty" lamp in the middle. There were two wooden armchairs by the fireside and under the window a large wooden chest with a box on top. The timber floor was partly covered with an animal skin in front of the fire. William was glad to put the trunk down, he hoped for the last time.

He thought the room looked very cosy, even if it was a bit dark, for not much light came from the fire and the small window. A young girl was standing by the fire attending to a pot hung over the burning embers. She was slim with dark hair, her plain, blue, cotton frock, reached her ankles, with full length sleeves and a white knee length, sleeveless apron. Her straight hair was gathered under a white bonnet tied with a bow below her chin.

'This is the maid, Martha,' Margaret said.'Martha, this William Durgy, come to live with us.'

Martha turned towards William and gave him a little bow.

'How do. Pleased to meet you,' she said.

William nodded back. 'How do you do. Martha. Pleased to meet you.'

'Martha goes home for the night. You can sleep upstairs, William,' Margaret said. 'Come with me and I'll show you.'

He followed her into the porch again, carrying his gunny sack.

'Bring the trunk, William,' she said, 'and you can put it in that room there,' Margaret pointed to the room to the left of the entrance. 'That is our sleeping room. There's a fire there for the winter.'

William lifted the trunk, with his gunny sack on top, and carried it into the bedroom. He put it down definitely for the last time with relief. He had time to see that the bedroom had a large double four-poster bed with curtains, two wooden chairs and a mahogany sideboard.

Margaret climbed the stairs and William followed. At the top was a large space covering both rooms below, with the chimney piece built in the middle. There was no window and it took him a second or two in the poor light to see that it was full of stores of all kinds.

'You can clear a space in the middle next to the chimney it'll be warm there and we'll find some straw, to fill a sack for bedding. You see there are gaps between the floorboards, this allows heat from below to come up; you should be comfortable enough.'

'It looks very suitable Mistress Bishop. Thank you.'

'I'm glad you like it. Soon ye'll meet our sons, John and Samuel. They're out in the field now. I expect ye'd like a wash, ye'll find a bucket out at the back.'

William went out of the front door, as there was no back door, and round to the back of the house. Here he found there was an allotment with vegetables, fruit trees, a small wooden barn, a chicken run and some pigs. He looked inside the barn but found it was empty. Presumably the horse was with the boys. The leather bucket full of water was on a table. He washed his face and hands in the cold water, then returned to the main room.

'This is a fine house you have here, sir,' he said to Thomas Bishop. 'How long have you been here?'

'Well, Ipswich was first settled in 1634, the Indians called the place Agawam. We arrived here twenty-five years ago and built a bark-covered wigwam, like you'll see Mistress Harfield still has. Her husband died soon after they came and she has never built herself a house. We built this house, with this one room at first, which we call the hall; we built the bedroom ten years later. Many of the houses you will see here still have only one room, but some do have a lean-to built at the back. We find it comfortable enough.'

'You mentioned Indians. Do you see them at all?'

'Very seldom. The local ones are friendly, but it is still dangerous to travel too far inland. There are other tribes which are not so friendly – they'd have your scalp!' He laughed.

'Don't tell him such things!' Margaret exclaimed. 'William, he does tell tales. We've had no trouble with the Indians here. They trade peacefully with us. Bring us their furs and we give them knives and sugar.'

Soon it was dark and Margaret Bishop lit the betty lamp. William had not seen one of these before. It had a round, wooden base with a screw post, attached to which was a crossbar with two small metal containers for oil or grease with a wick. It gave off a flickering light, enough to see by, and a smell which William would have to get accustomed to.

The table was laid with six pewter plates, each with a pointed knife and a spoon. Martha carried a large bowl of food from the fireplace which she placed on the table in front of Margaret. Just then young Samuel and John came in.

'You're just in time, boys, your father's home,' she said. 'Have you washed your hands?'

'Yes, mother,' they both replied.

'This is William Durgy – he's going to help us on the farm.' Thomas said.

The boys nodded to William but paid more attention to their father.

'Father, glad to see you back. Did you have a good voyage, sir?' John asked.

'Yes, thank you. A good load of cotton, sugar, rum and tobacco which I sold in Boston. Meet my sons, William; this is Samuel, my eldest and this whipper-snapper is young John.'

'Father, I'm no whipper-snapper!' John complained.

William shook hands with the two boys. He thought Samuel looked about eighteen and John fifteen.

'Glad to meet you, what have you been doing today?'

'John looked after the sheep and I ploughed some land for our wheat crop.'

'Sit you down at the table, we must not let the food get cold,' their father said. 'We'll say grace. Lord, we thank you for our victuals and for guiding us safely home again. Amen.'

Mistress Bishop ladled out the food, a stew with mixed vegetables, boiled pork and a slice of bread.

'Are you from Barbados, William?' Samuel asked.

'Yes, I was with your uncle Job, at Farley Hill plantation.'

'What was it like there?'

'I found it fair enough. I was the groom. The weather was warmer than it is here.'

'Were you in Barbados long?'

'Yes. Sixteen years, not counting the time I went to Jamaica.'

'Jamaica! What were you doing there?'

William explained all about his experience in Jamaica.

'My! You've had an exciting life!' John said, 'You must tell us all about it. We've never been further than Boston!'

After the meal, Martha cleared the plates away and took them outside to wash. Thomas brought the box over from the chest. He opened the box and took out a large Bible.

'William, we brought this Bible with us from England and we read from it every night before going to bed. I usually open it at random. Tonight I see I have opened it at Luke, Chapter 6:

"But I say unto you which hear," he read. "Love your enemies, do good to them which hate you. Bless them that curse you and pray for them which despitefully use you. And unto him that smiteth thee on the one cheek offer also the other; and him that taketh away thy cloak forbid not to take thy coat also. Give to every man that asketh of thee; and of him that taketh away thy goods ask them not again. And as ye would that men should do to you, do ye also to them likewise." This is the word of the Lord. Amen.'

'Amen,' they all muttered.

After a pause, William said, 'Sir, I find that lesson hard to follow. I fought the Commonwealth men at Drogheda, should I love them? They killed my father, my mother, my two brothers and my sister. I find it very hard in my heart to love them.'

'Perhaps, William,' Bishop replied, 'you could in time forgive them. Remember, even Christ himself on the point of death asked His Father to forgive his persecutors, "for they know not what they do".'

'Maybe, sir, in time I might learn to forgive them. A priest taught me to have faith and I believe that helped me through the years in Barbados. Then another priest told me I was mixing faith with hope. That I could hope for something, but if I did not get it that was no reason to abandon my faith.'

'Faith, hope and charity go together,' Thomas said. 'God is love, charity, forgiveness. You are not a complete Christian if you only have faith and hope without charity.'

'I often wonder why I was not killed in Ireland or Jamaica. I believe I was meant to come here, for what purpose I do not know.'

'I am sure you are right, William. Now, I think we should go to bed and save Mistress Bishop's light. We rise early at dawn.'

Martha came back into the room and said,'I'll go now, Mistress

Bishop. Goodnight to ye.'

'Thank you, Martha, good night. Give my respects to Mistress Cross and Goodman Cross.' Martha bobbed and went on her way.

William said 'goodnight' and went up to his attic. He found he had a bare board to sleep on for that first night, but promised himself he would find some straw the next day! Thomas and Margaret Bishop went to their bedroom and he could hear young Thomas and John settling down on the floor in the room below by the fire.

The next morning, William awoke when he heard movement down stairs. He could not tell it was dawn for it was still dark in his attic. He rose, dressed and went to wash in the bucket at the back of the house.

Breakfast was fried pork, bread and a mug of water. After the meal John took William round the village to meet some of the villagers. At the front of the house was a track leading through the village.

'We call this Mill Street,' John explained.

The house in the next allotment was occupied by Mary Bishop, Job's wife, which surprised William as he did not know Job Bishop had a wife, although he had on occasions left the plantation at Farley Hill to return to Ipswich with his brother. He had never mentioned his wife to William.

'William Durgy! Welcome to Ipswich,' Mary said. She was a tall, thin woman with grey hair and a kind smile. 'Job has mentioned you to me. Good with horses, you be, he told me.'

'How do you do, Mistress Bishop,' William replied, 'Mister Bishop was very good to me in Barbados. It was my good fortune to be serving him.'

'I hope ye'll be well satisfied here.'

'Across the stream there is the Cross's house, Martha's home. Robert and Hanna have a big family of children.' John explained. 'Next door is the Nelsons, William and Elizabeth, she is one of Robert Cross's daughters, then the Searls house and then William Cogswell.'

Further up the village John pointed out the village meeting hall. 'That is where the councillors meet. Father is a member of the council. We also have our prayer meetings there on Sundays. Theophilus Wilson, the constable, lives on the right of the meeting hall and Robert Lord, the marshall on the other side.'

At the top of the village was the bark-covered wigwam, the home of

Mistress Harfield. It looked out of place with the rest of the houses, small as most of them were. They did not go any nearer than fifty yards away and William saw an old woman with long, grey hair standing outside the entrance, leaning on a stick. She had a hump back and her long brown cloak, almost reaching her bare feet, looked from this distance to be made of sacking.

'No-one has anything to do with Mistress Harfield,' John said. 'The children think she's a witch!'

They met many people who all greeted John and were introduced to William, but by the end of the morning he had met so many he could not remember all their names.

'And that building there,' said John, pointing across the street, 'is the village beer-house. Moses Maverick makes beer. I should not drink too much of it if I were you, it's pretty strong but he sells a lot at Thanksgiving! Would you like to look inside? Father won't allow me to go in, but we could look.'

'Yes, I don't mind having a look.'

They went up to the entrance and William saw the notice inside the door, setting out the conditions required of Moses Maverick to "sell drink without doors" and as an innkeeper:

"He shall not suffer any unlawful play or games, in said house, garden, orchard or elsewhere, especially by men servants or apprentices, common labourers, idle persons, or shall suffer any Town Inhabitants to be in said house drinking or tippling on ye saturday night after ye sunset or on ye sabbath day, nor wittingly or willingly admit or receive any person notoriously defamed of for theft, incontinency or drunkenness, nor keep or lodge there any stranger person above ye space of one day and one night together, without notice thereof, first given to such Justice or Selectman as above said."

When they got back to the house William saw Martha had arrived and was helping Margaret. He thought she looked very pretty and was unaccustomed to be in close contact with such a young girl.

That afternoon William was shown the small flock of sheep John had been looking after the day before. They were grazing on the common land just outside the village.

'I haven't seen the horse yet,' William remarked to John.

'Samuel is ploughing, come with me I'll show you.'

They walked through a small copse of trees and on the other side found Samuel ploughing with the horse. He stopped at the end of the furrow and William looked at the horse with interest. It was a small horse and he thought was about six years old.

'What's the horse's name?' he asked.

'Agawam, after the name the Indians called Ipswich,' Samuel told him.

'Yes, your father told me that last night. Well, Agawam, I look forward to riding and looking after you.' He stroked the horse's head and patted his neck.

'You like horses then?'

'Oh, yes. I had my own mare in Ireland and spent most of my time in Barbados looking after horses.'

'Agawam is a good worker. Now I must get on,' Samuel said, 'I want to finish this patch today.'

William soon settled down to his new surroundings. He chopped the firewood, fetched water from the stream, fed the chickens and the pigs, groomed and fed the horse and watched Margaret Bishop making candles. He had little contact with Martha.

On the first Sunday, William left the house early and went down to the jetty to do some fishing. It was peaceful here, out of sight of the village. He could see the Redemtioneer still riding at anchor, the sand pipers pecking in the mud along the foreshore, and sea gulls flying around. He thought how lucky he was to have been accepted by such a contented family and friendly people in the village. He was sure he was going to be happy here.

When he came back to the house at midday, Thomas Bishop looked very annoyed.

'William Durgy! ' he shouted, 'where have you been?'

'Fishing, sir. Look I have three large ones here.'

'Fishing! On the Sabbath! Man, you should have been at the prayer meeting. Don't you understand, everybody must attend the prayer meeting on the Sabbath? No one fishes on the Sabbath! That is sacrilege! This will be raised at the next council meeting, what am I going to say?'

'You will have to say I am a stranger and did not know.'

'I doubt they will understand that. I'm sure I don't know what they'll say. The punishment for missing prayer meeting is several lashes of the whip. I don't know!' he shook his head in despair.

William was confused. He had never heard of prayer meetings being compulsory, not in Ireland nor in Barbados. In fact, for the last five years he had virtually held his own prayer meeting with his Bible and rosary.

'I'm sorry, sir. I did not know. I've never had to attend before.'

A special council meeting was called the next day. Theodor Wilson, the constable, put the case before the council.

'Mister Chairman, members of the council, I have to report that on Sunday a newcomer to the settlement, one William Durgy, a servant of goodman Bishop, failed to attend the prayer meeting.'

'This is a serious matter,' Robert Lord, marshall and chairman of the meeting said. 'Goodman Bishop, he is your servant, what have you to say on this matter?'

'Sir, I regret to say that William Durgy was unaware of our custom and did not know he should attend the prayer meeting. He has only this past week come with me from Barbados where he says prayer meetings were not attended by everyone.'

'How extraordinary!' Robert Lord exclaimed. 'Do you believe that?'

'I have no reason not to believe it. He was not in the house when we left and we did not know where he was. I can assure you, it will not happen again. I have advised him of his duty and in future he will attend.'

The members of the council discussed the matter and finally decided William Durgy should be given five lashes of the whip or pay a fine of three pounds.

'As he is my servant, I will pay the fine,' Bishop replied.

'William,' he said on returning home, 'The council decided to award you five lashes of the whip for failing to attend the prayer meeting. What do you say to that?'

'Oh, William,' exclaimed Margaret Bishop, 'you were let off lightly!'

William was not sure he agreed.

'I am sorry to have caused so much trouble,' he said. 'When do I receive the punishment?'

'Don't ye worry, William. The alternative was a fine of three pounds, which I paid. I will have to take it off your wages for the next, let me see, it'll be about a year!'

William was very relieved not to be flogged, but still thought the fine to be harsh although he had the common-sense not to say so.

'Thank you, sir. I will go in future,' he said meekly.

The next Sunday he attended the prayer meeting with the rest of the family. All the males sat on one side of the hall and the females on the other side. Every eye of the congregation was on him for the whole meeting. The sermon lasted three hours and if the stool had not been so uncomfortable and if it had not been so cold that his hands and feet felt as if they were dead, he would have fallen asleep. He had no idea what the sermon was about, he lost the drift of it after the first hour.

CHAPTER 15
MARTHA

William liked to go fishing whenever he had the chance. He used to sit on the end of the wooden jetty and look across the river, it was quiet and peaceful here. There were the sea gulls and curlews to watch and the sand pipers pecking along the river edge. The *Redemtioneer* had sailed back to Boston for a cargo of skins and timber to take to St. Kitts and Barbados, bringing back the usual sugar, tobacco, cotton and rum. Thomas Bishop did not go with the ship every voyage, only when he wanted to see his brother, or to arrange a special business deal.

William spent his time thinking of the future. He realised he had started on the wrong foot by not going to the prayer meeting. The villagers were friendly when he arrived and now he sensed they shook their heads at him.

'That's the man who didn't attend prayer meeting,' they whispered. Or was he imagining it? Anyway, he knew he would have to tread carefully in future. They did not know he was a Catholic yet. Thomas knew, but had apparently kept it to himself. What would the villagers do if they found out?

He knew he had to serve Thomas Bishop for five years, after that he would be on his own. He thought he would concentrate on horses, after all he knew about horses and they were of vital importance in this country. At present the roads between the settlements were mere tracks through the heathland and forest and there were rivers to cross. It was easier to reach Boston by sea, but the country was growing. soon bridges would be built across the rivers and the tracks would become dirt roads. The demand for horses would grow.

His thoughts were interrupted by the sound of foot steps along the jetty. He looked back and saw Martha approaching him.

'Good day to you, William' she said. 'Are you fishing?'

'Aye, that's right. Good day to you.'

'You didn't attend prayer meeting. You were fined three pounds!'

'That's right,' he replied. 'Quiet now, I've caught a fish!'

He played the fish and landed it on the jetty.

'Oh, that's a big one! Do you do a lot of fishing?'

'Whenever I can after I've done my work.'

'You came from Barbados?' she asked.

'Yes, that's right, but before that my home was in Ireland.'

'Where's that?' she asked thoughtfully.

'The other side of the ocean, next to England. Didn't they teach you that at school?' He looked up at her and could not help thinking how pretty she was.

'I never learned that at school!' she exclaimed. 'I learned my numbers and how to read the Bible and that's all. I can cook, weave and make candles.'

'I suppose that is all you need here?'

'I can knit and make clothes too.'

'How long have you been here?'

'I was born here.' William cast his line out again. He wanted to ask when that was, but thought it better not to.

'How long were you in Barbados?' Martha asked.

'About fifteen years. I went with Cromwell's army to Hispaniola and Jamaica.'

'Ooh!' Her eyes widened with excitement, 'You have had some adventures! You'll find it quiet here.'

'It's nice to live a quiet life for a change. It's beginning to get dark now, I'd better get back to my meal.'

'I'll carry your fish for you. You'll let me come again and help you fish?' She asked. 'You can tell me all about your adventures.' She stared at him and he gazed into her deep blue eyes. Yes, he had to admit she was beautiful and she reminded him of Olivia. He hoped she was not going to tease him like Olivia did.

'If you like,' he said, rolling up his line, 'I don't mind.'

'Will you be fishing tomorrow?'
'Perhaps, if the weather is good and I've finished work.'
'Then I'll come tomorrow.' They walked back together.
The next evening he was fishing again and Martha joined him.
'Why didn't you go to the prayer meeting on the first Sunday, William?' she asked.
'I didn't know it was compulsory.'
'Was it not in Barbados?'
'Well, yes, we did have Mass every Sunday.'
'Mass? What's that?'
'That's what we call it.'
'Who calls it mass?' she asked mystified.
'Catholics. I am a Catholic.' Suddenly he realised he had let slip a very dangerous piece of information. Really, he must be more careful!
'Ooh,' she gasped with alarm, 'I've heard of them! I don't think they like Catholics here. Five years ago they hung a woman from a tree on Boston Common for being a Quaker. Mary Dyer was her name, I remember the talk about it. She came from England. You'd better not tell anyone else you're a Catholic.'
'No,' he replied, regretting he had said the word "Mass". 'We'd better keep that to ourselves. Goodman Bishop knows.'
'Don't worry, William. I'll keep your secret. You can trust me.' He hoped he could.
'It's getting dark, Martha. We'd better go home now.'
'Oh, let's stay a bit longer. Tell me about your travels to, where was it, Jamaica?'
'It's a long story. I went with Cromwell's fleet, there were over sixty ships and thousands of soldiers. I did not do much fighting, though. I was glad to be sent back to Barbados. It was then I met Goodman Job Bishop. Martha, I do think we ought to go now.'
'We must meet here again and you can tell me more.'
'Yes, Martha, perhaps we can.' He was not too enthusiastic.
They walked back together, Martha carrying the fish. They met her sister, Elizabeth Nelson, and brother-in-law, William. Elizabeth, Martha's eldest sister, was twenty-eight. She was short and dressed in a plain brown frock with white apron and white bonnet.

'Elizabeth,' Martha said, 'meet William Durgy. He is working with me for Mistress Bishop. He has travelled to many places and is full of stories. William, this is my sister Elizabeth Nelson.'

'How do you do, Mistress Nelson,' William held his hand out.

'Good day to you, William,' she smiled and they shook hands. 'This is William, my husband.'

'Good day,' said Nelson, not looking at all pleased. 'You'll be the Bishop's servant, then.'

'Yes, that's right. Pleased to meet you.' He held out his hand to Nelson but it was ignored.

'We've been fishing and look what William's caught.' Martha held out the catch.

'Should you be out alone like this?' Nelson queried.

'Oh, mother doesn't mind.' Martha assured him.

'You had better be on your way home now. Good day to you Durgy.' Nelson took Elizabeth's arm and walked on.

When he returned home William did not mention these meetings with Martha after work. He did not consider it important, after all he was now over thirty years old and he thought Martha appeared to be only about twenty. It did not occur to him to wonder why Martha should be alone after work in the evening. The younger children, both boys and girls, played around by themselves, but not the older girls. Obviously Nelson disapproved of her action, the older girls were always escorted by their mother or father. Why was Martha roaming around on her own? She was attractive enough but a bit naive for his liking; on the other hand, she was probably the only eligible girl in the village. All the others he had seen were much younger or married!

'William,' Thomas Bishop said, while they were eating supper, 'we've been discussing the possibility of building an extension to the back of the house. We could build a store there and empty the attic. This would give more room upstairs for you and the two boys. It will mean felling some timber, have you done any tree felling?'

'Yes, sir. That was my first job when we arrived at Barbados. Also I did some timber splitting from a saw pit with a two handled saw.'

'Excellent, then you can help me and the boys. There will not be much work on the land in the winter. We might even finish most of it before the snow comes.'

The next day they went to the nearby forest with the pony Agawam to select suitable timber for the building. They could choose from pine, white oak, spruce or hickory.

'We'll take the oak for the uprights and pine for the cross beams. That hickory is used for furniture and axe handles,' Bishop explained.

'We used hickory for making chairs in Barbados. I learnt some carpentering and can make a chair.'

'We'll see what sort of job you make of one later. Which tree do you think we should start with?'

'We'd better start with the hard one – the oak.'

They felled and trimmed two oaks on the first day. The trees were hitched behind the pony and dragged back to the homestead. They managed to get the timber they wanted moved to the house before the first snow fell. William was busy for several days and did not have time for fishing.

Two days after Nelson met William and Martha he told Robert Cross he had seen Martha alone with William. Robert was furious and decided to speak to Martha. He was a tall man with a severe countenance, had been in Ipswich since 1634 and considered himself as the senior resident. He had a large plot of land as well as twelve children, a strict Protestant, stern and domineering with his family.

'I hear Martha has been seen out alone with that man William Durgy,' he complained to his wife, Hannah.

'You mean the Bishop's servant, father? Well, they work together in the same house. I see no harm in it. Where did you hear this?'

'Goodman Nelson told me. Says he met them the other evening walking alone.'

'I don't think there is any harm in it, Father.' Hannah Cross replied. A short, slim, grey haired, forty-six years old woman, Hannah had been married for twenty-eight years, given birth to all of Robert's twelve children and was completely dominated by him.

'She should not be out alone, woman. And with that man Durgy. He's an ex-slave, isn't he? Surely I'd be happier if she chose one of Goodman Bishop's sons and not his servant. I forbid her to see him after work and I'd be obliged if you'd see she doesn't roam about alone.'

'I've so much to do in the house, Father, I cannot see what all the children are doing all the time. I cannot keep all nine inside the house all day, they play about outside on their own.'

'You've got Anna to help you. I'll talk to Martha and tell her to stay at home after work.'

He called Martha in from the garden.

'Martha, I hear you were seen walking alone with William Durgy.'

'Yes, father,' she replied, 'he is a very interesting man. He has travelled a lot and had an exciting life.'

'I'd rather you spoke with the Bishop's sons than his servant. He's an ex-slave and no good for you.'

'But Samuel and John are so boring, father. All they talk about is the farm and the sheep. I am with William all day and he has a lot to talk about.'

'I forbid you to see him after work. Do you understand that? If I hear you disobey me I shall have to punish you. Understand?'

'Yes, father.' She consented unwillingly.

'I'd have thought you had enough to do helping your mother look after the younger ones.'

'Yes, father.' She replied reluctantly. She was fascinated by William and determined to see him as much as she could when she could talk to him away from the Bishop's house.

One day Mistress Bishop asked Martha to bring some logs in as she thought William was not about. She went outside and started to lift a log. William was in the garden and came over to her.

'What are you doing, lifting logs?'

'Mistress Bishop asked me to, William.'

'Leave it to me. I'll do it.' He bent down next to Martha to to take the log from her. It was the closest contact he had had with her and he looked closely into her lovely blue eyes. She gazed back at him and he realised he was falling in love with her and the way she looked at him, perhaps she felt the same.

'Give me the log,' he said,'I'll gladly do it for you.'

'Thank you, William,' she said smiling.

Normally, he had little chance to speak to Martha during the day. She worked in the house and he worked outside.

She had to wait until late January before William had time to go fishing down by the river.

'William.' she said, 'you've been busy for weeks. I've waited for a long time for ye to come down here. Are you clamming?'

'Yes Martha. Yes I'm digging clams. No, I haven't been down here for several weeks while I've been busy felling trees for the building.'

'I know. Can I help you and we can talk?'

'If you like.'

'William, what is the difference between a Catholic and a Protestant? I've been thinking about it and I can't ask any one else.'

'I'm not sure that I know, Martha, except that Catholics consider their's is the true religion and all the others are those that broke away. I think it was King Henry the eighth who broke away from Rome.'

'Why did he do that?'

'Well, he wanted to divorce his queen and the Pope wouldn't let him. Altogether he had six wives – not all at once, but one after the other.'

'My, he must've been a bad man!'

'I don't think he was bad. He just liked the women he met. You don't know any history then?'

'No, William, I didn't learn history at school. But I am now learning to weave wool. That'll be more useful, don't you think?'

'Yes, I suppose so. Knowing history is not going to clothe you, is it?'

'My brother, Robert, is getting married next month.'

'Oh, yes. How many brothers and sisters have you got?'

'Eleven. Elizabeth, my eldest, you have met. She's mistress Nelson. Then there's Anna, and Mary, she's married to Ephraim and is mistress Herrick. Then Robert, John...'

'Hey. Stop,' William interrupted her, 'I'm lost with so many names.'

'Did you have lots of brothers and sisters, William?'

'I had a sister and two brothers but they were all killed by Cromwell's men in Ireland.'

'Oh, William, that was sad. I am sorry.'

'It all happened a long time ago. I want to forget it.'

They were bending down to put the clams in the bucket and once again he was in close contact with her. They looked hard at each other.

'William, I do like you,' Martha said, 'do you like me?'

William thought she was young, but attractive; those deep blue eyes were looking up innocently at him and she was smiling so sweetly. He was sorely tempted to kiss her.

'Yes, Martha, I like you.' He bent towards her and kissed her lightly on the cheek.

'Oh, William!' she protested. 'You shouldn't do that!'

They stared at each other, then she turned away from him and ran along the path, reaching the village well ahead of him.

He stood and watched her running. What have I done? He thought. Is she going to tell everyone I tried to force myself upon her? He realised the people in the village were very prim and they would not approve of him kissing a young girl like that. He could imagine the Church elders discussing it with relish and deciding to award him another five, or even ten, lashes of the whip! And the Bishops would not approve their servants behaving in this way. But it had been nice; he wouldn't mind another if she was really willing.

The wedding of Robert Cross to Martha Treadwell on the 19th February 1664 was a big event in the village. Everyone attended in the Cross's house including the Bishop family, but William was not invited. He spent his time in the garden. He had seen Martha Treadwell before at the prayer meetings. She was younger than Martha Cross and he did not think she looked nearly as attractive.

The snow was not too bad that winter. William was pleased as he had not been in such cold weather since he left Ireland. By the end of February they had built the store at the back of the house, cleared the attic of all the stores and made it into a bedroom.

During March he spent most of his time digging the plot of garden ready for the vegetable seeds; it made him think of poor old Josh. As the daylight began to get longer he had time to do some fishing, or digging for clams.

Occasionally Martha came to join him and he resisted the temptation to kiss her again. The opportunity did not arise until several days later when he was grooming Agawam in the stable. Martha came in.

'Mistress Bishop has gone out and I have nothing to do in the house, so I thought I'd come and talk to you. You don't mind, do you William?'

'No, I don't mind, Martha.' He smiled at her.

'You like horses, William, don't you?'
'Yes. I had my own horse at home in Ireland.'
'Do you miss your home in Ireland?'
'Well, yes, of course. But my family are now all dead and my home was burned down by Cromwell's men. So I have nothing left in Ireland.'
'Oh, William. I am sad for you. Did you have a girl in Ireland?'
'Yes,' he admitted, 'I had a girl in Drogheda. But I saw the Commonwealth soldiers shoot her in the battle.'
'Oh, William, that was must have been terrible, I am sorry. Did you love her?'
'Very much.'

During March Martha took every opportunity she could to talk to William. He told her all about his home in Ireland, about the battle of Drogheda, his voyage to Barbados and his life there. She was growing fonder of him every day and he was growing fonder of her. The temptation to kiss her was strong. Whenever they met during the day, which was not as often as William would have liked, they smiled at each other secretly.

One day Martha came to the stable to see William. He looked at her and said, 'Martha, I'm falling in love with you.'

'Oh, William, I am in love with you too. I would not have any other man.' He took her in his arms and gave her a passionate kiss on the lips. She did not resist him.

He led her to the pile of hay in the corner of the barn and pulled her down to lie beside him. They hugged and fondled each other. William was getting very sexually excited.

'William,' Martha said at last. 'This is very nice, but I must go.'

'Let me kiss you once more,' he said. She did not refuse, but then pulled herself away from him and ran out of the barn.

He thought,'That was very nice. I wouldn't mind doing it again if she is willing.'

One day in April they were alone in the stable again.

'Come on Martha, let's lie down.' She obediently lay down and he lay over her and kissed her. She was beginning to enjoy this!

'Martha, I wish I could make love with you.'

'William, I know nothing about making love but Martha tells me it's lovely. What do we do?'

'Martha, do you really want me to make love.'

'Oh, yes, William, please. I love you and you say you love me. Will you not trust me?'

This was too much for William to resist. He had been without love for too long, but he did not have to wait much longer. They lay down full length on the hay.

'All right then, if you're sure, Martha.'

'Oh, yes William. I'm sure. But how?'

He was quick to show her and she was very eager to learn the art of making love. He was a good teacher. Agawam whinnied to her cry as William entered her.

Afterwards she said, 'Oh, William, that was lovely.' He kissed her again and she responded eagerly. He lay back and wondered. What have I done? Kissing this young girl was one thing, but going this far! What would the village say? Could he marry her? No, not yet. He was in no position to support a wife. Really, he must control himself and not do it again.

'William, you do love me, don't you?' she asked.

'Yes, Martha, I do love you.'

'Will you marry me, William?'

'Well, yes. But not now, we must wait until I can care for you. I have to serve Goodman Bishop for five years.'

'I can't wait that long, William.'

'We'll see, Martha.' He was bound not to commit himself too early.

It was one day early in May when Martha failed to attend the breakfast table.

'Where's Martha? Has she gone to work?' Robert Cross asked.

'She's poorly, not well this day.' Hannah Cross replied.

'What ails her, woman?'

'I don't know. She's been sick, I don't think its much.'

'Sick? What's she eaten ?'

'I don't know. Don't worry about it, I'm sure its nothing. I'll go and tell Mistress Bishop.'

The next morning the same thing happened again.

'But she was all right yesterday, after the morning.' Robert declared.

'She can't be sick every morning without some reason can she? What can it be?'

'I'm sure, I don't know! What are you thinking?'

'Woman, I'm thinking she's with child!'

'How could she be? What a suggestion!' Hannah was horrified at the thought and prayed it was not true. The shame of it would be unbearable.

'Find out! Ask her.' Robert demanded.

She was afraid of asking, for fear of what the reply might be. Robert Cross left to work in his field and Hannah went to see Martha, still lying in bed.

'How are you, Martha?' she asked.

'I still feel very sick.'

'What do you think it is? What have you eaten?'

'Nothing, mother.'

'Your father thinks – we are wondering – it can't be, can it? Surely not! Daughter – you are not with child are you?'

'Could I be, mother?'

'You tell me! Have you bled this month?'

'No, mother.'

'The Lord help me, it must be! I think you are. Who have you been with?'

'William – William Durgy, mother.'

'William Durgy! Did he force himself on you?'

'No, mother! I love him and he said he loved me. I want to marry him.'

'The Lord help me! What is your father going to say! What will Mistress Bishop say! Child, how could you do it? The shame of it! I can't believe it!' She burst into tears and Martha starting crying too.

'Mother, help me. I'm frightened,' she cried.

'So am I! There's only one answer – you'll have to marry him, but what your father is going to say I do not know.'

When Robert returned to the house at midday he found Hannah sitting by the fire still weeping.

'What's the matter, woman?'

'Father, she's – she's with child!'

'She's what? I knew it! I knew it, woman. I told you. Who's the man?'

'William – William Durgy!'

'William Durgy! That Catholic, slave, scum!' Robert's face went red with fury.

'Catholic?' Hannah asked, horrified. This was even worse than she thought.

'Yes, Catholic. Thomas Bishop told me in confidence. I'll kill him! Yes, I will, I'll kill him with my own hands!' He clenched his fists and shook with rage.

'Father, you can't! You couldn't kill him. Leave our daughter with no husband!' Hannah beseeched him.

'Daughter – daughter? She's no daughter of mine any longer. Whore, fornicator! I'll whip her!'

'Robert, no! You can't say that of our daughter!'

'I suppose he took her by force!'

'No, father. She says she loves him and he said he loved her. She wants to marry him. 'Tis best to let them marry.'

'Love? She doesn't know the meaning of the word! Stupid girl. My God, I'll have to report this to the council. Yes, that's what I'll do. Report it to the council and sue him. They'll have him hanged, for a Papist if nothing else!'

'No, Robert. I beseech you. Let her marry him! It's our own grandchild we have to think of!'

'Marry? Marry that scum! Never! Never, woman, I tell you, never! It will be no grand child of ours!' He strode out of the house to see Theophilus Wilson, the constable.

Martha came creeping into the room, still weeping.

'Your father is furious!' Hannah said.

'I know, mother. I heard every word! Oh, mother, I'm frightened. What shall I do? I'm too frightened to see father.'

'I don't know what you can do, daughter. I just don't know!' Hannah hid her face in her hands.

'I know. mother. I'll go and see Elizabeth. I'll go now before father comes back.'

Martha ran out of the house and went to see her sister, in the house next door.

Elizabeth was busy making candles when Martha rushed into the house, sobbing bitterly.

'Sister, what ever is the matter?'

'Oh, Elizabeth, help me. I am with child and my father is going to whip me! Help me!'

'How did this happen? Are you sure?'

'Yes, I've been sick these many mornings and Mother says I must be.'

'Who is the father then?'

'William Durgy. I love William and he says he loves me. We only made love once. Why can't we get married? Father is going to sue him and the council will have him hanged because he's a Catholic!'

'Catholic? My God, did you know this?'

'Yes, of course. What difference does it make? Elizabeth, I want to die this very day!' She sat on the stool and tears flooded down her cheeks.

'Come, come, Martha, calm down. Surely it is not as bad as that. There must be something we can do?'

'You'll never get father to change his mind. He has disowned me. Called me a whore and a fornicator! Oh, what do I do?'

'You can stay here with us until this matter is settled. Remain here now and I'll go and see mistress Storie.' She put on her shawl and walked next door to the Storie's house.

'Sarah, Good day to you,' she said. 'Our sister, Martha, is at my house sorely distressed. She says she's with child and that William Durgy is the father. Father is furious and is going to sue William. What can we do?'

'Is she certain?'

'Oh, yes. Can you come with me to Mistress Bishop and we will see William?'

'Yes, I'll come with you. Perhaps he will deny it.'

She put on her shawl and the two women crossed the stream to the Bishop's house.

'Good day to you, Mistress Bishop,' Elizabeth said as she and Sarah entered the house. 'Martha is at my house in much trouble. She says she's with child and William Durgy is the father.'

'William! And Martha!' Margaret Bishop exclaimed. 'I can't believe it. They are here together every day, of course, but I've never seen any affection between them. I know Martha has not been well these last few days. Do you wish to see William?'

'Yes please Mistress Bishop.'

'He's working in the garden. I'll call him.'

William took off his muddy shoes at the back door and walked into the hall in his bare feet. Elizabeth Nelson and Sarah Storie were standing at the head of the table. They stared hard at him, but said nothing. He looked at Margaret, but she gave no indication what she wanted him for. In the silence, he could hear the clock ticking. He was puzzled.

'Good day, Mistress Nelson, Mistress Storie' he said. 'Is anything the matter?'

'There certainly is! Martha is at my house crying her eyes out in a terrible state.' Elizabeth explained. 'She says she is with child and you are the father. Can this be so?'

William was horrified. Martha had not been to work for two days and he had wondered what was the matter with her. Should he admit it, or deny it? How could he deny it? He had made love to her once and he was sure she had been with no other man. He would have to admit it.

'She never told me. Yes, I suppose it could be my child.'

'You suppose it could be? Do you say you laid with her? I)o you think she had another man?' He was bombarded with questions.

'My God, William!' Margaret Bishop exclaimed. 'How could you? Don't you know what they'll do to you?'

'No, I don't.' What could they do to him? What would happen now? He hated to imagine.

'Goodman Cross is furious. He has threatened to whip Martha and has disowned her. He is going to sue you,' Elizabeth explained. 'The case will come to the court and you will be tried. Do you know what they do to fornicators?'

'No.' He dreaded to think what they could do.

'They hang them!'

Chapter 16
MONTHS OF SCORN

William sat bowed in the chair by the fireside, his head in his hands. The women had gone to see Martha, he was left alone with his thoughts. What would happen now? He had been so happy to be with this family and he thought he had a great future before him. Had he ruined it all? By failing to control his desires, had he lost any chance of a future here? Would they really hang him?

He remembered Martha telling him about the Quaker, Mary Dyer; they'd hung her on Boston common just for being a Quaker! What would they do with a Catholic, and one who had committed fornication? Death on both counts!

'Dear God, forgive me! Help me!' he prayed.

Did he really want to marry Martha? How could he with no money and no house? How could he get out of it? Would her father ever agree? He thought it most unlikely; and if he would not agree to the marriage, what would happen then? He was completely confused.

The door burst open and William Nelson strode into the room.

'William Durgy!' he shouted, his face red with anger. 'What have you done to my sister-in-law? Stand up man and answer me!'

William stood and faced Nelson.

'I'm sorry – I said the child – could be mine,' he said weakly. On the spur of the moment he could not think of anything else to say.

'Sorry, man! Are you saying she's a whore? How dare you!'

'No!' William exclaimed.

Nelson swung his right hand out and hit William's cheek with his clenched fist. William felt a tooth come loose in his mouth. He sat down again and nursed his face.

'No, I'm not saying she's a whore. I have eighteen meals a week. For the sake of the child I'll give six meals.' He was in no position to fight back. Indeed, he did not want to fight, he merely wanted this dilemma to somehow disappear.

'Is that all you can say? What about the girl?'

'I cannot marry her. I cannot keep her!'

'You should have thought of that before you laid her! By God is my witness I'll see you hang for this!'

'Would that help Martha or the child?'

'You're just scum. A slave you were, a slave you still are. Call yourself a man? You're just a fornicating bastard! You're not fit to marry Martha. I'll see you hanged first! Think on it, man. Think hard. Take a rope out and hang yourself and save us the trouble! I'll have nothing more to do with you, you scum!'

With that as his parting word he left the room and slammed the door shut behind him.

William spat his broken tooth out and threw it on the fire. He buried his face in his hands and wept.

Half an hour later he realised the Bishops would soon return. He could not face them. He rose and went to the stable at the back of the house. He saddled up Agawam and rode off behind the homestead, through the trees surrounding the village, across the open heath and up the hill overlooking the inlet. He halted the horse, sat in the saddle and looked at the view. It was a bright, sunny day and the country looked green and fresh. The water in the bay was deep blue and calm. It was a good country to be in.

He thought of his home in Ireland. His mother, his father and his brothers and sister. Once again he heard the guns pounding the walls of Drogheda, the shouts of the Roundheads and the screams of the wounded. He could smell the dust of the ruins and the powder of the weapons. He stood again along the wall of the city and looked out over the buildings as they counted, one, two, three, 'Dear God. Not me please,' and heard the skull of the man standing next to him split open. I was saved then, shall I be saved now?

He relived the dreadful voyage from Drogheda to Bridgetown,

shackled in chains. 'Now thank we all our God...' he remembered the hymn Father O'Neill sang when they arrived in Barbados. The years of slavery; some not so bad, some very bad. He felt the lash of MacGregor's whip, the scar from which still showed. He recalled the death of Peter Cusack tied to the post all night after that savage beating. He thought of poor old Josh and wished he could see his grave. He saw that man in the cage, strung up high, at the point of death, being pelted with tomatoes and eggs. He faced death again in Hispaniola and Jamaica.

'Have faith, my son.' Father O'Neill had told him. Faith or hope? He was not sure. But what he was sure of was that he had been saved from death all these years for some purpose. What purpose was it? Was he meant to make love to Martha – or had he merely fallen to temptation? He could grow to love her, he knew she loved him. She was young, but a nice enough girl. Surely, he must marry her, somehow, and create a family here. Here in this beautiful country. But he could not do that, they were going to hang him.

'Dear God,' he prayed, 'save me! Be with me in my hour of need.' He took his rosary from his pocket and prayed.

He had sat there all day. The light was failing and the sun was sinking behind him casting a long shadow before him. He reigned the horse and slowly rode back home. He stabled Agawam and gave him a feed of oats. He crept into the house and up the stairs to his dark attic. He heard the family below talking; probably discussing him, but he could not face them now. He undressed and lay on his bed of straw and prayed again, using his rosary. 'Holy Mary, Holy Mother..' He fell into a fitful sleep. He dreamed of a rope round his neck and woke in a sweat. The house was quiet, apart from Samuel snoring at the other end of the attic.

The next morning he woke when he heard movement downstairs. He rose, dressed and went to wash out of the bucket behind the house as he did every day. He let the chickens out and fed them, he fed the horse and the pigs. He picked up two leather buckets, filled them from the stream and carried them to Margaret Bishop as usual. The family were just starting breakfast and he joined them to say grace. They ate in silence.

After breakfast the boys left to work and Thomas Bishop looked straight at William.

'William,' he said, 'you disappoint me. We take you into our house and treat you as one of the family. Then you let us down like this. Whatever were you thinking of to go with an innocent girl like Martha? I find it hard to believe. Where did it happen? Not in this house?'

'No sir. She used to follow me down to the jetty when I went fishing. I'm sorry, sir. I've had years being alone with no one to love and the temptation was too great. I'm sorry sir.' He did not like to admit the assignations in the stable.

'Sorry isn't going to help you. The council will discuss this. Goodman Cross is suing you. I don't know what they'll do.'

'They say they will hang me.'

'I don't think they hang fornicators now, nor Catholics. But I don't know what they will do to a Catholic fornicator. That is too much! One thing for certain, there will be a court case.'

'Yes, sir. I suppose they will want me to attend the court?'

'I would think most certainly they will. The constable will be round very soon. You'd better prepare yourself for the first trial. Robert Cross is a hard man to deal with. Always taking matters to court. He sued Cornelius Waldo for debt, he is always having court cases over the hay in his meadow. A hard man to deal with. If he has said he will not allow you to marry Martha, nothing will change his mind.'

'I see,' William said lamely. 'I'll be working in the garden while I wait for the constable to come. I will not be far off, sir.' Bishop nodded agreement and let William go.

'I feel sorry for him, woman,' he said to Margaret.

'He's a good man, father. I cannot believe what he has done. Martha is a wayward girl, always has been. Gets her own way and disobeys her father. I think she must have been a great temptation for William. As he said, he has been many years living a hard life and he must have been sorely tempted if she did not refuse him.'

'I think you're right. I feel we should do what we can to help him, but how I cannot see now. If only we could persuade Goodman Cross to agree to them marrying, that would solve the whole matter.'

'I hear Mistress Cross wants that. Could you see Goodman Cross, father, and talk to him.'

'Not today. He's a difficult man and he is very angry over this matter. I'll talk to him later, perhaps he will calm down.'

Theophilus Wilson, the constable, arrived later in the morning.

'Good day to you, Goodman Bishop.'

'Good day to you, Constable Wilson. You want to see William Durgy.'

'Yes, please. I have to serve him with this writ to attend the court.'

Bishop called William and he took his muddy shoes off at the door came in bare foot looking very nervous.

'Are you William Durgy?' the constable asked, unnecessarily.

'Yes sir.'

'I have to serve you with this writ to attend Hampton Court on the Tuesday of next week. You need say nothing to me now, but I want your assurance you will attend.'

'Yes sir. I will attend the court next Tuesday.'

Theophilus handed over the document and departed. William stood looking at the writ.

'At least we have a few days to think the matter over,' Bishop said. 'What does the writ say?'

'Sir, it says Goodman Cross is suing me for alienating his daughter's affections.'

'I see. How will you plead?'

'I think I'll plead not guilty, sir.'

The next Sunday all the family attended the prayer meeting as usual. Robert Lord read the first lesson from Ephesians 5.

'Be ye therefore followers of God, as dear children; and walk in love as Christ also hath loved us and hath given himself for us an offering and a sacrifice to God for a sweet smelling favour. But fornication,' Robert raised his voice in emphasis,' fornication and all uncleanness or covetousness let it once not be named among you as becometh saints. Neither filthiness nor foolish talking nor jesting which are not convenient but rather giving of thanks. For this ye know that no whoremonger nor unclean person, nor covetous man, who is an idolater hath any inheritance in the kingdom of Christ and God.'

The second lesson was from Proverbs 7. and when this was finished William thought the whole village must know for whom this was intended. He looked across at Martha with Elizabeth and saw she sat with her head bowed in shame.

The sermon which followed, lasting at least two hours, was on the same subject. William felt that he and Martha were being tried, accused and sentenced here at the prayer meeting before the court was held. What chance of a fair trial did they have?

The Hampton Court was held on the Tuesday. William attended with Thomas Bishop and pleaded not guilty. Evidence was heard from Robert Cross, Elizabeth Nelson and Sarah Storie.

After hearing all the evidence the Court ordered William to be whipped not exceeding twenty stripes and put in security of twenty pounds, for the care of the child. William was very relieved to hear that at least they did not think of hanging him.

Thomas Bishop leaned over and whispered to William, 'Plead for an appeal.'

William stood and said, 'Sir, I ask for an appeal.'

'Granted. The case will then be heard at the Court to be held in September.'

'That gives us some time to persuade Goodman Cross to change his plea and give permission for you to marry,' Thomas said on the way home.

William was not at all sure that Robert Cross would ever agree, but at least he had until September to try to do something to make him.

During the next week he had to go to the village to buy some chocolate for Margaret Bishop. He went up the back way instead of Mill Street to avoid meeting people. The children were coming out of school and there was little room to pass them on the narrow track by the stream.

'Fornicator!' one of the boys yelled, 'they be goin' to hang ye!'

'Fornicator!' they all cried out and one boy picked up a handful of mud and threw it at him. He held his hand up to shield his face. He could not retaliate, it would not help his cause if he threw clods of earth back at them. Several other boys, and one or two girls, picked up stones and started pelting him. He pushed his way past as fast as possible and walked quickly out of range. After he had bought the chocolate he waited to see the path was clear before he returned home.

Am I not going to be able to walk safely up the village? he thought.

How am I going to live in this place like this? Martha stays indoors at the Nelsons every day, except Sunday. She never ventures outside.

So William was very surprised one night, about two weeks later, when there was a knock on the door. The family had just finished their evening meal and were about to read from the Bible. 'Whoever could that be at this time of night?' Margaret queried. She opened the door and saw Martha and Elizabeth standing there with their shawls on. 'Mistress Nelson and Martha! What a surprise, do come in.'

'Good evening to you, Mistress Bishop, I am sorry to disturb you at this time of night, but Martha would like to talk to William, if that is possible. Father has forbidden Martha to see or talk to William, so we had to come when it was dark.'

'Of course. Come in, can I take your shawl?'

'Good evening, Goodman Bishop.' Elizabeth said as she entered, 'Good evening Samuel, John and William.'

The boys acknowledged the greeting. William looked embarrassed and muttered his own greeting as he stood up.

'Do sit down, Mistress Nelson and Martha,' Margaret said, 'We do not have seats for everyone, but the boys will not mind standing.' They all sat down round the table with the open Bible waiting for the reading. The two boys stood by the fireside.

'We are very worried about this affair, Goodman Bishop,' Elizabeth said, 'Martha is fretful and cannot sleep at night. Has anyone approached her father to ask him to let them marry?'

'I saw Goodman Cross last week,' Bishop replied, 'but he refused to talk to me about it. Said he did not own Martha as his daughter and it was nothing to do with him.'

'William,' cried Martha wiping the tears from her eyes with the corner of her apron, 'why don't you show you love me as I love you? Why don't you see father and ask for my hand?'

'I don't think he'd talk to me. I passed him the other day and said "Good morning, Goodman Cross" and he looked the other way and walked on. Martha, I don't know what to do.'

'Why did you tell Goodman Nelson you were sorry you said the child was yours? Whose else could it be? You know you are the only man I'd marry, I won't have anyone else.'

'I'm sorry I said that, Martha. I was distraught and didn't know what to say. I said "I'm sorry. The child is mine."'

'William, you will marry me, won't you?'

'Of course, Martha. But how are we going to get married without your father's consent?'

'I don't know. What shall we do?'

'I think we shall have to leave the matter for a while,' Bishop said, 'We have two months before the trial. We can only hope that in that time your father will relent and agree. If we press him too hard now we may only make matters worse. In time he may calm down. I know your mother is trying her best to make him change his mind.'

'I'm sure Martha will be happier now that she has heard William say he will marry her, aren't you Martha?'

'Yes, Elizabeth. At least that is comforting. You do mean it William, don't you?'

'Yes, Martha, I mean it. But how we are going to live, I don't know.'

Thomas Bishop looked at Margaret. 'Of course we will accept you both to live her with us a servants. T'will be as before, but Martha will have her home here.'

'Oh yes, Father, of course you must both live here with us.' Margaret approved with delight,'That is what we expect. After you are married you can both live here, William is a great help and I know Martha works well'.

'Oh, thank you, Mistress Bishop, Goodman Bishop. I will be very happy to continue to be your servant. I can make candles, weave and knit I'll do anything you want.' Martha said eagerly.

'She certainly can knit and weave,' Elizabeth observed, 'she's done nothing else for the baby these past weeks!'

'Then that is agreed,' Thomas said. 'All we can do now is to hope your father will change his mind before the court sits in September.'

'I see we are interrupting your Bible reading, Goodman Bishop,' Elizabeth observed, 'We must must not tarry any longer. Come Martha, let us say good night and be on our way home.'

'Thank you, Mistress Bishop, for all your help,' Martha said, 'I pray father will in time give his permission for William and me to be married and look forward to living with you.'

Martha and Elizabeth left and William sat down feeling that somehow events were moving in his favour without him doing anything about it. But what could he do? He could not make Robert Cross give his permission for them to marry, and without it all the plans anybody made would be useless. The court would decide that he should be whipped, and that would be the end of it!

He did not hear the Bible lesson that night, he was too wrapped up in his own despairing thoughts. He muttered 'Amen' with the rest of the family, said 'good night' and went to bed. He lay awake, tossing and turning, for ages as he did every night these days before finally falling into a fitful sleep.

In the light June evenings he went fishing whenever he had the time. He could cross the little bridge in front of the house and go down the track to the jetty without meeting anybody. It was peaceful down there and out of view of the village.

Whilst fishing there one evening his peace was disturbed by the sound of someone walking along the jetty. He was reminded of the day Martha met him, and he looked to see if it was her. But it was a boy, a young boy about twelve, he thought. He recognised him from the prayer meetings, but did not know him. The boy came right up to William.

'Good day to you' he said, 'I know you are William Durgy, I am William Butler.'

'Good day, William. I've seen you at prayer meetings. Where do you live?'

'I'm Goodman Cogswell's servant. I wanted to talk to you because I hear you come from Ireland.'

'That's right. I was taken prisoner by Cromwell's men at the battle of Drogheda.'

'My father and mother came from Ireland. They were persecuted by Cromwell and transported here in 1650. Conditions were much harder here then and I believe they did not do very well. I was born here in 1653 but my mother died when I was born, so I never knew her. My father died when I was six and Goodman Cogswell took me into his house. What I wanted to know was, what was Ireland like?'

'Before Cromwell came it was a good country to live in. My ancestors had lived there for hundreds of years and my mother was Lady

Durgy and my father Sir William Durgy. We lived in Patten Hall near Drogheda and I had my own mare to ride. I trained it as a foal. But when Cromwell came all my family were killed in the fighting. That was when I was sent to Barbados as a slave in chains.'

'Were you in Barbados long then?'

'About fifteen years. Some of it was hard, some of it was not so bad. It was better when I was bought by Job Bishop, Goodman Thomas Bishop's brother. I was his groom as well as working on the plantation.'

'I was sorry to hear about the trouble you are having with Goodman Cross. I hope it will be solved happily for you. Thank you for telling me about Ireland. I would like to go there one day and see where my father and mother came from, but I don't think it will ever be possible.'

'I would like to go back too, but I hear our home has been burnt down and I have no family there now apart from an uncle I hardly know. I think we will have to stay here.'

'Yes, I suppose you're right. I hope we can be friends.'

'I am sure we can be. Do you like fishing?'

'I've never done any.'

'Well, come down here in the evenings, you may find me here and I'll show you how. There now, I've got a catch. You have to play the line in gently, if you jerk it too hard you'll lose your fish. Here he comes, now I lift it nice and steady, there you are a nice big one. Catch hold of it firmly and take the hook out of its mouth, knock it on the head with this stick and you have your supper. Would you like it?'

'Oh, thanks. I'll take it home. Will you be here tomorrow?'

'Probably, if I have no other work to do and it doesn't rain.'

Butler left with the fish and William cast his line out again. He thought Butler was a bit young for a friend, but he was short of friends these days and he knew he would be glad to talk to anyone.

They met several times during June and July. William talked about his life in Ireland and young Butler talked about school and what he was learning and his chores as servant to Cogswell. William felt sorry for him, having lost his parents so young. He had never had a happy family life with brothers and sisters.

One evening late in July he was surprised to see several children coming down the pathway to the jetty. They were all boys and they were laughing and playing about. They came along the jetty and he saw William Butler following them.

'You're William Durgy, aren't ye?' the boys asked.

'That's right. And who are you?'

'Fornicator! They be going to hang ye!' they taunted him.

William ignored them and carried on fishing.

'What shall we do with him?' they asked. One of them kicked him in the back as he sat on the edge of the jetty. 'He deserves a good kick!' William continued to ignore them. He knew it would be no good to stand up and chase them off, although he would dearly have loved to do so.

'No fight, eh?' they shouted. 'Let's see if he can swim?'

Suddenly William felt several hands on his back and before he could do anything he was given a good push and he left the jetty and joined his fishing line in the water. The boys cheered with delight and ran off without waiting to see if he could swim. William could not swim and was thrashing about in the water trying to grab one of the piles supporting the jetty.

Butler did not run away with the other boys. He picked up a long stick and, kneeling on the edge of the jetty, offered it to William. He grabbed it and Butler pulled him towards the jetty where he took hold and heaved himself up out of the water.

'Thank you William. You saved my life, I can't swim!'

'That's all right. I couldn't leave you there to drown. Those boys don't know what they're doing, always getting up to mischief.'

'I would've liked to have given them a good hiding, but it would not make the people in the village think any better of me.'

'Are you all right now? You're very wet.'

'Yes and I've lost my line. Suppose I'd better get back and dry my clothes.'

'I'll come with you.'

They walked together up the path, William's shoes squelching with water and his clothes sodden from head to foot.

'I wonder how you learn to swim, William?' Butler asked.

'I don't know, but I don't think you can learn by just being pushed in like that. I can't teach you to swim, but I could teach you how to ride a horse. Can you ride?'

'No. I've never been taught to ride, but I would like to learn. Can you teach me?'

'I'll ask Goodman Bishop if I can teach you on Agawam. He's a gentle horse and you'll soon learn on him.'

'Oh, thank you, William. I'll look forward to that.'

'Here we are, you go on home, and thanks again for fishing me out.'

'See you again tomorrow evening?'

'If I'm not laid up with a cold and I have time to make another line, yes, William.'

'My God, you're all wet, William!' Margaret greeted him.

'Yes. I slipped off the end of the jetty,' he explained. 'Young William Butler pulled me out.'

'How lucky he was there,' she said, 'you'd better get those clothes off and I'll dry them by the fire.'

While the family were at supper, William asked Bishop if he minded him teaching William Butler to ride on Agawam, 'he pulled me out of the river today when I fell in and I'd like to do something to thank him.'

'Fell in did you? I've heard another story, I've heard a bunch of young lads pushed you in!'

'Did they really?' the boys asked together laughing, 'that must have been funny to watch!'

'Not funny at all,' Margaret said, 'if William couldn't swim he could have drowned.'

'Why didn't you chase them off, then?' John asked.

'I tried to ignore them. I didn't think it right for me to fight mere boys.'

'Anyway, young William pulled you out, did he?' Bishop asked.

'Yes, sir. And I'd like to teach him to ride, if you don't mind.'

'I don't mind, William. I'm sure you are a good teacher and the horse and young Butler will come to no harm. Goodman Cogswell takes good care of him, but I suppose he feels it is not up to him to teach his servant how to ride. A boy needs to be able to ride. You go ahead and I'll be interested to see how your pupil progresses.'

'Thank you, sir. I've been able to ride as long as I can remember. I think I must have been sat on a horse as soon as I was born!'

One evening a few days later William Butler came for his first lesson.

'Now William you must get to know your horse. After all you're going to sit on his back and if he doesn't know you or thinks you're afraid of him, he's going to play up and be awkward.'

'I must say I know very little about horses, William. How do I get to know him?'

'Stroke his head, like this, put your face close to him and talk to him. Pat him gently and even offer him some hay. Hold the hay with your flat hand, if you offer him a fistful he'll maybe take your fist as well, but he wouldn't mean to harm you.'

Butler gave Agawam a handful of hay and stroked his neck.

'Now do you think I've made friends with him?'

'That's a good start. In time you will groom him and he'll get used to you. Now I'm going to put a halter round his neck and show you how to mount. When you're up and comfortable I'll lead him round gently in a circle and show you how to sit.'

He saddled the horse, showed Butler how to mount and the first lesson began.

William enjoyed these lessons; it took his mind off the eternal problem which worried him every day and night. September seemed a long way ahead and each week that passed Robert Cross gave no indication that he would give way. Thomas Bishop tried to talk to him several times, but Robert was either too busy on his land or just refused to see him. Elizabeth tried too, but she only got as far as talking to Hannah, who was just as keen as she was that William and Martha should be allowed to marry, and as quickly as possible.

William spent as much of his spare time as he could fishing or riding, sometimes with young Butler on the horse with him. They would go across country, often as far as Chebacco, the nearest village to Ipswich.

'You told me one day your father was Sir William and your mother a Lady,' Butler said on one of these excursions, 'would you mind if I told my friends at school?'

'No, I don't mind.'

'I was thinking about Martha and Goodman Cross. Does he know about your past life?'

'I don't think so. I told Martha, but I don't suppose she told her father.'

'Its just that I thought the more everyone knows the truth about you the better chance you've got that Goodman Cross may approve of the marriage. Now you see all the children call you names, and the rest of the village ignore you. Goodman Cogswell said he was surprised I was going out with you so much, I tried to tell him what I know of you and I think he may think better of you. '

'Thank you, William. But the court will just look at me as a fornicator and a Catholic.'

'I don't think being a Catholic these days is looked upon as badly as it used to be. My parents were Catholics and I was brought up as one. Although now I attend the prayer meetings and I suppose I am really a Protestant. Some years ago, you know, the Council agreed people should follow their own religion, although we are all made to attend the prayer meetings.'

'I know. I missed the first Sunday and was awarded a beating or a fine, which Goodman Bishop paid.'

'Oh, yes, I heard about that. But you attend every Sunday now.'

'I've no choice. I don't think it makes all that much difference, after all we all pray to the same God.'

'I don't know much about the different religions. I've been taught to read the Bible and I say my prayers and that's about all I know.'

'As you grow older it will mean more to you. I was told to have faith, and I believe my life has been spared for some purpose. I believe I was meant to come here for some reason.'

'I am sure you're right and I hope you win your case at the court and marry Martha.'

'Yes, William, I hope so too.'

CHAPTER 17
THE COURT CASE

'Silence in court! Silence in court! Be upstanding for Marshall Robert Lord.' Theophilus Wilson, the constable, was also the clerk of the court. He was a small, inoffensive man but in court he held himself as upright as possible and was proud of his exalted position. He was in charge here and the people obeyed him.

'Silence in court!' and there was silence.

The meeting house was crowded one day in September 1664 and the whole village was eager to hear full details of the case to be tried. The accusation of fornication was rare and this made the case well worth attending and listening to. No one was going to miss a word, so they were all agog in silence and impatience.

Robert Lord sat in his seat of judgement and the crowd waited with excitement for the case to begin..

'The clerk will read the charge of the first case.' Robert Lord ordered.

'Sir, this is the charge of Robert Cross against William Durgy, for alienating his daughter's affection.' Theophilus Wilson read out to the court. The villagers looked at one another and shook their heads at the thought of such a dreadful thing happening.

'How pleads William Durgy?'

William was sitting next to Thomas Bishop feeling nervous. The last four months had been a great strain to him. He had not slept well and the abuse and derision he had suffered had deeply affected him. How could he have a fair trial in this court?

He looked across the room at Martha, sitting next to her sister, Elizabeth, hanging her head down in shame her face hidden under her bonnet. He had not seen her except on Sundays at the prayer house and that one evening when they came to the Bishop's house. Her father still rejected her and was not in court. He had forbidden her mother to come.

'How pleads William Durgy?' Robert Lord asked again.

William slowly turned and faced the Marshall.

'Not guilty, sir,' he replied. 'Not guilty, sir! We wish to marry.'

'Call the first witness.'

'Call Mistress Margaret Bishop.'

Margaret Bishop took the witness stand, held the bible in her hand and read the oath.

How say you, Mistress Bishop?'

'Mistress Nelson and Mistress Storie came to see me one day in May and said her sister, Martha Cross, was at Mistress Nelson's house in sore distress as she found she was with child by William Durgy and that her father had called her dreadful names and threatened to beat her. William Durgy was digging in the vegetable plot and I asked him to come and talk to Mistress Nelson and Mistress Storie. He said the child could be his.'

'What happened next?' asked the Marshall.

'After some discussion Mistress Nelson and Mistress Storie decided to see Goodman Cross and plead with him to let Martha marry William Durgy.'

'Is that your testimony?' Robert Lord asked.

'Yes sir.'

William was sorry she could not say any more. But what more could she say? William is an honest man and a good worker. He has had a hard life going many years without a woman, and now this little hussy comes along and seduces him! She could not really say that, could she? But it was the truth, the whole truth and nothing but the truth.

'You may stand down. Call the next witness.'

'Call Mistress Nelson.' Theophilus Wilson cried.

Elizabeth Nelson took the witness stand, held the bible in her hands and read the oath.

'How say you, Mistress Nelson?' Robert Lord asked.

'Martha Cross came to me one day in May crying bitterly. She said she found she was with child and I asked her who the father could be.

She said it was William Durgy and that she loved him and he had said he loved her. She said our father was very angry and had threatened to kill William Durgy and beat her and he called her bad names. She was so upset she said she wanted to die that very day. I told her she could stay with us until we could decide what to do. I went to my neighbour Mistress Sarah Storie and we went to Mistress Bishop where we saw William Durgy. He said he knew nothing about it, but perhaps the child could be his.'

'Did he admit he had been with Martha?'

'We didn't ask him, but we all thought he had.'

'What did you do next?'

'Mistress Storie said I should go and see my father, Goodman Cross and plead with him. I said I was fearful of going on my own and she agreed to come with me. We went to my father's house and found my father and mother very distressed, not knowing which way to turn or what to say. We pleaded with my father to let Martha marry William but he refused. He said he no longer had a daughter called Martha, and if he did he certainly would never let her marry that slave, William Durgy.'

'Is that your testimony.'

'It is sir.'

'Is there another witness?' Robert Lord asked.

'Yes sir.' said Theophilus Wilson, 'I call Goodman William Nelson.'

William Nelson took the stand and read the oath. William wondered what this witness was going to reveal – would he admit to hitting him and telling him to go and hang himself?

'I saw William Durgy later in the day, after my wife and Mistress Storie had left and he told me he was sorry he had said the child was his. I asked him what he meant, did he think my sister-in-law was a whore?'

'And what did the defendant say to that?'

'He said he was sorry and I said that was no good. I said he was just scum and ought to be hanged. I said he was not fit to marry Martha.'

'What did he say to that?'

'He said if he was hung that wouldn't help Martha or the child and then he added that he had eighteen meals a week and, for the sake of the child, he would give six meals.'

'So, what did you say to that offer?'

'I left in disgust. I haven't spoken to him since.'
'Is that your testimony?'
'That is my testimony sir.'
'What else is known of this case?' Robert Lord asked.

'Sir, the Hampton Quarterly Court considered the case after Goodman Cross made his complaint,' Theophilus Wilson explained, 'and they ordered William Durgy, being presented for fornication, to be whipped not exceeding twenty stripes and to put into security of twenty pounds to save the town of Ipswich from the charge of keeping the child, or else go to prison.'

'Is Goodman Cross in court?'
'No, sir.'
'So we do not know if he still wishes to pursue his complaint?'
'The court has not had any further notice from him, sir.'
'Has the defendant anything to say?'

William was not expecting this question but he supposed he should have thought he might have an opportunity to say something. He stood up and looked round the court. Every eye was on him, except Martha's.

'I can only say I plead not guilty, sir. Goodman Nelson misunderstood what I said. I said I was sorry – but I had admitted the child was mine, not that I was sorry I had said the child was mine. We wish to be married and beseech Goodman Cross to give his daughter leave to marry. Had he given his consent in May this court would not now be troubled with this case. That is all I can say, sir.'

'The Court will adjourn for half an hour, while I consider the verdict.' Robert Lord announced.

'Be upstanding in court. Marshall Robert Lord adjourns for half an hour.' Constable Theophilus Wilson announced.

Robert Lord retired to a small room at the back of the hall and consulted those members of the council not concerned with the case.

'The whole village is demanding the maximum penalty for fornication. Also, it is known, this man Durgy is a Catholic.' Captain Appleton said.

'Has he attended the prayer house every sabbath?'

'He missed the first sabbath and was fined three pounds which Goodman Bishop paid. We would be well rid of him if we could hang him.' Robert Lord was advised.

'On the other hand,' Robert said, 'the Hampton Court ordered he be whipped and put in security of twenty pounds, for the care of the child. I do not see where this twenty pounds is coming from. Obviously, Durgy is a man of no means, I assume Goodman Bishop is not going to pay. Goodman Cross disowns the child and his daughter. If we hang Durgy, there will be no one to care for the child and the cost will be on the town. We cannot support orphans and vagrants. I recommend Durgy be left to care for his own child and I support the Hampton Court order. It is a pity Goodman Cross cannot be persuaded to allow them to marry, that would solve the matter finally. I cannot see where this twenty pounds is coming from.'

'Fornication is still fornication and an abominable sin even if the couple marry later. We think Martha Cross is as guilty as Durgy and should be whipped for the same offence after giving birth. We must make this order to satisfy the public opinion.'

'And what sentence should we impose on the girl? She is not on trial, remember.'

'But she is as guilty as he is. We think she should be whipped not exceeding ten stripes after the birth of the baby.'

'Very well, I agree with reluctance,' Robert Lord decided.

Meanwhile, William and Thomas Bishop were outside the court discussing the case. Elizabeth, William Nelson and Martha stood some distance away.

'I don't think it helped when Goodman Nelson misunderstood you when you said you were sorry you had admitted the child was yours, William.' Thomas said.

'No sir. I was bewildered at the time and didn't know what to say. He misunderstood what I said. What will happen next?'

'We must wait for the verdict first.'

Inside the court some of the villagers were discussing the case among themselves.

'Of course, Durgy is right,' Grace Searl said, 'if Goodman Cross had only given his consent in May this case would not have come up. How many of us were married while pregnant?'

'Mistress Searl! Speak for yourself, not many I would say!'

'Well, I wasn't you can be sure; but I wager some of us were.' No-one agreed with her.

Half an hour later they were all back in court.

'Be upstanding in court.' Theophilus Wilson sounded as if he was enjoying his job, 'Marshall Robert Lord will announce his verdict.'

Robert Lord entered the court and took his seat.

'I have considered this case carefully. The defendant does not deny the offence and has shown some remorse. The plaintiff clearly refuses to allow the young couple to marry. I therefore have no alternative but to find for the plaintiff and uphold the order of the Hampton Quarterly Court.'

There was a general murmer of approval.

'Furthermore,' Robert Lord added, 'it is the order of this court that Martha Cross be whipped, not exceeding ten times, for fornication, or pay a fine of three pounds. Punishment to be given after the child is born.'

There were murmurs of surprise in the court. Martha burst into tears and Elizabeth tried to console her. William was horrified at this latest order and looked across the court to see Martha crying. Her distress dismayed him and he wondered what he could do to help?

He turned and looked appealingly at Thomas Bishop.

Thomas leaned forward and whispered, 'ask for an appeal.'

'How say the defendant?' Robert Lord asked.

'I ask the court's permission to appeal,' William pleaded, hopefully. 'I am willing to marry Martha Cross if only Goodman Cross will give his consent.'

'Permission to appeal granted. Case will be deferred to next Quarter Sessions in December.' Robert Lord agreed with relief. 'Call the next case.'

Somewhat pleased by the permission to appeal yet again, Thomas, William and the Nelsons with Martha departed to their homes. William had no opportunity to speak to Martha who was still crying.

Thomas was fairly satisfied with the outcome.

'Well, that will delay the order of the Hampton Court.' he said. 'What do we do next?'

I think somehow we must persuade Goodman Cross to allow the

marriage,' Margaret Bishop replied. 'The next time the case will be heard will be in December and Martha will be near her time. I was very relieved when you said you would marry, Martha.'

'Well, I didn't see how I could until you offered to take her as a servant. I'm sure we are both very grateful to you for that.'

'I know Mistress Cross is in favour of the marriage for the sake of the child,' Margaret said. 'I only hope in the time we have left she can persuade Goodman Cross to agree.'

'Robert Lord looked very relieved when William asked for an appeal. I wonder if he would approach Goodman Cross? He might have more influence with him than any of the family.' Thomas said. 'I think I'll have a word with him.'

The next day he went to see Robert Lord. After the usual greetings he said, 'I would like to discuss the Durgy case with you, if you don't mind.'

'Certainly, Thomas, how can I help you?'

'I do not think the execution of the court award is going to help the case at all. I realise there must be some punishment for what they have done, but after that, who will look after the child and where is the fine of twenty pounds coming from?'

'As to the fine, I agree with you, I do not see where it can come from. You paid the three pounds for the failure to attend prayers on the sabbath, I understand you are not prepared to pay the twenty pounds?'

'I do not see why I should. Durgy can't pay. He has offered to spare six of his meals a week for the child and I suppose that is something.'

'Yes, that was stated in court. What I wanted was evidence that the two were really able to marry and that Durgy was capable of supporting a wife. I did not get that impression from either the witnesses nor from his statement.'

'If they could marry my wife and I have offered to employ both of them as servants. We can accommodate them.'

'That is very generous of you.'

'It is the least we can do. We feel that is the only answer and to be able to do that we must have Goodman Cross's approval. I came to ask if you would approach him on the matter. You would have more influence on him than the members of the family who have already tried their best. I attempted to speak to him, but he refuses to see me.'

'I agree with you that is the best solution. I will see Goodman Cross if you think it will do any good. I can't say I like the man, he has done well in the village and built up a decent farm, but he is short tempered and too strict for my liking. However, I will see him and let you know the result.'

'Thank you, sir. I hope you are successful.'

'God willing, but do not depend on it.'

Thomas went home and told Margaret the result of his talk with Robert Lord.

'When is he going to see Goodman Cross, father?'

'He didn't say.'

'I shall be waiting every day for good news. If only he can persuade Goodman Cross – that would be wonderful!'

William was told as well and he added a prayer at night for Robert Lord's success. Margaret went to see Elizabeth and Martha and told them too. Martha was delighted, she was sure her father might pay attention to what Goodman Lord had to say.

They had to wait another week before they heard the result of Robert Lord's efforts.

He went to Robert Cross on a Sunday afternoon. He considered that the best day to find him not working and free to see him.

'Good day to you, Goodman Cross,' he said on entering the hall. Cross was sitting in his chair, he stood and offered Lord his hand.

'Good day to you, Marshall Lord. To what do I owe the honour of your visit?' They shook hands.

'I would like to discuss the marriage of your daughter to William Durgy.'

'I do not own a daughter marrying that scum. He is only a slave, a Catholic one at that, you cannot expect me to approve.'

'Yes, I understand he is a Catholic, but he now regularly attends the prayer meetings every Sabbath and so I do not think we should take the fact that he is, or was, a Catholic into account. What I would like to point out is that even if the award of the court was carried out, they would still be unable to marry and we would have a bastard in the village.'

'That is no concern of mine, sir.'

'Durgy has no means of paying the fine of twenty pounds. Where is that to come from?'

'That again, sir, is no concern of mine. Durgy must be left to solve his own problems. You cannot expect me to help him. He has even denied that the child is his, according to Goodman Nelson.'

'At the court, Durgy said Goodman Nelson misunderstood him. He said he was sorry and added that he had admitted the child was his. He said he had eighteen meals a week and offered six for the sake of the child. I had hoped to persuade you to be more reasonable in the interest's of the village.'

'Reasonable, sir! For what reason should I give a fornicator permission to marry a girl who was my daughter. After his actions I have lost my daughter and you expect me to be more reasonable! Sir, I suggest you are wasting your time and I expect to be left in peace on the Sabbath. I wish you, good day, sir!'

'I'm truly sorry to have disturbed your day of rest. But I hope you will think carefully on what I have said and in time give your permission. You have until December to think on it.'

'I can assure you, sir, I shall not give it another thought. Good day to you, sir.'

Robert Lord had no alternative but to leave and replied, 'Good day to you, Goodman Cross.'

He told Thomas the result of his visit which Thomas considered, knowing Robert Cross, was not to be unexpected.

William was naturally very disappointed to hear Robert Lord's efforts came to no avail. He decided to occupy his mind as much as possible apart from fishing and giving William Butler riding lessons.

'Would you like me to show you how I can make chairs, sir?' he asked Bishop.

'Yes, you can use my tools. If they are good enough to sit on we shall be needing them when Martha joins us.'

William smiled. 'I was thinking the same thing. I can assure you they will be good enough to sit on, and if they aren't they will go on the fire.'

It took William a week to make two chairs and they were tried out by Samuel and John who passed them as safe to use.

'I think William really turned his hand to making those chairs to take his mind off Martha,' Margaret said.

'I'm sure you're right, woman. I should go to see Job, it is a whole year since I last went. Do you think William should come with me? It will give him a complete change and we'll be back before the end of November.'

'What a good idea, father. I'm sure he would like it.'

'Can you spare him?'

'I'll have the boys to help. The hay is in and there's only the ploughing for Samuel to do. John is just as good with the animals as William. You take him with you.'

'I will have to discuss it with Goodman Lord and give him an assurance William will return with me.'

So Thomas went to see Robert Lord the next day and told him he wanted to take William with him for a visit to Barbados.

'Goodman Bishop,' Robert Lord said thoughtfully,'I do not think I can agree with that proposal. Suppose he absconds? We will be left with an unmarried woman and bastard child in the community.'

'I am sure that William will not abscond. He loves Martha Cross and wishes to marry her.'

'Suppose he meets with a fatal accident? He could be washed overboard, anything could happen.' Robert Lord persisted.

'I think that hardly likely. He will not be a member of the crew. In any case, if it did happen, though God forbid, we would take Martha and the child as part of our family.'

Robert Lord gave this statement some thought. Finally he said, 'That is very generous of you. In that case, I will, with some misgiving, agree. I wish you a safe passage.'

William was pleased when Thomas told him he was going to Barbados and wanted him to go with him. No one thought of telling Martha.

They sailed on the *Redemtioneer* on the third of October. It was a wet and windy day and they had a rough passage to Boston.

William went ashore while the ship was being loaded with cargo for St. Kitts and Barbados. It was a year since he had been to Boston and he was surprised to find quite a few new buildings and the place seemed very busy and prosperous. He was able to buy himself a new pair of shoes. Thomas had continued to pay William each month, even though he had said the fine for not attending the prayer meeting on the first Sunday would take him a year to repay. He had spent very little money in Ipswich so was able to save most of his wages. He had a drink and went back to the ship.

Two days later they sailed again. The weather continued to be bad and for several days they had to proceed under shortened sails. William was glad he was a good sailor as the small ship rolled and tossed all day and night. After a week they reached St. Kitts on a beautiful calm sunny day. There was not much cargo to unload here so William did not go ashore. They raised the anchor and put to sea again the next day and had a smooth passage to Speightstown. William spent his time doing some of the wood work Thomas wanted done on board..

Thomas and William went ashore and hired two horses to ride to Farley Hill. The plantation had not changed much and Job was pleased to see William again.

'Welcome back, William,' Job said, 'Are you visiting or are you coming back to work for me?'

'No sir, I am content in Ipswich, thank you. How are you working without me?'

'Oh, we are managing somehow. I must say Oduduwa is much better with the horses after your training. He'll be pleased to see you.'

'Is there anything I can do for you, sir, before I go to the stable?' he asked Thomas.

'Just take my bag inside and then you can go and see your old friends the horses.'

On the way to the stables William met John Harper, the foreman.

'Ah, William Durgy. Nice to see you again,' he said, 'are you coming back to work for us?'

'No, sir, just visiting with Thomas. How have the crops been this last year?'

'Not as good as the year before. Not enough rain and too much wind. But we struggle on. Oduduwa will be glad to see you. One of the horses is not too well.'

'I'll go and look at it then.'

He found Oduduwa in the stable.

'Hullo, Oduduwa, I hear one of the horses is sick.'

'Oh, sar, have you come all de way from America to see sick horse?'

'Not really. I'm just visiting but Harper told me about the horse. What is the matter with it?'

'He is old, sar, and just will not work. Come and see him.'

William was shown the horse, the one he called Black Beauty. He ran his hand over his head, patted him and inspected his fore legs. He opened his mouth and looked at his teeth.

'Yes, Oduduwa, poor old Black Beauty is old, isn't he? I don't think you can do much with him except to put him out to graze and let him retire gracefully. He must be well over twenty years old.'

'He's been here longer than I have and I've been here twenty five years.'

'Twenty five years?'

'Yes, sar, I was one of the first slaves to be brought here. But I'm not unhappy. I've a good job, a loving woman, and five children. Have you found a woman in Ipswich?'

'Yes, Oduduwa, I've found a woman in Ipswich.'

'I'm glad for you, sar. Marry her and make a good home.'

'I hope to, Oduduwa.'

He looked round the tobacco field and the drying shed and saw things had not changed. As he was passing the slaves quarters on the way back to the house he saw Eshu, Oduduwa's wife.

'Hullo. Eshu. How are you?'

She looked at him with surprise, smiled coyly and turned her face away. She was too shy to say anything and walked quickly away to her house – one room of a dozen in a row where the married slaves lived.

'Afraid there is no room for you to sleep in the house, William,' Job said, 'but you can find somewhere in the stable like you used to, can't you?'

'Yes, sir. I'll be all right.'

William slept in the stable and ate with the slaves as he had done for many years. It made him appreciate the comforts at Ipswich all the more.

Apart from washing and ironing Thomas's clothes, and Job's as well while he was about it, he had little to do and plenty of time to think. He realised the only reason he had been brought here was to give him a change from Ipswich and his problems with Martha. But it was not going to solve the matter. He must do something to make Martha's father change his mind. Why was it that Robert Cross objected to him so much, apart from making love to his daughter before they were married? Robert called him a slave and scum and obviously hated Catholics. He could not deny his religion, but he did not consider himself a slave. Perhaps if Robert was told he was a prisoner of war, taken in battle fighting for his King and country, and he was the son of Sir William and Lady Durgy, would that impress him?

They stayed at Farley Hill for a week and then went back aboard the ship, loaded with sugar, cotton and tobacco and sailed for St. Kitts again. Here they picked up more sugar and tobacco and proceeded to Boston. They took four days to unload and were back at Ipswich by the first week in November.

'Martha will be glad to see you back,' Margaret greeted him. 'When she heard you had gone back to Barbados she came round here in a terrible state. She thought you had deserted her and she would never see you again. I reassured her you would be back by November. Father, I have been considering, do you think we could take Martha back from now? She can live with Elizabeth and come here every day. That might even persuade Goodman Cross to give his consent.'

'An excellent idea. I agree.'

'Thank you mistress Bishop.' William was delighted at the idea. 'Do you think I should go and see her and tell her she can come back to work?'

'I don't see it would do any harm. I know Goodman Cross has told her to have nothing to do with you, but she is not living with him. You'll find Elizabeth there and perhaps Goodman Nelson.'

'I'm not very keen on seeing him, but I think I should see Martha and put her mind at rest.'

He went to the Nelson's house that night and found the door shut as the weather was cold. He knocked on the door and William Nelson opened it.

'What do you want?' Nelson asked angrily.

'I'd like to see Martha please, Goodman Nelson.'

'I don't want you in my house,' he shouted.

Elizabeth came to the door.

'Whatever is all this noise?' she asked. 'Oh, William, its you! You want to see Martha? Do come in.'

'If he comes in I go out.' Nelson declared. Elizabeth ignored him and let William in. Nelson stalked off down the path.

'Hullo, Martha.' William greeted her as she sat by the fire knitting.

'Oh, William, am I glad to see you. I was afeared ye'd gone back to Barbados and left me.'

'No Martha, I wouldn't do that. I just went with Goodman Bishop to see Farley Hill again. During the voyage I had some woodwork to do. Before I left I made two chairs and Goodman Thomas was well pleased with them. Also I think they sent me so that I should forget our problems here. But I had so much time on my hands with little to do, I had plenty of time to do some thinking. I have a plan to help make your father change his mind. I won't tell you what it is now, I don't want to build up your hopes too much. But I just want to say I love you and I want to marry you.'

'Thank you, William,' she got up, put her knitting down, and came over to him. The fact that she was pregnant was very evident now. They embraced and kissed. The first time he had had the opportunity to kiss her again for six months.

'And I have some good news for you. Goodman Bishop and Mistress Bishop want you to come back to work for them. You can stay here and come over each day. They think it may help your father to consent to the marriage.'

'William, that is wonderful. Yes, I'll come tomorrow.'

'Now you two, afraid I've got to stop this. Martha is not supposed to see you. I wonder what father will think if you are working together? I hope it does have the right effect. Thank you for coming, William, but I think you'd better leave now.'

'Thank you for letting me in, Elizabeth. I hope Goodman Nelson will not be too angry'.

The next day Mary Bishop came to see William and Margaret.

'How was Job at Farley Hill?' she asked.

'Very well Mistress Bishop. He said he was pleased to see me and asked if I had come back to work for him.'

'Thomas brought me a letter from Job and he says he's well enough, but it is nice to hear from someone who has seen him apart from Thomas. I wish he'd sell the plantation and come here.'

'The foreman, John Harper, told me the crops had not been as good this year. I think the island would have to be very prosperous before he could sell.' William thought he had never heard Job say he would sell one day, but kept that to himself. He wondered why he never came to Ipswich and this couple seemed to be content to live apart.

'I see Martha is here. Has Goodman Cross given permission for you to marry yet, William?'

'No,' said Margaret, 'there is no change. Goodman Lord went to see him again last week, but with no success. We decided to let Martha come back to work, hoping it would influence her father. I hear Hannah beseeches him almost every day – surely he must give way soon!'

'While I was in Barbados I had time to think on this matter,' William said. 'I think Goodman Cross objects to the marriage because he thinks I am only a slave, a Catholic one at that, and calls me mere scum. Apart from the fact that I made love to his daughter without his permission, that is. I wonder if he could be convinced that I am not a slave and never have been, he might think better of me and agree I am a fit person to marry his daughter? You see, really I was captured while fighting for my King and country in Drogheda and taken prisoner. I was sold in exchange for sugar, along with over a hundred others, and we were sent in chains to Barbados. My father was Sir William Durgy and my mother Lady Elizabeth Durgy, a Lady in her own right; my ancestors have had large estates in Ireland for hundreds of years. If Goodman Cross thinks I am not of good enough family for his daughter, he'd have difficulty finding a man with a family history like mine anywhere near here. I don't want to boast, but I want Goodman Cross to know who I am and where I come from. Mistress Bishop, many people have approached Goodman Cross but I don't think any have told him what I have just told you. Could you see him and tell him this? You could also tell him I have worked for Job for over five years and I think he was very satisfied.'

'I have never had much to do with Goodman Cross,' Mary answered. 'I know and like Mistress Hannah, I could see her and perhaps she would tell her husband. I will do what I can, if you think it will be of any help.'

'Perhaps you could say I have just returned from a visit to Farley Hill and Job was sorry to hear Goodman Cross had refused permission for his daughter to marry me?'

'That is quite a good reason for seeing him. I will think it over and let you know how I am received.'

A few days later Mary Bishop called in again.

'I saw Mistress Cross yesterday and told her what you told me about your family and history. When I had just about finished Goodman Cross came in and Mistress Hannah asked me to repeat it all over again to him. I also told him Job was very impressed with your work and sorry to hear William could not marry Martha. He thought William would make an excellent husband.'

'That was nice of you, Mary,' Margaret said. 'What was Goodman Cross's reply?'

'At first he did not want to listen at all. Went on about he'd lost his daughter and would never accept William. When I had finished he just grunted and thanked me for coming and wished me "Good day". So I had to leave without a positive reply, but I think I impressed Mistress Hannah and possibly she may persuade Goodman Cross to change his mind. I can't really say one way or the other.'

'Thank you very much, Mistress Bishop,' William said, 'I'm sure you did your best and we can only hope that it has done some good.'

William had to wait another six weeks for the court to hear the case again. He continued to teach William Butler to ride and one day showed Thomas Bishop the result of his efforts. He made Butler ride Agawam while Bishop watched. He had put up low fences for William to jump and made him gallop some distance.

'First rate, William,' Bishop decided, 'You've done a good job there, he can ride well and sits perfectly, even takes the jump with ease.'

Finally the eighteenth of December arrived.

Well, William. Court tomorrow. How do you feel?'

'I pray to God it will go well.' William replied.

That night he did pray to God, as he had never prayed before. He used his rosary three times and before he fell asleep he was sure in his mind that God was going to help him. He felt an inner happiness he had not felt for months. He slept well without any disturbing dreams and woke the next morning feeling happy. Happy that he was going to face that court again? He could not believe himself, but was sure it was the result of his prayers. Everything was going to be all right, he told himself.

Chapter 18
THE APPEAL

Theophilus Wilson called for silence and there was silence in the court room while Marshall Robert Lord took his seat.
'The clerk will read the first case.' Robert Lord ordered.
'This is the case of William Durgy against Robert Cross appealing to the defendant to give permission for him to marry his daughter, on the evidence presented at the previous Quarterly Session.' Theophilus Wilson read out in a clear, loud voice which echoed round the small, crowded hall.
William was sitting next to Thomas Bishop and he looked across the hall to see Martha with Elizabeth and William Nelson. Martha looked up at William and smiled.
William was pleased to see Martha smile, but surprised.
'She knows something,' he thought, 'perhaps she knows her father has at last approved? Please, God, let it be!'
'Call the first witness.' Robert Lord ordered.
'Sir, there is no witness, but I have a statement made and signed by Robert Cross.'
'You may read the statement to the court.'
The whole village was in the court-house, eager to hear the outcome of this case. Everyone sat quietly waiting for the statement to be read out. Would Robert Cross persist in refusing to allow the marriage, or had he finally given way?
'Sir, the statement is addressed "For Her much respected friend Mister Robert Cross at Ipswich in New England. These present with care" and reads, "Neighbour Bishop: to you and your wife this is to let

you understand our minds to the case standing as it does. We leave your servants to your disposal and for the marriage you may put to any period as soon as you wish; we shall in no ways hinder it. Our hearts are sore oppressed, we are full of sorrow. Honoured Sir, you may easily understand how the case stands concerning my daughter and I give them leave to marry. Your servant Robert Cross.'"*

Everyone accepted this evidence in silence waiting for the judgement. Martha raised her head and smiled again at William. He smiled back and heaved a great sigh of relief.

'I find for the plaintiff. Defendant will give his daughter in marriage or pay five pounds damages. William Durgy and Martha Cross you are free to leave this court.' Marshall Robert Lord was pleased to declare without any hesitation.

A few people clapped and William rose and walked across the hall towards Martha. She rose from her seat and met him in the centre, where they embraced and kissed. The clapping increased and continued for several minutes, until Theophilus Wilson decided enough was enough.

'Silence in Court. Silence in Court!' He shouted.

Gradually the hubbub subsided and there was silence while those interested in the case filed out. William heard Robert Lord call for the next case, while he and Martha walked hand in hand to freedom outside.

'Well, William, now we will be able to marry tomorrow,' Martha said.

'Has it all been arranged, then?'

'Oh yes. It was arranged yesterday.'

'Nobody told me. Oh Martha, I'm so happy. This is a great relief to me.'

They walked down the dirt track to the Bishop's house, Martha's hand tucked over William's arm, while the Bishops and Elizabeth followed them. William Nelson went to his own home.

'I'll not be seen dead in the same house with that man,' he declared as he parted. Elizabeth made no comment, she was used to her husband's often repeated opinion of William.

'I am so happy for them,' said Elizabeth, 'they make a lovely couple and I'm sure they will make a success of their marriage.'

'I'm sure William will do his best for her,' Margaret replied, 'I'm glad we were able to make the arrangements for the wedding tomorrow.'

* As taken from the Boston Records and Files.

'Father won't be there, he still disowns Martha and forbids her to go home. I wish he could find it in his heart to forgive them.'

'Perhaps he will in time,' Margaret tried to console Elizabeth. 'Who will give Martha away? We must have someone, if your father won't be there.'

'William won't. He won't even come now to be under the same roof as William!'

'I suppose Thomas could do it, but it seems strange. I'll ask him.'

'I can't think of anyone else.' Elizabeth agreed. 'Look, Margaret, they've gone inside the house. Shall we wait a few minutes to leave them together?'

'A good idea. I'll show you our vegetable patch at the back. I'm sure you've always wanted to see it!'

'One vegetable patch is much the same as another, as far as I'm concerned. But let's go and see it.' There were not many vegetables to be seen under the light cover of snow but they looked at the chickens and the pigs.

Once inside the house William took Martha in his arms and gave her a long passionate kiss.

'Oh, William, I'm so happy and I do love you. All these months apart have been terrible. I've been much happier since I started working here again and could see you every day.'

'I love you too, Martha. We'll be all right now. Our room is ready in the attic. Its a bit dark up there, but we shall be together.'

'And I thought you'd left me when you went back to Barbados. I was so angry and disappointed. I couldn't sleep and cried all night. Then Elizabeth went to see Margaret and told me you had only gone with Thomas for the visit. I was so relieved, you couldn't imagine.'

'Fancy you thinking I would desert you, Martha!'

'But you didn't seem too eager to marry me at first. I wondered what you really felt for me. I couldn't understand it when Goodman Nelson said you were sorry you said the baby was yours.'

'He misunderstood what I said. I said I was sorry then added the baby was mine. He struck me and I lost a tooth.'

'Oh, William, I am sorry. I didn't know that.'

'I couldn't see how I could marry you without somewhere to live and how to keep you. When Thomas and Margaret agreed to take you back and both of us to live here, that solved everything, apart from you father's permission. When did you hear he had changed his mind?'

'Only yesterday. Mother came round and told us he was writing to the court. I don't think he will ever really accept you, but he was finally convinced that to let the court carry out the first order would not solve anything. Mother was so happy.'

They were still embracing when Margaret and Elizabeth came in.

'Can we come in now?' they asked.

'Oh, Elizabeth, I'm so happy,' Martha rushed up to her and kissed her. 'Thank you for all you've done for me all these months.'

'It has been a long time, Martha, but I'm glad it is now all over.'

'And Mistress Bishop, thank you for taking me in your house.'

'We are happy to treat you as one of the family, Martha. But no Mistress Bishop, please, Margaret from now on.'

'Thank you, Margaret.'

'Now we should get the meal ready. Father and the boys will be in immediately. See, William has made two chairs, they're quite sound so we can all sit down.'

Thomas Bishop came in followed by Samuel and John.

'Well that was a short session in the court, William. I'm very pleased for you. I heard Robert Lord had received Goodman Cross's letter last night, but I did not tell you. I let you wait to hear it yourself this morning.'

'You might have told me! But when I saw Martha smiling in court, I guessed something good had happened.'

'Welcome to our home, Martha.'

'Thank you, Goodman Bishop.'

'Thomas to you, Martha.'

They sat down and Thomas said grace.

'Lord, we thank you for our good fortune. May we live in peace and enjoy your benefactions. Amen.'

'Amen,' they all muttered.

'Now tomorrow the wedding will be here in the morning at eleven,' Margaret said while dishing out the food, 'Father saw the Marshall last evening and asked him to perform the service and forego the banns in view of Martha's condition. But we have a problem.'

'What is that, wife?' Thomas asked.

'We have no one to give Martha away. Her father refuses to come and Goodman Nelson won't do it. Who do you think we can find?'

'I've not thought about it,' he replied, 'who do you think?'

'Father, I wondered if you'd do it?'

'Me?' he queried, surprised, 'Why me?'

'There's no one else, father. You'll have to do it.'

'It seems strange, but if Martha doesn't mind I will.'

'Goodman Bishop, Thomas, you are my new father – please do it for me!'

'Very well then, I will. I have no daughter so it will be an opportunity for me to do something I never thought I would!'

'Now, we've made a division up in the attic, Martha, so you and William will be on your own.' Margaret said. 'The two boys are in the other half.'

'And please don't snore so much, Samuel.' said William.

'I don't snore.'

'You should hear yourself. Nearly lifts the roof off!'

'Quite right, William,' said John, 'he keeps me awake too.'

After the meal Thomas got up from the table and said, 'Well, some of us can spend all day talking, we have work to do. Come on boys, we'll leave them to discuss the wedding. By the way, how many guests are coming?'

'Father, you know very well there'll just he us. But I hope Mistress Cross will be there and we will be glad to see any friend.'

'Mother told me she would come,' Martha said. 'Thank you Margaret for the lovely meal, now if you don't mind I'd like to go back with Elizabeth. I feel so tired, I'd like to lie down. I expect it's the excitement. William, you will excuse us, won't you?'

'Of course, Martha. You get your rest and be fit for tomorrow. I'll see you at eleven.'

'You'd better be here, William! Don't you go fishing.'

'I'm not likely to go fishing. But I know what I forgot.'

'What's that, William?'

'A ring. We must have a ring!'

'William,' said Margaret, 'we do not have a ring in our wedding

* As taken from the Boston Records and files.

service. That is a Catholic custom.'

'Oh, I see. I didn't know that.'

Martha and Elizabeth made their way to the door and Martha turned and said, 'Now good bye, William, and thank you again, Margaret.'

William kissed Martha and she left with Elizabeth.

'I'm so happy for you, William,' Margaret said after they had left. 'What a pity the wedding wasn't last June. We'd have had all the village present and a big meal. Never mind, you are going to be wed and that's the main thing. It won't be long before Martha has her baby. What do you want, a boy or a girl?'

'I haven't really thought about that. I don't mind so long as Martha is all right and the baby is perfect.'

'I don't suppose you've thought of names, either, have you?'

'No. My mind has been too much on the result of the court case.'

The next day, Hannah Cross was getting ready to go to the wedding, putting on her best dress.

'Where are you going, woman?' Robert asked.

'To our daughter's wedding, father,' she replied.

'I have no daughter being wed today. Your place is here to look after your own family.'

'But father, I promised Martha I'd be there. Please let me see my daughter on this important day.'

'I tell you woman, we have no daughter being wed today. You stay here, this is your family, not with that fornicator!'

'Oh, father! Will you never accept them?'

'Never. Not ever so long as I live. That's my final word. I don't want it mentioned in this house again!'

Hannah turned so that Robert would not see her silent tears. She had so wanted to see her daughter married, but she was the mother of twelve children by this strict husband and she knew better than to go against his will.

The hall of the Bishop's house was beginning to fill with the family to celebrate this happy occasion. Elizabeth Nelson was one of the first to arrive, William Nelson still refusing to come. Sarah Storie and Mary Bishop then came in.

William and Samuel, as best man, stood in the middle of the hall and greeted the guests. There were not enough seats to sit on, but everyone seemed happy to stand. William could not help thinking how different his wedding was going to be from his sister's in Drogheda.

Thomas Bishop came in with Martha holding his arm. She was wearing a long, brown, cotton dress and a sprig of mistletoe on her head.

Then old Sarah Harfield, who lived in the bark covered wig-wam up the village, came shuffling in. She was a short, thin woman with a bent back and grey hair, her clothing smelled of damp and her toes stuck out from her worn-out shoes. Slowly, she walked up to Martha and handed her a small bunch of garlic, 'to keep the evil spirits away from you, my dear,' she said.

'How thoughtful of you, Mistress Harfield. Thank you.' Sarah then quietly shuffled out again.

Robert Lord entered the hall and greeted everybody. He was very pleased to perform this ceremony after the many court cases. He was sorry for William and Martha and glad the matter had been settled at last.

He read through the wedding service with great emphasis.

'William wilt thou have this woman to thy wedded wife to live together after God's ordinance in the holy estate of matrimony? Wilt thou love her comfort her honour and keep her in sickness and in health; and forsaking all other keep thee only unto her so long as ye both shall live?' He asked.

William looked into Martha's eyes and replied, 'I will.'

'Martha wilt thou have this man to thy wedded husband to live together after God's ordinance in the holy estate of Matrimony? Wilt thou obey him and serve him love honour and keep him in sickness and in health; and forsaking all other keep thee only unto him so long as ye both shall live?'

Martha looked up to William and smiling replied, 'I will.'

'Who giveth this woman to be married to this man?'

Thomas replied,'I do.'

William and Martha then held their right hands and pledged their marriage vows.

Robert said, 'Repeat after me, "With my body I thee worship, and with all my worldly goods I thee endow: In the Name of the Father, and of the Son, and of the Holy Ghost. Amen."'

He then said, 'Those whom God hath joined together let no man put asunder.' He closed his prayer book and congratulated William and Martha, shaking their hands.

'We hope you will stay and share our food with us?' Margaret asked.

'Thank you, Mistress Bishop, I will be pleased to.'

William took Martha in his arms and they kissed.

'William, now we are married.' Martha said with a sigh of relief. 'What do you think of my posey of garlic?'

'Yes, a bit smelly. I was thinking of my sister's wedding. Still, as you say we are married and we are not likely to forget this day.'

Margaret brought out the food she had been preparing earlier in the morning. It was only bread and cheese and slices of cold chicken, but everyone enjoyed it and toasted William and Martha with cups of chocolate for the ladies and glasses of beer for the men.

The family happily chatted together for over an hour after eating and expressed their sorrow that Mistress Cross was absent.

When all the guests had departed William took Martha upstairs to show her their room. She climbed the narrow, steep stairs with difficulty and looked around in dismay.

'Oh, William, it is dark isn't it? And that's our bed – straw filled sacks in the corner?'

'That's where I've slept for the last year. Its up against the chimney and is nice and warm. I suppose I'm used to sleeping on the ground after fifteen years or so. I did have a bed of my own at home in Platten Hall.'

'William, you made those chairs in the hall, could you make a bed for us?'

'I've never made a bed, but I suppose I could. Yes, Martha, I'll make a bed for us. But I don't think I can do it before the baby arrives.'

'Never mind. Perhaps you'd better make a cradle first?'

'I can see I'm going to be busy carrying out my wife's orders.' he said laughing.

'Oh, William, you don't mind do you?'

'Of course not,' he took her in his arms and kissed her again. 'I'll do anything for you, Martha. I've longed for this day.'

'So have I, William. Now I think we'd better go down and I'll see if there is anything I can do for Margaret.'

The hall was now empty and Margaret and Elizabeth were busy

washing the dishes.

'Can I help you, Margaret?' Martha asked.

'No, my child, you sit down. Elizabeth is helping. This is your wedding day, you rest and enjoy it.'

'Thank you, Margaret. I do feel tired after all that standing. I've done so much just sitting down these last nine months, I'm not used to standing for long now.'

'Robert Lord was pleased to perform the service, I asked him the night before last and he said he would be glad to. I was happy he stayed for the meal.' Thomas said.

'Yes, he read the service very well.' Elizabeth said.

'William and Martha I am glad you are now married, and that's the important thing.' Thomas declared.

'William, you'll have to make more chairs.' John said.

'I've already been told to make a cradle for the baby and a bed for us.'

'Are you making a bed? Can you make one for us too!' John pleaded.

'One cradle, two beds and two chairs. I can see I'm going to be busy!' William laughed. 'Now I think I should go over and thank your father for his permission, Martha.'

'If you like, William, but he is very angry and still disowns me. I don't know if he'll even talk to you, but you can try.'

He crossed the stream and walked up to the Cross's house. He had never been to the house before, which was bigger than the Bishop's house, and had hardly spoken to Robert Cross beyond passing the time of day which was always ignored. He knew he was a very hard man to deal with, not violent, but he had fixed ideas and was a strict Protestant. His manner was brusque and William was nervous to meet him. He knocked on the door and Hannah opened it.

'Hullo, William. I am so sorry I could not come to your wedding.'

'We were sorry too, but we understood, Mistress Cross.'

'How is Martha?'

'Very well and happy now we are wed, thank you. Could I see Goodman Cross please.'

'Come in, William. He is in the hall. I don't know whether he will see you.' She gently knocked on the door, opened it slightly and said,

'Father. Here is William Durgy to see you.'

'What does he want?' Robert shouted.

William entered the room and saw Robert sitting in an arm chair, reading a book. He did not get up, but glared over the top of his book.

'Sir,' William said quietly, 'I want to thank you for your permission to marry your daughter.'

'Durgy! What are you doing here? How dare you come into my house! You have married no daughter of mine,' Robert exclaimed, going red in the face and still sitting down, he was not going to stand for this scum. 'If you want to marry a whore that is your affair. I'd be obliged if you'd not mention it to me again, and I'd be obliged if you would take your leave at once.' He raised his book and continued reading.

William did not reply, he felt there was nothing more he could say so he turned and left the room. Hannah was standing by the front door.

'I'm so sorry, William,' she said quietly, 'But he is still very angry. I'm afraid he'll never forgive you. I'll try and come over to see Martha. Tell her, will you please? I still love her.'

'Thank you, Mistress Cross. I understand and I will tell her.'

He returned to the Bishop's house. He was glad that visit was over; he did not expect the response would be other than what it was, but he felt he had to thank Robert and it was remotely possible he would be better received.

'I saw your father, Martha, and thanked him for his permission for us to marry,' he told her, 'but he did not want to see me. Your mother said she was sorry she could not come to the wedding and she will try and come over to see you. She says she still loves you.'

'Thank you, William. You've done your best and I'm glad you saw him. It must have been difficult.'

'It was not very pleasant, but I'm glad I've done it.'

He then went out to look for some wood to make the cradle and the bed. He hoped to be able to at least make a cradle before the baby arrived. He found a plank of oak left over from building the extension earlier in the year.

While he was working in the shed, William Butler came.

'Hullo, William. I've brought Goodman Cogswell to meet you'.

William looked up from his work and saw John Cogswell standing behind Butler. A short man with a pleasant smile. William had seen him at the prayer meetings but had never spoken to him.

'How do you do, sir?' he said, offering his hand.

'How do you do, William,' Cogswell shook his hand, 'William has told me a lot about you and how you taught him to ride. May I offer my congratulations on your marriage? I hope ye'll both be very happy.'

'Thank you, sir.'

'And Martha, of course I'm pleased for her too.'

'Thank you, sir. She is resting now.'

'What are you doing?'

'I'm trying to make a cradle for the baby, sir.'

'Is there nothing you can not do? Riding teacher and carpenter!'

'I can't swim.'

'Ah, yes. I heard all about that. Well, we'll leave you to your work, William. Just wanted to wish you well.'

'Thank you, sir.'

On the first night of their wedding William and Martha nestled together on their straw filled sacking on the floor of the attic.

'William, I do love you and I'm so happy now,' Martha said.

'And I love you too, Martha. I only hope that in time your father will forgive us and make our happiness complete.'

They clasped their arms round each other and fell to sleep.

William finished the cradle before the end of the month. He made the sides and bottom with mortices at the ends which slotted through tenons in the head and foot boards, drilled holes in the mortices and secured them with pegs. The head and foot boards were rounded at the base so the cradle would rock sideways. He had no means to make the inside surface completely smooth, so lined the cradle with leather. Finally he carried the finished article into the hall and put it on the floor.

'There you are, Martha. One cradle. Where is the baby?'

'Oh, William, that is lovely. Margaret look at this – isn't it lovely?'

'My, William, you are getting good at making things. It is very nice, but a bit big, don't you think? The baby will be lost in that!'

'He'll grow,' said William, wondering whether, after all, it was a bit big but he had no idea what size a cradle should be.

'He?' asked Martha, 'how do you know it will be a boy?'

'I felt him kicking last night, I know it must be a boy!'

Margaret laughed, 'I don't know about girls, but I do remember my two kicked a lot, maybe you're right.'

After the cradle William started making a bed. This was a more difficult job and he had to look for more wood. There had been a fall of snow and he walked half a mile before he found a suitable tree. It was very cold, but he soon warmed up chopping it down.

On the 3rd January 1665, Martha felt she was near her time. Margaret sent John to tell Hannah. She was putting on her shawl when Robert came into the house.

'Where are you going, woman?' he asked.

'Across to Mistress Bishop, our daughter is having our grandchild,' she replied.

'Woman, I've told you not to mention that again in this house. That is no daughter of ours and the child will be no grandchild of ours. Your duty is here in this house to look after our children. You stay here with your own family,' Robert ordered.

'Oh, father, I did so want to go and help Martha. She's having her baby, father.'

'You stay here, or go to her and stay with her for good.'

Once again, Hannah knew when she could not go against him.

'I'm sorry, John, you'll have to tell your mother I can't come.'

John went home and told his mother. So she sent him to fetch Elizabeth who returned with him and she and Margaret attended to Martha, upstairs in the attic. They took several candles to give light in the dark room.

Thomas, the two boys and William were told to keep well away – this was women's work! All the men were asked to do was to see there was plenty of hot water on the fire.

William was concerned to hear Martha crying out in pain.

'Don't ye fret yourself, William,' Thomas assured him. 'They always cry out when the baby is coming. She'll be happy enough when it is over.'

It seemed a long time, but eventually Margaret came down the stairs into the hall.

'It's a boy, William. A fine bonny boy. Martha is ready for you to see her now.'

William went upstairs and found Martha lying on the straw bed on the floor and she smiled up at him.

'It's a boy, William,' she said, 'are you glad?'

'Of course, Martha. How are you?'

'Fine now, William. But it was a long time coming. Don't you want to see him?'

'Yes, please,' he glanced down into the cradle and saw the red faced little baby with fine strands of dark hair, a tiny mite lost in the large cradle.

'Isn't he small? – but perfect. The cradle does look too big for him. Martha, what shall we call him?'

'I want to call him John. Do you like that name, William?'

'Yes, Martha we'll call him John. I like that name too.'

'Don't you worry about the cradle, he'll grow and soon fill it.'

William knelt down, kissed Martha on her forehead and took her hand in his.

'Now thank we all our God, with heart and hands and voices. Martha, I know now why I was saved at the battle in Ireland,' he said. 'My brothers and my father were killed then. After the battle a hundred of us were lined up on the wall round Drogheda and one in ten was knocked on the head. I prayed to God not me. I heard the man next to me being hit. Then I was sent in chains to Barbados. When we arrived there my friend, Father O'Neill sang that hymn. I served fifteen years in Barbados. Then I was spared in Jamaica. I could have died of marsh fever, but I came through safely. And now I know why I came to America. I came here to meet you and to start a family in New England. I pray they may all live happily and serve their country well. I was told to have faith, Martha, faith and hope gave me the strength to survive and now I have love too. Martha, I do love you.'

'Oh, William, I love you too. Try to forget the past, William, and live for the future. You're a good man. the future is ours and together we'll live here and have a God fearing family.'

They smiled happily at each other and were contented.

THE END

EPILOGUE

William and Martha lived happily in Ipswich and had ten children. He was appointed a short seat on the council.

John was born 3rd January 1665. He became a weaver and also served as a deacon in the church. He married Elizabeth Parsons and had eleven children. After Elizabeth's death he married Hannah Bennett. John died in Windham, Connecticut on 11th September 1739.

Thomas was born in 1666. He married Elizabeth Ford (or Lord). They had ten children. After Elizabeth's death he married Rebecca (Tilton) Lamb, the widow of John Lamb. She had three children by her first marriage and two with Thomas. Thomas died in Woodbury, Connecticut about 1757.

Martha was born in August of 1668. She married Thomas Fuller as his second wife. They had one son, Stephen. Martha died in Hampton, Connecticut on 30th January 1748.

Elizabeth was born about 1670. She married George Martin, Snr as his second wife. They had no children. Elizabeth's death date is not known, but she likely remained in Ipswich after her husband's death there in 1734.

William Jnr was born in 1672. He married Rebecca Gould in 1704. They were the parents of eleven children. William also served in the church as a deacon. He died in Windham, Connecticut on 2nd March 1731.

Jane was born in January 1674. She married John Martin, a son of George Martin, Snr., husband of her sister, Elizabeth. She had six children. Her death has not been found.

Mary was born in April 1678. She married Joseph Peck in 1709. They apparently left Ipswich, but no further information has been found.

Anna was born in October 1680. She married Samuel Palmer in 1727 as his second wife. She had no children. Anna died on 7th February 1761 in Windham, Connecticut.

Henry was born in May 1682. He apparently died at an early age.

Mercy was born in 1684. She married George Martin, another son of George Martin Snr. as his second wife. They had four children. Mercy died on 1st. August 1730 in Windham, Connecticut.

Robert Cross died after 1695 in Ipswich. His wife, Hannah, died on 29th October 1677.

William and Martha are recorded as having a house next to the Bishop's on a list of the inhabitants of Ipswich in 1678. He purchased about one quarter acre of land from the town in 1693. He had previously had his barn on part of this land.

The last reference to William in Ipswich was in 1705 and infers that he had died about that time. The actual date and place of his burial are unknown.

Martha moved with the family to Windham, Connecticut about 1712. She lived with Thomas and his family. She had 45 known grandchildren. She died on 11th January 1726/27 and was probably buried in the Old Litchfield Cemetery, although no gravestone remains.

The name of Durgy was used for several generations but gradually became Durkee. The most famous Durkee was Col. John Durkee who fought in the Indian Wars and founded the Sons of Liberty. He served with distinction in the Revolution.

Phineas Durkee was one of the first settlers of Yarmouth, Nova Scotia, removing there on 9th June 1762. The 9th June is Durkee's Founder's Day in Yarmouth.

The Honorable Charles Durkee served in the Senate and as Governor of Utah.

Eugene Return Durkee was the founder of the Durkee Food Company and Henry Durkee invented Shredded Wheat.

Anyone wishing specific information on the descendants of William and Martha Durgy may contact:

The Society of Genealogy of Durkee,
c/o Bernice B. Gunderson, 4100 East Therasa Street,
Long Beach, California. U.S.A. 90804 -1758.

THE AUTHOR'S FAMILY TREE

William Durgy and Martha Cross 20/12/1664
b.1633? b.1643?
d.1704? d.11.1.1726

John and Elizabeth Parsons 22.3.1689
b.3.1.1665 d.23.9.1711
d.11.9.1739 md Hanna Bennett 18.10.1712

Children:
- John b.23.11.1689 d.11.9.1739
- Thomas b.1666
- Martha b.1668
- William b.1672
- Elizabeth b.1670 d.14.4.1734
- Jane b.1674 d.1760
- Mary b.1678 d.7.2.1761
- Anna b.1680
- Henry b.1682
- Mercy b.1684 d.1.8.1730

Stephen md Lois Moulten 19.3.1729
b.3.6.1706
d.18.8.1769

- Phineas md Phoebe Pearl 1751
  b.16.9.1730
- Andrew b.1692 d.5.1.1724
- Jeremiah b.1694 d.29.8.1752
- Elizabeth b.1697 d.17.3.1753
- William b.1699 d.26.12.1724
- Thomas b.1701 d.28.9.1724
- Patience b.1703
- Plus 4 others

Amasa md Ruth Robins 21.11.1776
b.26.9.1752 b.6.7.1754 md Martha Shurtliffe
Lois d.5.11.1801
d.13.13.1829

Children:
- Amasa b.31.8.1777 d.25.7.1779
- Ruth Lydia b.6.7.1779
- Sibyl b.10.11.1731 d.1747
- Robert (Capt) b.26.11.1733
- Lydia b.1735 d.1.11.1814
- Andrew b.1737 d.26.4.1814
- Lois b.1739 d.1845
- Stephen b.1769 d.1825
- Hannah b.1742 d.26.12.1724
- Pearl b.1769 d.16.4.1856
- Phoebe b.1745 d.28.3.1827
- Stephen b.1771
- Elizabeth b.1774 d.21.9.1754
- Amasa b.1747 d.28.9.1793
- Hannah b.1781 d.10.5.1754

Lyman James md Louisa Kelly 1845
b.13.12.1822 md Sarah Carol 1858
md Elizabeth Crosby 3.5.1886

- Olive b.18.7.1756 d.10.4.1812
- Amasa b.23.7.1782 d.18.9.1783
- Eleanor b.1758 d.5.1.1724
- John b.1760 d.30.3.1761
- James b.1788 d.Nov.1762
- Phineas b.1762 d.12.9.1867
- Robert b.1765
- Lyman md Hannah Kelly md Mary Payson
- Hannah Kelly
- Catherine
- Maria Anna
- Adeline b.1828 d.26.9.1910
- Lydia Bacon b.1830 d.1917
- Margaret b.1831 d.1832
- Plus 2 others

Frances b.1874

James Edward md Mary Walsh 18.7.1882
b.11.5.1865
d.17.7.1944

- Jack Lyman md Catherine Rowland
  b.2.3.1885
  md Galdys Irene Rose
  d.8.4.1962
- Clarissa b.1900
- Dora b.1891
- Josephine b.16.11.1882

John Lyman
b.19.9.1913
d.Oct.1990

Peter John
b.12.6.1918